MW01076808

SilverFast:
The Official Guide

SilverFast®:
The Official Guide

TAZ TALLY, PH.D.

SAN FRANCISCO | LONDON

SYBEX®

Associate Publisher: DAN BRODNITZ
Acquisitions Editor: WILLEM KNIBBE
Developmental Editor: PETE GAUGHAN
Production Editor: ELIZABETH CAMPBELL, DONNA CROSSMAN, ERICA YEE
Technical Editor: PAUL BUCKNER
Copyeditor: JUDY FLYNN
Compositor: KATE KAMINSKI, HAPPENSTANCE TYPE-O-RAMA
Graphic Illustrator: CARYL GORSKA, GORSKA DESIGN
Proofreaders: EMILY HSUAN, NANCY RIDDIOUGH, SARAH TANNEHILL
Indexer: TED LAUX
Book Designer: CARYL GORSKA, GORSKA DESIGN
Cover Designer: JOHN NEDWIDEK, EMDESIGN
Cover Photographers: TAZ TALLY: MOUNTAIN, ROSE, BUILDING WITH TREES,
JOHN NEDWIDEK: CHILD, SIGN, WOMAN IN POOL, AND BOAT, SILVERFAST/LASERSOFT: PLANE, HOUSE, CLOWN

Copyright © 2003 SYBEX Inc., 1151 Marina Village Parkway, Alameda, CA 94501. World rights reserved. The author(s) created reusable code in this publication expressly for reuse by readers. Sybex grants readers limited permission to reuse the code found in this publication or its accompanying CD-ROM so long as the author(s) are attributed in any application containing the reusable code and the code itself is never distributed, posted online by electronic transmission, sold, or commercially exploited as a stand-alone product. Aside from this specific exception concerning reusable code, no part of this publication may be stored in a retrieval system, transmitted, or reproduced in any way, including but not limited to photocopy, photograph, magnetic, or other record, without the prior agreement and written permission of the publisher.

LIBRARY OF CONGRESS CARD NUMBER: 2003104312

ISBN: 0-7821-4197-8

SYBEX and the SYBEX logo are either registered trademarks or trademarks of SYBEX Inc. in the United States and/or other countries.

Screen reproductions produced with Snapz Pro X. 1999-2003 Ambrosia Software Inc. All rights reserved.
Snapz Pro X is a trademark of Ambrosia Software Inc.

Internet screen shot(s) using Microsoft Internet Explorer 5.2 reprinted by permission from Microsoft Corporation.

TRADEMARKS: SYBEX has attempted throughout this book to distinguish proprietary trademarks from descriptive terms by following the capitalization style used by the manufacturer.

The author and publisher have made their best efforts to prepare this book, and the content is based upon final release software whenever possible. Portions of the manuscript may be based upon pre-release versions supplied by software manufacturer(s). The author and the publisher make no representation or warranties of any kind with regard to the completeness or accuracy of the contents herein and accept no liability of any kind including but not limited to performance, merchantability, fitness for any particular purpose, or any losses or damages of any kind caused or alleged to be caused directly or indirectly from this book.

MANUFACTURED IN THE UNITED STATES OF AMERICA

10 9 8 7 6 5 4 3 2 1

Dear Reader,

Thank you for choosing *SilverFast: The Official Guide*. This book is part of a new wave of Sybex graphics books, all written by outstanding authors—artists and professional teachers who really know their stuff, and have a clear vision of the audience they're writing for.

At Sybex, we're committed to producing a full line of quality books on a variety of digital imaging topics. With each title, we're working hard to set a new standard for the industry. From the paper we print on, to the designers we work with, to the visual examples our authors provide, our goal is to bring you the best graphics books available.

I hope you see all that reflected in these pages. I'd be very interested in hearing your feedback on how we're doing. To let us know what you think about this, or any other Sybex book, please visit us at www.sybex.com. Once there, go to the product page, click on Submit a Review, and fill out the questionnaire. Your input is greatly appreciated.

Best regards,

Daniel A. Brodnitz
Associate Publisher
Sybex Inc.

Software License Agreement: Terms and Conditions

The media and/or any online materials accompanying this book that are available now or in the future contain programs and/or text files (the "Software") to be used in connection with the book. SYBEX hereby grants to you a license to use the Software, subject to the terms that follow. Your purchase, acceptance, or use of the Software will constitute your acceptance of such terms. ■ The Software compilation is the property of SYBEX unless otherwise indicated and is protected by copyright to SYBEX or other copyright owner(s) as indicated in the media files (the "Owner(s)"). You are hereby granted a single-user license to use the Software for your personal, noncommercial use only. You may not reproduce, sell, distribute, publish, circulate, or commercially exploit the Software, or any portion thereof, without the written consent of SYBEX and the specific copyright owner(s) of any component software included on this media. ■ In the event that the Software or components include specific license requirements or end-user agreements, statements of condition, disclaimers, limitations or warranties ("End-User License"), those End-User Licenses supersede the terms and conditions herein as to that particular Software component. Your purchase, acceptance, or use of the Software will constitute your acceptance of such End-User Licenses. ■ By purchase, use or acceptance of the Software you further agree to comply with all export laws and regulations of the United States as such laws and regulations may exist from time to time.

Reusable Code in This Book
The author(s) created reusable code in this publication expressly for reuse by readers. Sybex grants readers limited permission to reuse the code found in this publication, its accompanying CD-ROM or available for download from our website so long as the author(s) are attributed in any application containing the reusable code and the code itself is never distributed, posted online by electronic transmission, sold, or commercially exploited as a stand-alone product.

Software Support
Components of the supplemental Software and any offers associated with them may be supported by the specific Owner(s) of that material, but they are not supported by SYBEX. Information regarding any available support may be obtained from the Owner(s) using the information provided in the appropriate read.me files or listed elsewhere on the media. ■ Should the manufacturer(s) or other Owner(s) cease to offer support or decline to honor any offer, SYBEX bears no responsibility. This notice concerning support for the Software is provided for your information only. SYBEX is not the agent or principal of the Owner(s), and SYBEX is in no way responsible for providing any support for the Software, nor is it liable or responsible for any support provided, or not provided, by the Owner(s).

Warranty
SYBEX warrants the enclosed media to be free of physical defects for a period of ninety (90) days after purchase. The Software is not available from SYBEX in any other form or media than that enclosed herein or posted to www.sybex.com. If you discover a defect in the media during this warranty period, you may obtain a replacement of identical format at no charge by sending the defective media, postage prepaid, with proof of purchase to:

Sybex Inc.
Product Support Department
1151 Marina Village Parkway
Alameda, CA 94501
Web: http://www.sybex.com

After the 90-day period, you can obtain replacement media of identical format by sending us the defective disk, proof of purchase, and a check or money order for $10, payable to SYBEX.

Disclaimer
SYBEX makes no warranty or representation, either expressed or implied, with respect to the Software or its contents, quality, performance, merchantability, or fitness for a particular purpose. In no event will SYBEX, its distributors, or dealers be liable to you or any other party for direct, indirect, special, incidental, consequential, or other damages arising out of the use of or inability to use the Software or its contents even if advised of the possibility of such damage. In the event that the Software includes an online update feature, SYBEX further disclaims any obligation to provide this feature for any specific duration other than the initial posting. ■ The exclusion of implied warranties is not permitted by some states. Therefore, the above exclusion may not apply to you. This warranty provides you with specific legal rights; there may be other rights that you may have that vary from state to state. The pricing of the book with the Software by SYBEX reflects the allocation of risk and limitations on liability contained in this agreement of Terms and Conditions.

Shareware Distribution
This Software may contain various programs that are distributed as shareware. Copyright laws apply to both shareware and ordinary commercial software, and the copyright Owner(s) retains all rights. If you try a shareware program and continue using it, you are expected to register it. Individual programs differ on details of trial periods, registration, and payment. Please observe the requirements stated in appropriate files.

Copy Protection
The Software in whole or in part may or may not be copy-protected or encrypted. However, in all cases, reselling or redistributing these files without authorization is expressly forbidden except as specifically provided for by the Owner(s) therein.

ABOUT SYBEX

Sybex has been part of the personal computer revolution from the very beginning. We were founded in 1976 by Dr. Rodnay Zaks, an early innovator of the microprocessor era and the company's president to this day. Dr. Zaks was involved in the ARPAnet and developed the first published industrial application of a microcomputer system: an urban traffic control system.

While lecturing on a variety of technical topics in the mid-1970s, Dr. Zaks realized there wasn't much available in the way of accessible documentation for engineers, programmers, and businesses. Starting with books based on his own lectures, he launched Sybex simultaneously in his adopted home of Berkeley, California, and in his original home of Paris, France.

Over the years, Sybex has been an innovator in many fields of computer publishing, documenting the first word processors in the early 1980s and the rise of the Internet in the early 1990s. In the late 1980s, Sybex began publishing our first desktop publishing and graphics books. As early adopters ourselves, we began desktop publishing our books in-house at the same time.

Now, in our third decade, we publish dozens of books each year on topics related to graphics, web design, digital photography, and digital video. We also continue to explore new technologies and over the last few years have been among the first to publish on topics like Maya and Photoshop Elements.

With each book, our goal remains the same: to provide clear, readable, skill-building information, written by the best authors in the field—experts who know their topics as well as they know their audience.

About the Author

Dr. Taz Tally is the founder of Taz Tally Seminars, a consulting and training company that specializes in electronic publishing. Taz is the author of *Avoiding The Scanning Blues*, a comprehensive guide to desktop scanning, which was chosen as a featured selection of the DoubleDay book club, as well as *Electronic Publishing: Avoiding The Output Blues*, a textbook on electronic publishing fundamentals and Postscript file preparation. He is also a frequent contributor to *Photoshop User* magazine, for which he writes a regular prepress column.

Taz has produced numerous instructional videos and CDs on scanning, prepress, Photoshop, Microsoft Publisher, font management, and keyboard shortcuts, and was the co-developer and instructor for the video training series DeskTop to Print. Taz has invented and produces a 10-step scanner and digital camera calibration target and kit. Taz is a frequent presenter at seminars and trade shows throughout the U.S., including GraphExpo, and appears as a member of the Photoshop Dream Team at the biannual Photoshop World conventions.

Taz is perhaps best known for his entertaining, content-rich seminars and his ability to present complex materials in a simple, easy-to-understand fashion. Taz is currently writing books on Acrobat & PDF, Digital Photography, Photoshop, and OSX, and is developing an on-line training print curriculum for Sessions.edu.

When Taz is not touring the country by plane or motor home presenting his seminars, he splits time between houses in Homer, Alaska, and Ft. Myers, Florida, with his fabulous partner Jaz and their Cardigan Welsh corgi, Zip. In their "spare time," Taz and Jaz generally head off to the outdoors. They can be found hiking or mountain biking in Alaska, skiing the powder snow in Utah or diving with the whales in the waters off of Hawaii.

Taz is available for custom training and consulting.

Contact Taz & Jaz at

Taz Tally Seminars
3616 Heritage Lane
Ft. Myers, FL 33908
239-433-0622 (Office)
239-267-8389 (Fax)
ttallyphd@aol.com or jazkatz@aol.com.

Dedication

To my Mom, amazing Rae, whose courage is an inspiration.
I will love you always.

Acknowledgments

Many people have contributed to the success of this book. First thanks go to Karl-Heinz Zahorsky and the other key members of the LaserSoft Imaging development team, who created SilverFast. Karl and his co-workers have for the first time provided us with a scanning-software standard, and an excellent one at that. Paul Buckner at LaserSoft Imaging deserves special recognition for spearheading the development of this project, providing technical review, and seeing it through to completion. ■ The editorial staff at Sybex has been a terrific team to work with. Pete Gaughan, the developmental editor, is the best I have worked with. Many thanks go to Judy Flynn, who has provided some terrific copyediting, which made this book easier to read and understand. Pete Gaughan, Donna Crossman, Erica Yee and Elizabeth Campbell all get gold stars for keeping the book on schedule. I would like to recognize the fine work done by Kate Kaminski in the layout of the final chapters; they look great! ■ I would like to acknowledge Hal Hinderliter for his fine contributions to this book, especially his input on the first three chapters. And finally, I want to thank my wonderful Jaz for all her help in preparing the Word files for submission and for running interference so that I could work on this project. She's the best.

CONTENTS AT A GLANCE

Contents

Foreword

Over the recent decades the role of images in the communication of information has steadily grown. The technological progress regarding the capture, storage and display of images has created a situation in which images have become a standard means of communicating information. The proverb "a picture is worth a thousand words" clearly demonstrates the unique significance and compactness that images have on the process of gathering and processing information with our brain.

When we realize that all living beings base every decision on what images they recognize, we become aware of the powerful impact of images in nature as well as in our personal life. All intelligent actions in the universe are guided by images. Bits and pieces of structures, patterns and colors are communicated through our senses and computed (or recognized) by our brain into a picture connecting the unrelated fragments into a meaningful oneness—a picture.

A few years back only professionals could work with images since the technology was very complex and costly. Drum scanners used to be $100,000 and more. Today the equipment is affordable for everyone but working with digital images still remains complex. We must not forget, color reproduction has been a science, where people have had an in-depth education. Using an imaging work station enables photographers to realize, for the first time, their projects in multi-purpose formats: the digital image which can be printed onto paper or fabric, projected as a presentation, e-mailed across the globe, or displayed on the World Wide Web. Digital imaging is on the way to rapidly replace the conventional photography and printing.

With the emergence of color publishing in the 90s, I was confronted with the complexities of high-end imaging with drum scanners as well as with the inadequacies of the early desktop scanners. At this time, software for scanners was either too complex or too simple. While a normal user could not use the complex software, the professional could not achieve acceptable results with simple software. This was the point where I saw the opportunity to bring these two opposites together into one piece of software; so beginners and professionals could work with the same package. This was the inception of SilverFast Ai.

SilverFast Ai version 1 appeared in early 1995 and was available only for a few scanners on the Macintosh. The two-level user interface with an automatic intelligence (Ai) image type presets was well received over the years and gained worldwide recognition through large bundles with PFU, Epson, Nikon, Microtek and others.

High-end drum scanners such as the Howtek scanners where supported very early in 1996 while low-end scanner bundles with SilverFast SE started to appear with the advent of Epson's Perfection 2450 in 1999.

With SilverFast Ai version 4, the *ScanPilot* was introduced. The *ScanPilot* was a contribution from myself being a pilot, where securing workflows by checklists safeguards using complex technology in flying.

With version 5.5 NegaFix¨ was launched, adding a complete solution for negative film scanning with over 120 different film types and a film type editor.

The early recognition of 48-bit raw data (a side note: I was involved in the development of the raw data concept of 48-bit tif with Leaf Systems in 1990) led to the development of SilverFast HDR in 1996 when several scanners could already write out raw data. The addition of a JobManager turned SilverFast HDR into a powerful production tool. In version 5.5 HiRePP was developed so users could open one Gb files in one second only.

SilverFast Ai 6 was introduced in August 2002 supporting the new Macintosh OS-X operating system with new features such as SRD¨ (dust and scratch removal), ACR¨ (adaptive color restoration), SC2G¨ (selective color to gray) and others.

The key to SilverFast Ai's success is based on having a clear vision of the future of imaging and maintaining a close relationship with many users all over the world from different areas of the industry. Since we have added our SilverFast Forum on our web site, the communication with SilverFast users has become so much more extensive and efficient. The "New Features Wish List" in our forum allows large numbers of users worldwide to discuss their suggestions for new functions.

Today SilverFast Ai 6 supports over 200 scanners on Macintosh and PC. The latest development dedicated to digital cameras is SilverFast DC-VLT. This package integrates the imaging power of SilverFast with the "Virtual Light Table" and permits photographers to effectively view, organize, edit, and process their pictures. By the time you read this, SilverFast DCPro-VLT will available supporting all digital cameras (SLR) with raw data capability.

SilverFast: The Official Guide has been a timely undertaking offering users a great guide to review basic principles of imaging and the application of SilverFast tools. I am glad that someone as competent as Taz Tally has undertaken the task to help all levels of users to better understand imaging and successfully use the various SilverFast tools.

The book nicely focuses on the essentials of imaging. What is the significance of highlight and shadow? How to use the histogram? How to remove a color cast? How do I use an ICC-profile? There are also excellent example pictures within the book that illustrate the relevant points while the author clearly explains the implications. Here is where you will get a good understanding of the important functions that constitute a brilliant image.

May all your images become brilliant now!

Karl-Heinz Zahorsky
President & Founder
LaserSoft Imaging

Introduction

Perhaps the biggest challenge in teaching scanning has been the lack of a standardized tool for controlling scanners. Each manufacturer had different software. The second challenge has been the inconsistent, and often low quality, of scanning software.

The development of SilverFast meets both of these challenges in grand style. LaserSoft Imaging creates versions of SilverFast that drive nearly all of the scanners made today, thereby providing the consistent scanner interface we historically lacked. SilverFast also provides us with one of the most capable scanning applications ever developed, offering levels of control often previously found only in very expensive custom software. Users of SilverFast can access some new and very sophisticated tools, such as these:

- MidPip, a multipoint neutralization tool
- GANE, for removing grain and noise
- SRD, for dust and scratch removal

What's more, dedicated versions of SilverFast address the specific needs of particular image types. SilverFast HDR allows us to work with high-bit-depth scanned images, and SilverFast DC-VLT provides a virtual light table for digital camera files and similar images.

All of this is available to us, as well as a host of color adjustment aids, including Global and Selective Color correction tools and, one of my favorites, the Selective Color to Gray Scale tool, never provided on the desktop before. Because of its breadth of coverage and the depth of quality it provides, SilverFast qualifies as the Photoshop of the scanner world. *SilverFast: The Official Guide* introduces you to all the wonderful tools that SilverFast provides.

The third and final challenge in learning to scan—and one that this book addresses—is the lack of good information (or, in fact, the supply of misinformation!) on key foundation topics such as resolution, bit depth, and just how scanners work. In the early chapters of this book, I address these critical topics.

Who Should Read This Book

Many scanner manufacturers now ship SilverFast software with their scanners. If you have a scanner that came with SilverFast, this book will provide you with a comprehensive guide to that software. If you have a scanner that does not use SilverFast and you would like to upgrade to full-featured professional-level scanning software, then SilverFast and this book will be for you.

A note on exercises in this book, images in the color section, and using HDR:

Although many of the color images used in this book appear in the color section, they cannot effectively be used for most of the scanning exercises performed in this book because they are screened images (made up of dots) and not true continuous-tone images like the originals. However, included on the CD-ROM that comes with this book are digital versions of all the pictures used in the exercises in this book. Also included is a trial version of SilverFast HDR (but you can use your own version if you have one). You can use HDR to open and manipulate these uncorrected images and follow along step by step. You can, however, use the printed (screened) images to practice using SilverFast descreening functions.

SilverFast: The Official Guide is intended for use by novices and experts alike. If you are a scanning novice, be sure to carefully study the first two chapters to make sure you are clear on topics such as resolution and capture bit depth.

How This Book Is Organized

SilverFast: The Official Guide takes you easily from the basics that you need to know about digital images to the most advanced and detailed improvements, and adjustments you can make to your images, and along the way you'll learn the quickest and most common settings in scanning with SilverFast

Chapter 1: The Basics of a Scanned Image This chapter provides a foundation in key topics such as image resolution, scaling, and capture bit depth and channels. Knowing about these topics will help guide you in controlling your scans and images.

Chapter 2: Behind the Magic: How Scanners Work Knowing how a scanner actually works will help you understand how your images are created.

Chapter 3: Up and Running with SilverFast: Quick Start This is a quick-start guide to help youperform a basic setup of SilverFast and create your first image fast. Use this chapter as a way to get acquainted with SilverFast and your scanner, but don't stop here or you will miss much of the power and control that SilverFast provides!

Chapter 4: Automatic Scanning: Working with the Prescan Image SilverFast has excellent automated scanning capabilities. This chapter provides you with the knowledge and skills required to take advantage of them. If you scan mostly standard-quality images with no unusual challenges, this may be all the training you need in SilverFast. For those who have greater challenges and want more control, read on.

Chapter 5: Manual Scanning: Working with the Prescan Image This chapter provides detailed information on how to control and tweak most of SilverFast's fundamental tools, such as the histogram and the Gradation Curve tool, and it covers basic techniques such as setting highlight and shadow points, controlling brightness and contrast, removing color casts, and making global color adjustments.

Chapter 6: Fine-Tuning the Color of Your Scans If your color changes are great and/or you want to learn about the details of color control, this chapter is the ticket. Here I cover densitometer use, color correction with curves, making selective color correction to portions of images, mask-based color adjustments, and how to use the really powerful and cool MidPip tool for neutralizing images with complex color casts.

Chapter 7: Getting Control with the Expert Dialog This chapter is for those with a yen for numbers. You will learn how to use the Expert Dialog tool to make, store, and recall all your adjustments numerically.

Chapter 8: Sharpen, Smooth, and Remove Once you have mastered the fundamentals and details of image capture and correction, you may want to learn about some special tips and techniques—that's what's covered here. At the very least you will want to learn how to control the sharpness of your image. Also covered here is dealing with screened, patterned, and noisy images, as well as images with dust and scratches.

Chapter 9: Seeing the World in Black and White This chapter covers scanning line art and other hard-edged images. I cover the challenges and techniques of capturing both black-and-white and color original images.

Chapter 10: Power User Tips If you want to work fast and be really productive with Silver-Fast, this is the chapter to read. Here you will learn how to use the many cool productivity enhancement tools provided by SilverFast, including the ScanPilot, saving and using scan frames, batch scanning, and the SilverFast Job Manager.

Chapter 11: Getting a Grip on Color Management and Output Color management is a topic that merits its own book. SilverFast provides a very sophisticated yet easy-to-control set of color management tools, and here you learn how to use them.

Chapter 12: Using SilverFast HDR, DC, and PhotoCD SilverFast not only provides a complete scanning solution, it also provides a set of specialty tools for dealing with prescanned images, including HDR for correcting high-bit-depth scanned images, PhotoCD for accessing and correcting PhotoCD images, and DC-VLT for accessing and organizing as well as correcting digital camera (DC) images with SilverFast's way-cool Virtual Light Table (VLT). You will also learn how to quickly open and work with multi-gigabyte files using HiRepp and even control color conversion to grayscale with one of my favorite tools, SC2GS.

     In addition to the chapters you see in the printed pages, I've provided the following special material on the companion CD-ROM:

Bonus Chapter 1: Making Slides Come Alive All of the tools and techniques covered in other chapters apply to capturing film-based positive images. But here we cover those issues specific to handling film in general and positive film in particular, including calibration for scanning color positives.

Bonus Chapter 2: Positive Experiences from Your Negatives As with film positives, most of the tools and techniques learned in the printed book apply to film negatives, but only after we have met the special requirements of negative images. Here you will learn how to adjust for the various film emulsions, which change from manufacturer to manufacturer, using the NegaFix and NegaFix expert dialogs.

Appendix A: Manual Calibration This provides step-by-step instructions on performing manual calibrations using a grayscale target.

Appendix B: Keyboard Shortcuts This is a list of shortcuts that will speed up your scanning work.

What's on the CD-ROM?

The CD-ROM that comes with this book is full of valuable tools that will improve the quality of your scans:

Software LaserSoft Imaging has provided both Windows and Macintosh versions of all of its software. The CD includes trial versions of the following:

- **SilverFast Ai** is LaserSoft Imaging's flagship product, designed for working with multiple types of scanner hardware.
- **SilverFast SE** is a version of SilverFast for low-end digital cameras and scanners.
- **SilverFast HDR** has the same look and feel as SilverFastAi but works with files on your hard drive. This includes raw data images from scanners and digital cameras (48-bit format).
- **SilverFast DC-VLT** is a limited version of HDR for 24-bit files, like the ones generated by most digital cameras.

Images and reference files You will also find a variety of resources for you to use while you are learning to use SilverFast with this book. You will find IT8 reference files for use in your calibration and color management exercises. I've also included digital versions of all the images that are used in this book. These images can be opened and manipulated in SilverFast HDR, which allows you to follow along step by step with the exercises performed in the book. You will find both uncorrected and corrected versions of files so you can start with the uncorrected version and compare your results with those of the corrected file.

Bonus chapters and appendices I've written bonus chapters on film scanning: Bonus Chapter 1 covers scanning film positives, and Bonus Chapter 2 deals with scanning film negatives. You'll also find the two appendices on the CD.

How to Contact the Author

You can contact me via e-mail at ttallyphd@aol.com or though my website, www.tazseminars.com. You can find a complete listing of all of my digital training and educational resources, including Taz's 10-Step Calibration Kit for scanners and digital cameras, at www.graphicauthority .com/home.htm.

CHAPTER 1

The Basics of a Scanned Image

Welcome to a new world of digital imaging! This book will serve as your guide to both the how and the why of digital imaging with SilverFast, with information on pixels, color correction, image restoration, and much more. The first two chapters are not specifically about the use of SilverFast, but the background information you'll obtain about the digital imaging process is absolutely essential if you're to make informed, appropriate choices during the scanning process. In this first chapter, the following topics are covered:

- **Bitmap vs. vector**
- **Parts of an image**
- **Capture bit depth, channels, and shades of gray**
- **The resolution concept**
- **Color theory and color modes**
- **File formats for print or the Internet**

Bitmap vs. Vector

In today's information-packed world, we are bombarded with graphic images from television sets, computer screens, billboards, and magazines. As you float in this stream of digital content, contemplate this fundamentally important bit of information: Despite the wide variety of visual communication methods used to disseminate these images, every graphic brought to you through digital processes can be placed into one of two categories; it is either *vector* or *bitmap*.

Vector graphics are composed of a series of points and lines connecting the points (see Figure 1.1). Although some of these lines may be perfectly straight, it is more likely that any two points are joined by a line featuring one or more curves. The specific shape of these straight or curving lines and the coordinates of all the points these lines connect can be expressed using mathematical equations. When the entire series of equations needed to describe a particular illustration is saved as a single file, other programs can access the illustration and make it a part of a new illustration or page layout document.

Don't be put off or confused by the words *pixel* and *vector*. They are just new terms for things you are already familiar with. Before the digital age, we had painting and drawing. And we still do. We paint with pixels, and we draw with vectors.

Drawing Applications

Software packages used to create vector graphics are often called drawing programs, because the concept of building a digital illustration through a series of connected lines is very similar to the process of drawing a graphic with pen and paper. Vector graphics are also known as object-oriented graphics because individual objects drawn in this way can be manipulated independently (i.e., they can be resized, skewed, repositioned, etc.). It's typical that the equations describing these graphics are expressed in an object-oriented programming language, such as Adobe's PostScript.

Common examples of vector graphics include Encapsulated PostScript (EPS) files created by drawing programs such as Macromedia FreeHand or Adobe Illustrator, as well as the outline component of digital fonts (such as TrueType or printer fonts from the Type 1 format).

Adobe® PostScript® 3™

Figure 1.1

Vector images consist of points and lines mathematically defined.

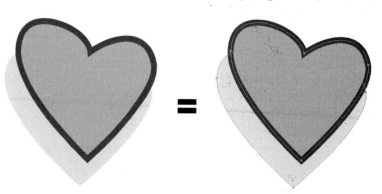

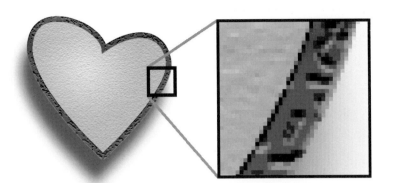

Figure 1.2

Bitmap images consist of thousands or millions of individually defined points.

The power of vector graphics is that they are not limited by size or resolution; they can be output as large or small as desired, and on devices of any resolution—the only restrictions on the quality of vector reproduction are the limitations of the output device itself. With that in mind, you might think that every graphic should be created and stored in vector format; unfortunately, that is simply not possible. Although vectors excel at reproduction of clearly defined shapes, they are not able to capture the incredible variety of shades and ambiguous details found in everyday life. For the storage of real-life scenes scanned from photographs or captured on digital cameras, we rely on graphics stored in the bitmap format.

Painting Programs

Painting programs such as Photoshop work with bitmapped or pixel-based images. The term *bitmap* refers to a collection of tiny squares called pixels, stored in an orderly rectangular grid akin to the sectors that make up a city map (see Figure 1.2). Each square pixel in this map can vary in hue (color), saturation (intensity), and brightness, but the entire square must be of a single value (for example, a single pixel cannot fade from dark at the top to a lighter shade at the bottom).

The appearance of each pixel can be expressed and stored as a specific set of numbers, and as with all numbers stored in computers, these values are stored as binary values. In the binary counting system, numerical values are represented as collections of 1s (ones) and 0s (zeros), which are called bits. Every bit must be either a 1 or a 0, and when bits are clustered together into groups of eight, they are known as bytes. A single byte (made up of 8 bits) expresses 1 of 256 possible values. The byte in Figure 1.3 shows the binary representation of the number 127, which could be used to designate a medium gray pixel in a grayscale image.

Figure 1.3

Pixel values are stored with bytes of data.

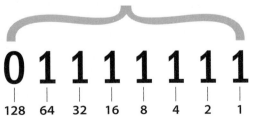

8 bits = 1 byte

0	1	1	1	1	1	1	1

Value = 128 64 32 16 8 4 2 1

Simple bitmap images are composed of pixels arranged in a maplike grid where the value of each pixel is described with a single bit (1 or 0), so these images can only contain a single color, or a single shade of gray, and are often known as line-art images. More complex bitmaps can use 8 bits (1 byte), 24 bits (3 bytes), or an even greater numbers of bits to describe shades of gray or specific colors within a complex rainbow of possibilities.

Parts of an Image

We often refer to tonal parts or areas of an image, in terms of both viewing it and measuring and adjusting it. It is the tonal ranges that we view and adjust when we capture an image.

Tonal Areas

There are five basic tonal areas: highlight, quarter tone, midtone, three-quarter tone, and shadow. Figure 1.4 shows representative locales for these five tonal regions in an image. The five basic tonal areas represent the entire tonal range of grayscale values found in an image.

Figure 1.4

Tonal areas of an image

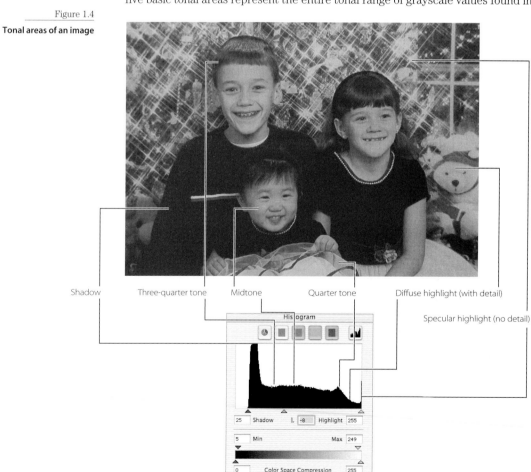

It is important to note that there are two kinds of highlights, specular and diffuse. Not all images contain both kinds of highlights, but this image does. Specular highlight, seen here as twinkles on the bulbs on the tree, have no detail in them, whereas a diffuse highlight has some image detail. We typically focus on finding and setting the diffuse highlight.

Histograms

Figure 1.4 also includes a *histogram.* A histogram shows the amount and distribution of tonal data from the highlight to the shadow end of the image. The histogram is one of the primary tools we use for viewing and adjusting the tonal data in an image.

Capture Bit Depth, Channels, and Shades of Gray

One of the most important characteristics of a bitmapped or pixel-based image is its bit depth. And understanding bit depth is the key to understanding the Scan Type choices in the SilverFast Scan Overview dialog (Scan Control window). Bit depth refers to the amount of information (represented by bits) that is stored in an image.

Bit Depth

As discussed previously, all digital devices work with only two values: 0 and 1. So all image data must be broken down into those two values. If we only worked with black-and-white images, all we would need to have would be 1 bit of information—a 0 for black and 1 for white or vice versa—stored in each pixel. All we would need would be images with a bit depth of 1. But this is not the case. We need to capture, store, edit, and output images with from hundreds to millions of values. So we need more bit depth, that is, more bits per pixel to represent more shades of gray and more colors.

The number of shades of gray or colors represented increases with the number of bits per pixel we have stored in our images in a geometric fashion. Every time we add another bit of information, we double the number of shades of gray or colors we can capture, store, edit, and output. The capture bit depth describes the number of bits of image data that can be captured by a scanner or digital camera. The minimum number of shades of gray we prefer to work with in printing is 256, which is $2 \times 2 \times 2 \times 2 \times 2 \times 2 \times 2 \times 2 = 256$, or 2^8. For the Web, we can often get by with fewer colors or shades of gray, such as 32 (2^5) or 64 (2^6). When we capture image data with a scanner or digital camera, we want to capture more than we might use on final output to allow us some data to work with in editing our images. Table 1.1 is a chart of the standard bit depths and the shades of gray controlled by each.

BIT DEPTH	COLORS OR SHADES OF GRAY
1 bit	2
2 bits	4
3 bits	8
4 bits	16
5 bits	32
6 bits	64
7 bits	128
8 bits	256
10 bits	1024
12 bits	4096
14 bits	16,384
16 bits	65,536

Table 1.1

Bit Depths

Image Channels

Once we understand that we can vary the bit depth and therefore the number of shades of gray in an image, we can address the second key variable, which controls the kind of image we have. This second key characteristic is the number of building block channels.

Pixel Bricks, Channels, and Capture Bit Depth

Pixel-based images are much like brick walls, with the pixels being the pixel "brick" building blocks. Just as brick walls can have multiple rows of bricks, pixel-based images can have multiple pixels. It is the number of rows of pixel-bricks (known as channels) that largely determines the kind of image with which we are working. And it is the number of channels and the bit depth of the pixels in each channel that determines the total bit depth and therefore number of shades of gray or color we have in our images. Table 1.2 is a list of some of the common image types and the number of channels and total bit depths they may have.

In the 32-bit CMYK image, black (K) substitutes for various portions of CMY, so more colors are not added, they are just built in a different way. See Chapter 11 for more information.

The 8-bit and 14-bit grayscale images will both have one channel. The 24-bit and 48-bit RGB images will both have three channels. The differences in each case will be the amount of bit depth present in each channel.

Figure 1.5 (and C1) breaks down the structure of various bit depths in images.

The image types are described as follows (all file sizes are given at 300 ppi):

1-bit line-art image Contains only one layer of pixels, with 1 bit of data per pixel. Each pixel is either black (1) or white (0). These are the smallest and simplest types of bitmapped images. The file size of this image is 285 KB.

8-bit grayscale image Contains only one layer of 8-bit pixels, each of which has the capacity to store and display 256 shades of gray. Grayscale file size is eight times larger than 1-bit images. This 8-bit-per-pixel file is also the basic building block for the RGB and CMYK images shown here. File size is now 2.2 MB.

24-bit RGB color (three-channel) image Contains three layers of 8-bit grayscale pixels, one for each color (R, G, and B). Each color can be shown in 256 shades, so the total number of colors possible is 256 red × 256 green × 256 blue = 16.7 million. This image is 24 times the size of the 1-bit image; file size is now 6.6 MB.

	IMAGE TYPE	TYPICAL COMPOSITION
Table 1.2	1-bit black-and-white	One channel, 1 bit/pixel/channel, 2 shades of gray
Some Common Image Structures	8-bit grayscale	One channel, 8 bits/pixel/channel, 256 shades of gray
	14-bit grayscale	One channel, 14 bits/pixel/channel, 16,384 shades of gray
	24-bit RGB	Three channels, 8 bits/pixel/channel, 16.7 million colors (256^3)
	48-bit RGB	Three channels, 16 bits/pixel/channel, 28 billion colors ($65,536^3$)
	32-bit CMYK	Four channels, 8 bits/pixel/channel, 16.7 million colors

Figure 1.5

Channels and pixel depth of images

1-bit black-and-white image
(single channel)

8-bit grayscale image
(single channel)

24-bit RGB color (three-channel) image

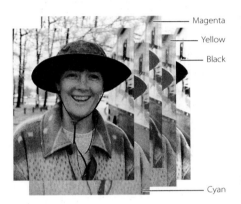

32-bit CMYK color (four-channel) image

32-bit CMYK color (four-channel) image Contains four layers of 8-bit grayscale pixels, one for each color. However, a 32-bit CMYK image produces the same number of colors as a 24-bit RGB image. The fourth, black channel (K) is substituted for various portions of the three color channels (CMY). This K channel improves contrast and shadow detail and reduces ink coverage but does not add any colors. A CMYK file is used for printing, is 33 percent larger than an equivalent RGB file, and is 32 times as large as a similar 1-bit image. File size is now 8.8 MB.

It is worth emphasizing here that your scanner and digital camera can capture only grayscale data. After all, they are digital devices that can "understand" only two values: 0 and 1, black and white. All color is actually provided by output devices such as monitors and printers. So when you capture 48 bits of data, you are capturing 48 bits of grayscale data, which you will use to control the color provided by an output device. Knowing that you are really only working with grayscale data will simplify the process of capturing and editing color values.

This book's companion CD has copies of the images seen here in Figure 1.5 so that you can open and view the channels that are present in each image. Look for Jaz_BW_200.tif, Jaz_GS_200.tif, Jaz_RGB_200.tif, and Jaz_CMYK_200.tif.

Why So Much Data?

In the image capture process during scanning or digital photography, we will typically capture more shades of gray/colors (12–16 bits per pixel) than we will use in the final output (often 8 bits). We will do this to provide ourselves more data with which to correct, manipulate, and edit our images. The final result is a very high-quality image. Capturing lots of grayscale data is particularly important if we intend to manipulate our image after the scan. Every correction you perform on an image results in image data being thrown out. And if you start with only bits of information (256 shades of gray) and edit your image after the scan, you may end up with far less than the 256 shades of gray needed for high-quality output. Figure 1.6 shows the results of editing an image after it is captured. There are missing data positions along the histogram on the bottom (after postscan editing). This is the type of data that also results from editing low-bit-depth images after the scan. Working with higher-bit-depth images will reduce or eliminate this type of image data degradation regardless of whether the image editing is performed during or after the scan.

SilverFast allows us to capture images at the highest bit depth allowed by the capture device. Higher-quality devices provide higher bit depth. Even if SilverFast delivers a 24-bit image, as it does in the 48 -> 24 Bit Color Scan Type mode, it will utilize all 48 bits during its corrections and then deliver a histogram full of high-quality data. Pay special attention to capturing all available image data if you choose to edit your image in the post scan rather than the SilverFast HDR and DC applications, because you will want all the data you can get your hands on for manipulation purposes!

Measuring Grayscale

Because capturing a digital image is all about capturing and controlling grayscale values, I should devote a bit of time here to introducing the concepts of measuring grayscale. You will see when you get deeper into the measurement of images that there are several scales and units of measurements for measuring grayscale. The details will be easier to understand when you are actually measuring your image, but a brief introduction is appropriate here.

The most important tool used to measure grayscale values in SilverFast is called the densitometer. In other applications, such as Photoshop, it is known as the info tool. But in all cases this tool is measuring grayscale value. Depending on which measurement mode you choose, you will see a variety of numbers. Perhaps the simplest and easiest measurement system to understand and relate to is the percent scale (see Figure 1.7). In the percent scale, we are measuring grayscale values from white to black on a scale of 0%–100% black, where %K, or black, is the unit of measurement.

Another common measurement scale is the 0–255 scale (representing the number of shades of gray in an 8-bit image). This is the measurement system used when measuring RGB values. In the 0%–100% scale, the highest value is pure black. The 0–255 scale is just the opposite. The lowest value, 0, equals black and the highest value, 255, represents white. So you can see that it is important that you know which scale you are using and what the values represent.

SilverFast provides value systems, including %K, RGB, CMY, Lab, HSL, HSB, and CMYK, to measure the internal grayscale and therefore the intended output color values. We will explore more fully these various measurement systems as we progress through the scanning exercises.

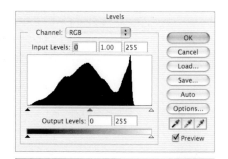

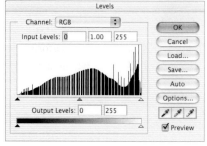

Figure 1.6

An 8-bit histogram (top) before and (bottom) after post scan editing

The Resolution Concept

SilverFast is a software program that aids in the capture and manipulation of bitmap (AKA raster or pixel-based) images acquired with a scanner or a digital camera. These bitmaps can be in full color or in black and white, but they must be made of pixels—SilverFast does not manipulate vector graphics. Although the advanced software functions of SilverFast provide a wide range of image enhancement techniques, there is no way to overcome the inherent limitations of bitmap images as compared to vector graphics. Pixels, unlike vectors, are resolution dependent, meaning that the size of the pixels, and therefore the effective resolution of the image, changes when we scale the image. Also, the resolution of an image controls the size and affects the quality of an image when it is viewed and printed. For these reasons it is important for us to understand and know how to assign and adjust the resolution of our images.

Input vs. Output Resolution

The treatment of resolution has been one of the most confusing areas of computer publishing for many people. One of the key reasons resolution is confusing is that there is more than one kind of resolution and we tend to misuse terminology. For instance, you will see the term *dpi* (dots per inch) used in nearly all discussions of resolution even when there are no dots involved. The debate about resolution terminology can proceed forever, but here is an approach I have found clarifying and therefore useful. I separate input from output resolution, and I use resolution terms that match the building blocks of the image.

Capturing an image with a scanner or digital camera would represent input resolution. And because the building blocks that result are pixels, we should use pixels per inch (ppi) instead of dpi. On the other hand, printing an image would involve output resolution. Here we typically have two kinds of building blocks: spots and dots. The spots are the smallest building blocks used to re-create an image. Spots are used to reproduce edge-based images such as vector line art and type. The smaller the spots are, the sharper the edge will be. The size of these

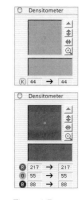

Figure 1.7

The densitometer using the %K grayscale measurement scale (top) and the 0–255 measurement scale (bottom)

image spots is controlled by the resolution of the output device (unfortunately referred to as the dpi of the device instead of spots per inch). A 300 dpi/spi laser printer creates spots that are 1/300′ across, while a 2400 dpi/spi platesetter creates spots that are 1/2400′ across. The true dot is the halftone dot, which is used to reproduce continuous-tone images. Halftone dots are actually constructed out of the much smaller image spots.

In a conventional halftone dot, the size of the dot controls the grayscale value it represents in the final printed image. Adding or subtracting the number of image spots used to create the dot controls the size of the dot. For output resolution, we have spots and dots, so it would make sense to use spots/inch (spi) and dots/inch (dpi). I wish it were so in common practice. Instead, we tend to use dpi when referring to spots per inch and lpi (lines per inch) when referring to the dots per inch. Lpi refers to the number of halftone dots per inch that will be used when an image is printed. The greater the lpi used to print an image, the greater the detail and the more shades of gray represented in the image (see Figure 1.8).

Figure 1.8

Building blocks of an image

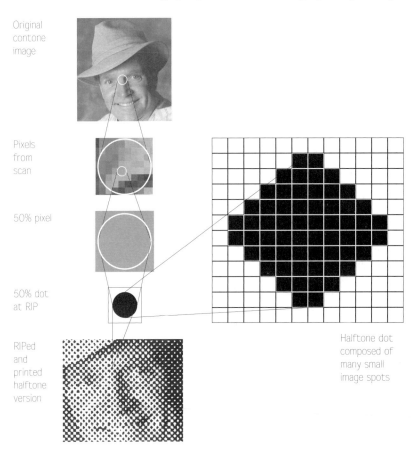

Original contone image

Pixels from scan

50% pixel

50% dot at RIP

RIPed and printed halftone version

Halftone dot composed of many small image spots

To further complicate matters, some scanning applications—and SilverFast is one of them—use output resolution, such as lpi, to set the input resolution of the scanner. In truth, using the output resolution you plan to use for your image to help determine the input resolution for scanning the image is not a bad approach to take. In fact, it is an enlightened approach. But using output terms to control input resolution can be confusing, and particularly if you are scanning an image for multiple purposes.

To add even more confusion, many applications use different terminologies to refer to resolution. Photoshop uses (correctly) ppi, many scanner software programs use (confusingly) dpi, and SilverFast uses lpi and a quality factor (Q-Factor) as well as dpi to represent input resolution.

Now That You Are Confused

So what to do. Until our industry establishes a common resolution lexicon (and this may never happen with so many options and so much ingrained usage), here are my two key suggestions:

- Keep input and output resolutions clear in your own mind and know what kind of building blocks you are working with.

- Evaluate each application you work with to figure out how it is referring to resolution and be sure you are clear about how that specific application handles resolution.

SilverFast's Resolution Terminology

- SilverFast uses dpi to refer to pixels per inch. So a 300 dpi scan will result in the creation of a 300 pixel per inch (ppi) image.

- SilverFast uses printing resolution (lpi) and a quality factor to determine the final input resolution. So an lpi of 150 and a quality factor of 2 will yield a final scanned image resolution of 300 lpi × 2 = 300 ppi.

Resolution, Image Dimension, and Quality

Unlike vectors, bitmaps have a specific physical size. As an example, you might scan an image that is 30,000 pixels wide and 24,000 pixels high. The term *resolution* refers to the decision of how great an area a specific set of pixels should cover; if this image was used at a ratio of 300 ppi (pixels per inch, as measured along a straight line), it would cover an area 10 inches wide and 8 inches high. If the same image were to be used at a resolution of 72 pixels per inch, however, its size would increase to more than 40 inches by 32 inches. Keep in mind that although you typically adjust the settings within your scanning software by requesting an area of coverage and a ppi rate, the end result is really just a specific number of pixels wide by a specific number of pixels high. If the image is displayed or printed at a rate that crams hundreds of those pixels into each linear inch of space, the image is said to be high resolution. If the same image is spread out over a larger area (as shown in Figure 1.9), so that the rate of pixels per linear inch falls to less than 100, it can be called a low-resolution image.

So you may ask, "How much resolution do I need?" When setting up to make a scan, begin by determining whether the scan will be for monitor viewing only (such as for a website or a PowerPoint presentation). If the answer is yes, then make your scan at 96 pixels per inch.

> Although you may have heard that scans meant to be viewed on a monitor were best made at 72 ppi, that information is now outdated. Due to improvements in monitor technology that have lead to finer pitch rates, the World Wide Web Consortium (W3C) now recommends 96 ppi as the default resolution for web page graphics.

If your scan will be for print reproduction, consider using 2 × lpi as your guideline. This widely accepted tenet stipulates that 2 pixels should be provided for every halftone dot of your output. In other words, if your goal is to output your image to film through an imagesetter with a halftone dot size of 150 lpi (lines per inch), then your scanning resolution should be 300 ppi (this would represent a quality factor of 2 in SilverFast's resolution setup). Some commercial printers, however, prefer an output scenario of 200 lpi, requiring a 400 ppi scan. If your intended goal were a color laser printer with a halftone dot size of 100 lpi, then 200 ppi would be sufficient. In practice, however, most people seldom scan images for print at less than 300 ppi; this way, if you decide to output your image on a higher-quality output device at some point in the future, you'll avoid the need to rescan. Three hundred ppi is also the resolution most often selected for inkjet printers and other output devices that utilize stochastic screening instead of halftone dots.

Keep in mind that all of these examples refer to scanning the image at the same width and height required for output. If you don't scale the document correctly during the scanning process, you run the risk of actually capturing a far lower resolution than you intended. For example, you might scan an image at 300 ppi for 150 lpi output, but upon placing the image into a QuarkXPress document, you decide to enlarge the image to 200% (twice the original size). Spreading the original number of pixels out over twice the area cuts the resolution in half; the result is that your effective scan resolution has fallen to 150 ppi. To avoid this dilemma, always be sure to determine the size at which you want to use the image before making the scan; then set this amount of enlargement (or reduction) into the scanning software prior to capturing the image.

Output to desktop printing devices, for the same-sized image, does not require as much input resolution as does commercial printing. But there is no clear numeric relationship

Figure 1.9

This bitmap image could be high resolution at a small size or low resolution if used at a much larger size.

300 ppi at 100%

75 ppi at 400%

between input and output resolution, as there is for commercial printing, due to there being so many different printing technologies used in desktop printing devices. A good rule to follow is to capture images for use with the highest resolution output, typically commercial printing, and then downsize for less demanding devices. I will address this issue more completely at the end of Chapter 11.

SilverFast's stated preference for a quality factor is a minimum of 1.4. The industry standard quality factor, as stated above, is 2.0. So who is right? My suggestion is to treat 1.4 as a minimum quality factor for truly continuous tone images. If your images have lots of high contrast edges or, even more to the point, logos and other line art in them, scan with a Q-Factor of 2.0. As we will discuss in Chapter 11, for output devices that do not use line screens (which includes an increasing number of desktop printing devices), some testing will be in order to find the right match of input and output resolution.

Color Theory and Color Modes

Now that you understand how a scanned image or digital photograph reveals the details of the subject (by displaying little squares of information called pixels), let's examine how these same images are able to describe a wide variety of shades of gray or colors. The many ways in which a digital image can display color information are known as color modes. Full-color reproduction is possible through modes such as RGB, CMYK, or Lab. Single color (usually referred to as black-and-white) images are rendered in either grayscale mode (which allows shades of gray to be displayed) or line-art mode (no shades of gray, only pure black or white).

Monochrome Modes

Confusingly, Adobe's popular Photoshop image editing software labels line-art images as being in the *bitmap mode*, because only 1 bit is used to describe the tonal value of each pixel (1 or 0, corresponding to white or black). However, these high-contrast images should properly be described as line-art mode (see Figure 1.10), because the term *bitmap* has traditionally been used to refer to any image (black-and-white or color) made from pixels.

Grayscale mode images (Figure 1.11) are another form of black-and-white bitmaps. In this mode, each pixel is represented by a single *byte* instead of a single *bit*. Because each byte of information is capable of expressing 256 different values, grayscale images can show black (0), white (255), and 254 different shades of gray between these extremes.

Both grayscale and line-art images are commonly used to reproduce black-and-white images, but the grayscale mode is appropriate for photographs and anything else with a range of tonal values, whereas line-art mode is used mainly for reproduction of drawings or other high-contrast artwork. Another point of confusion is that we commonly refer to grayscale and line-art as "black-and-white" modes, but these single-color images can actually be assigned to print with any color of ink (such as Pantone 286 blue or Rhodamine red).

Figure 1.10

This line-art mode image can contain only black or white pixels, with no shades of gray.

Figure 1.11

Grayscale mode images are used when you want to reproduce shades of gray.

RGB Mode and the Additive Spectrum

To truly render a lifelike range of colors, you'll want to choose a full-color mode for your digital image. For many people using desktop scanners, the most appropriate choice would be RGB mode. This widely used color mode provides three different channels to store color information about each pixel—one channel for red data, one channel for green data, and a third channel for blue. You might ask how only three channels can re-create the full range of color found in a photograph; the answer is that red, green, and blue are the primary colors of the additive spectrum (see Figure 1.12, and more importantly, see the color version, Figure C2, in the book's color section). Our eyes are most sensitive to these additive primaries, so blending these colors together can re-create almost all the remaining colors that we are capable of seeing. With one byte of data per channel for each pixel, RGB images can render 256 shades of red, 256 shades of green, and 256 shades of blue for a total of more than 16.7 million possible colors ($256 \times 256 \times 256 = 16,777,216$). Because RGB images can display most of the colors the human eye is capable of seeing, we say that the RGB color mode displays a wide *gamut* (range of colors).

The more colors that are used in an additive color (RGB) image, the brighter the image appears. If you combine all three primary colors at their maximum value (red + green + blue), the resulting total is white light. This is a very important observation because it means that the white light we use in our everyday lives is actually a combination of all the possible colors in the additive spectrum. In other words, white light—whether it comes from the sun or from a light bulb—contains red as well as green and blue and all the shades of color that can be made by combining these primaries. Beyond the wide gamut of the RGB mode, another advantage of RGB is that it's the native color mode for displaying information on computer monitors and televisions and it's the native mode of the scanning process (more on this in our next chapter).

CMYK Mode and the Subtractive Spectrum

In addition to scanning and monitor display, there is another area of great importance for users of digital images: print reproduction. In order for your scanned images to be output on a desktop inkjet printer, a color copier, or an offset printing press, the RGB color mode data captured by your scanner must be converted into CMYK mode (Figure 1.13 and Figure C3). Understanding how to make this conversion is relatively easy: home users can simply allow the print driver software furnished with their printers to make this conversion automatically, while professional users (such as print shops and service bureaus) who need more control over this conversion use tools such as Adobe Photoshop. To understand why this conversion from RGB into CMYK is needed, we'll have to examine the relationship between reflected light and the subtractive color spectrum.

In order to create a printed version of your document, you'll have to deposit some sort of ink onto the surface of a sheet of paper. This ink actually works as a filter, subtracting out unwanted colors contained in the light source and reflecting only some of these colors. For example, yellow ink on a sheet of paper looks yellow to us because yellow ink filters out the blue content of the light it reflects. This reflected light is made primarily of red and green light, which combine to create the color we see as yellow. These colors that can filter out the additive (RGB) primaries are known as the primary colors of the subtractive spectrum: cyan, magenta, and yellow. As already mentioned, yellow filters out the blue content from the light source, cyan filters out the red light, and magenta filters out the green light. Because using more colors in a subtractive color document results in filtering out more of the reflected light, the image gets darker as color content increases (see Figure 1.14 and Figure C4). This means that the subtractive color (CMY) gamut is smaller than the additive color (RGB)

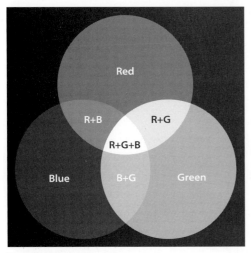

Figure 1.12

Red, green, and blue primaries make up the majority of the visible light spectrum.

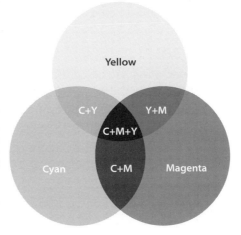

Figure 1.13

Combining the subtractive color primaries produces black ink.

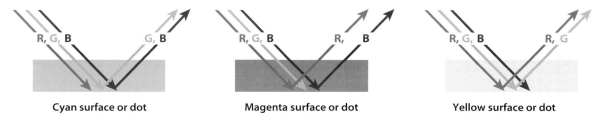

| **Cyan surface or dot** | **Magenta surface or dot** | **Yellow surface or dot** |

Figure 1.14

For each subtractive color used, more light is absorbed and less is reflected.

gamut, so printed images that must depend on reflected light to be seen cannot display the same range of colors as an RGB computer monitor, which is actually a light source.

Theoretically, if you combined all three of the subtractive primaries (C + M + Y), the total effect would be to absorb all the red, green, and blue so that no color could reflect from the sheet. We know this absence of reflected light as the "color" black. In reality, however, black ink is needed to compensate for the less-than-perfect light absorption properties of the inks and toners used in most printing processes. In essence, we use black to extend the tonal range of the printing process and obtain deeper, richer shadows. To distinguish this four-color ink set from the subtractive primary color set, we use the term *process color*. Images in process color mode are also known as four-color process or CMYK mode images; CMYK is an acronym for the names of the four process colors: cyan, magenta, yellow, and black. (The letter K is used to designate black because the B is already in use for the color blue.) Digital images saved in CMYK mode have four channels for each pixel, one for each process color.

Lab Mode

Recently, there has been great interest in another color mode, one that is not specifically tied to either additive or subtractive color: Lab mode. With a gamut that includes every color visible to the human eye, Lab mode is useful for analyzing and editing color images. Very often, RGB mode scanned images are converted to Lab mode for "color correction" processes and then converted again to CMYK for printing. The L in the name of this mode represents *Lightness* (what shade of gray is contained in the color, on the scale between white and black), and the a and b represent coordinates on a color wheel (see Figure 1.15 and Figure C5). See this book's color section for a color version of this graphic.

Figure 1.15

A model of the Lab color space

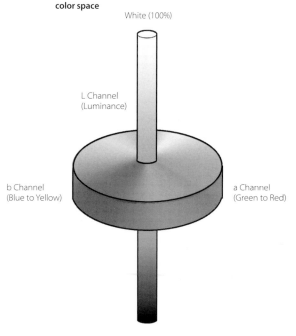

White (100%)

L Channel
(Luminance)

b Channel
(Blue to Yellow)

a Channel
(Green to Red)

Black (0%)

Lab mode is also known as CIELab mode, in reference to its development by the French organization Commission Internationale de l'Éclairage (International Commission on Illumination).

The Lab color wheel is arranged so that yellow is near the top and cyan is near the bottom; the hues (colors) are distributed *perceptually* so that the colors we can perceive the best (such as green and blue) take up the most space, while the colors that are more difficult for us to perceive (such as yellow) occupy less of the wheel. Additionally, colors near the perimeter of the wheel are the most saturated (vivid); moving toward the center of the wheel, the same hue is maintained but increasingly more gray is mixed into the colors, reducing their saturation. This means you can specify a certain color hue at a specific saturation by designating its a and b coordinates and then determine how light or dark that color should be by specifying an L value. For example, the red of a stop sign might be L33, a56, b47, and a light blue sky could be L44, a–8, b–46 (see Figure 1.16).

Look on the CD for a Lab version (`Jaz_Lab_200.tif`) of the Jaz images used in Figure 1.5 earlier in this chapter.

Indexed Color Mode

The Lab color mode is heralded for its capability to describe every color that is perceptible to the human eye, but there are times you might choose to use the very restrictive Indexed Color mode. Describing only a limited range of colors uses less information; as a result, the file size of a particular image can be kept small to allow for fast Internet downloads. This can be especially useful when the image is a simple graphic comprising only a few colors, such as a navigational button or background texture. Indexed Color mode uses only a single channel to contain the color information (instead of three channels as used by RGB mode images or the four channels used for CMYK images); this is possible because the available color choices are held in a specific palette (Figure 1.17), where each numerical value specifies a unique color selection.

There are multiple ways in which the Indexed Color mode palette can be determined; if you use the default System palette, a wide range of colors is available but subtle changes in color will be impossible to render. (System palettes differ between Windows and Macintosh computers, with the Windows palette utilizing more bold graphical colors and the Mac palette featuring more pastel color choices.) The Web palette is even more restrictive because it includes only the 217 colors that can be consistently displayed in all web browsers. For the most accurate rendition of your image, you'll want to choose the Adaptive palette option, as shown in Figure 1.18.

Figure 1.16

Identifying Lab color values

Adapting the colors in the palette to that image's specific range of colors means that every single color in the palette will be used somewhere within that image. Unfortunately, it also means that the description of this unique palette must be stored within the image, increasing the file size and slowing down the speed with which that image can be rendered on the viewer's monitor.

I've provided an Indexed Color version (`Jaz_Index_200.tif`) of the Jaz images used earlier in this chapter.

Figure 1.17

Several variations of Indexed Color palettes

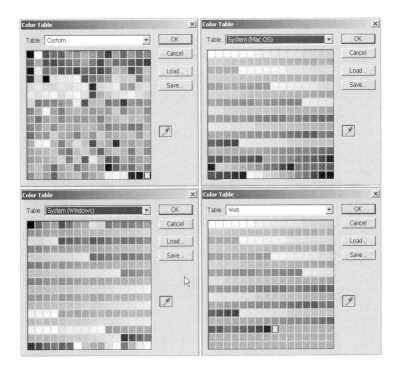

Figure 1.18

These examples show the difference between rendering an image using the Web palette versus an adaptive palette.

File Formats for Print or the Internet

After you've determined the color mode required and made your scan at a specific resolution, you'll need to save your image to your hard drive or a floppy disk. Doing so will require you to choose one of many available *file formats* (see Table 1.3 and Figure 1.19). Although the selection of a file format is not specifically linked to the color mode or resolution of an image, these factors do influence which file format might be the most appropriate for a specific circumstance. You could save the image in Photoshop's native file format (PSD), but it would be more appropriate to use a standard file format (such as EPS, TIFF, JPEG, or PNG) if you plan to use the image in a printed document, on a website, or as an e-mail attachment.

Adobe's Photoshop document file format is designated by the filename extension .psd and is the appropriate choice if you plan on continuing to edit the image. Photoshop files can contain many additional features, some of which are not supported in other file formats (including multiple layers, layer masks, Alpha channels, and multiple paths). A few years ago, you were required to convert Photoshop files into some other format before they would be compatible with any other software programs, but today PSD files can be placed directly into Adobe Illustrator and Adobe InDesign documents.

For use in documents that are destined to print, you'll want to select either the TIFF or EPS file formats. Typically, TIFF is seen as the default choice because its simplicity makes it easy to output or to share between computers running Microsoft's Windows or Apple's Macintosh operating systems. However, TIFF does not support a few specialized functions that are of interest to advanced users, such as duotone reproduction, true clipping paths, or anti-aliasing during PostScript output. To gain use of those specialized functions, you'll want to save your files in the EPS format. Keep in mind, however, that the platform-specific nature of the EPS preview means that these files do not easily move from PC to Mac (or vice versa).

Most of the photographic images traveling across the Internet are embedded in web pages or attached to e-mails using the JPEG format. Although RGB would be the most appropriate mode for displaying a color image on a computer monitor, you can also use the JPEG file format to save CMYK or grayscale mode images. JPEG images feature compression technology that reduces file size, allowing for faster downloading. However, this *lossy* JPEG compression also reduces the quality of the image, reducing the number of colors in use and obscuring detail (especially in the shadow areas of the image). This is why it's perfectly acceptable to convert TIFF or EPS images into JPEGs, but is not a good idea to convert JPEG images into TIFFs or EPS images for print reproduction (see Figure 1.20).

Figure 1.19

Adobe's Photoshop software offers a variety of file format choices.

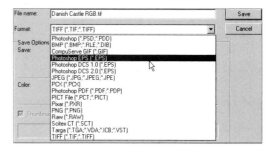

Table 1.3

Image File Formats

FORMAT	ABBREVIATION	FILENAME EXTENSION
Encapsulated PostScript	EPS	.eps
Graphics Interchange Format	GIF	.gif
Joint Photographic Experts Group	JPEG	.jpg
Photoshop	PSD	.psd
Portable Network Graphics	PNG	.png
Tagged Image File Format	TIFF	.tif

Buttons, banner ads, and other web graphics are often saved in the GIF format developed by CompuServe. GIF images typically take up less disk space than JPEGs because they utilize the single-channel Indexed Color mode as well as LZW (Lempel-Ziv-Welch) compression. In addition to faster download times, the GIF file format allows for transparent areas within an image—useful when you want to overlap one graphic on top of another or allow the background color to pop up through a portion of a logo. Unfortunately, the Indexed Color mode required by the GIF format means that only a small range of colors can be used to render your image. This can lead to poor results on complex photographic subjects. As a result, you should never scan an image and save it directly into the GIF file format; instead, save the scan as an

Figure 1.20

Comparison of detail between an uncompressed TIFF and a moderately compressed JPEG

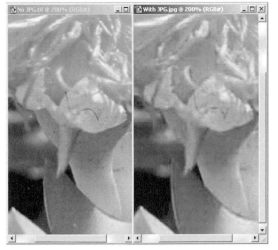

RGB TIFF image first so you can compare the results from selecting a variety of GIF and Indexed Color settings.

PNG is a relatively new file format that is slowly increasing in popularity for web page images. This file format is available as both PNG-8 (offering a maximum of 256 colors) or PNG-24 (which can display a full range of over 16 million colors). The advantages of PNG include the ability to create transparent areas within the image (where the background color of the web page can show through) and its use of a lossless image compression (the image quality is not harmed). However, lossless compression does not reduce the file size as effectively as JPEG's lossy compression, and not all web browser and e-mail reader software programs have been updated for compatibility with the new PNG file format.

CHAPTER 2

Behind the Magic:
How Scanners Work

If you've read through Chapter 1, you've certainly got some idea of what scanners can do; you've already learned about the process of converting an original (a piece of artwork, such as a photograph, slide, or drawing) into a digital computer file. This scanning process is also known as the *digitization* of an original. Knowing more about this process can help you appreciate the capabilities and limitations of your scanner, so let's look more closely at the hardware that can magically capture virtual representations of our physical reality. In this chapter, the following topics are covered:

- **Converting light into digital signals**
- **Common CCD configurations**
- **Understanding your scanner's resolution**

Converting Light into Digital Signals

Just as we experience a photograph or slide through our sense of sight (as opposed to our sense of touch or taste), scanners use white light to examine the originals we digitize. This color-balanced beam of light (composed of equal amounts of red, green, and blue wavelengths) either reflects off the surface of opaque items (such as a color photographic print) or travels through transparent items (such as a 35 mm slide). Once light has bounced off the reflective original or passed through the transparency, a measuring device analyzes the brightness as well as the amount of color contained in the light, as shown in Figure 2.1, and these measurements are captured as digital information. This digital data is then acquired by SilverFast 6 Ai or whatever other software package might be used to operate a particular scanner.

Figure 2.1

Original artwork, whether reflective or transparent, is converted to electrical signals.

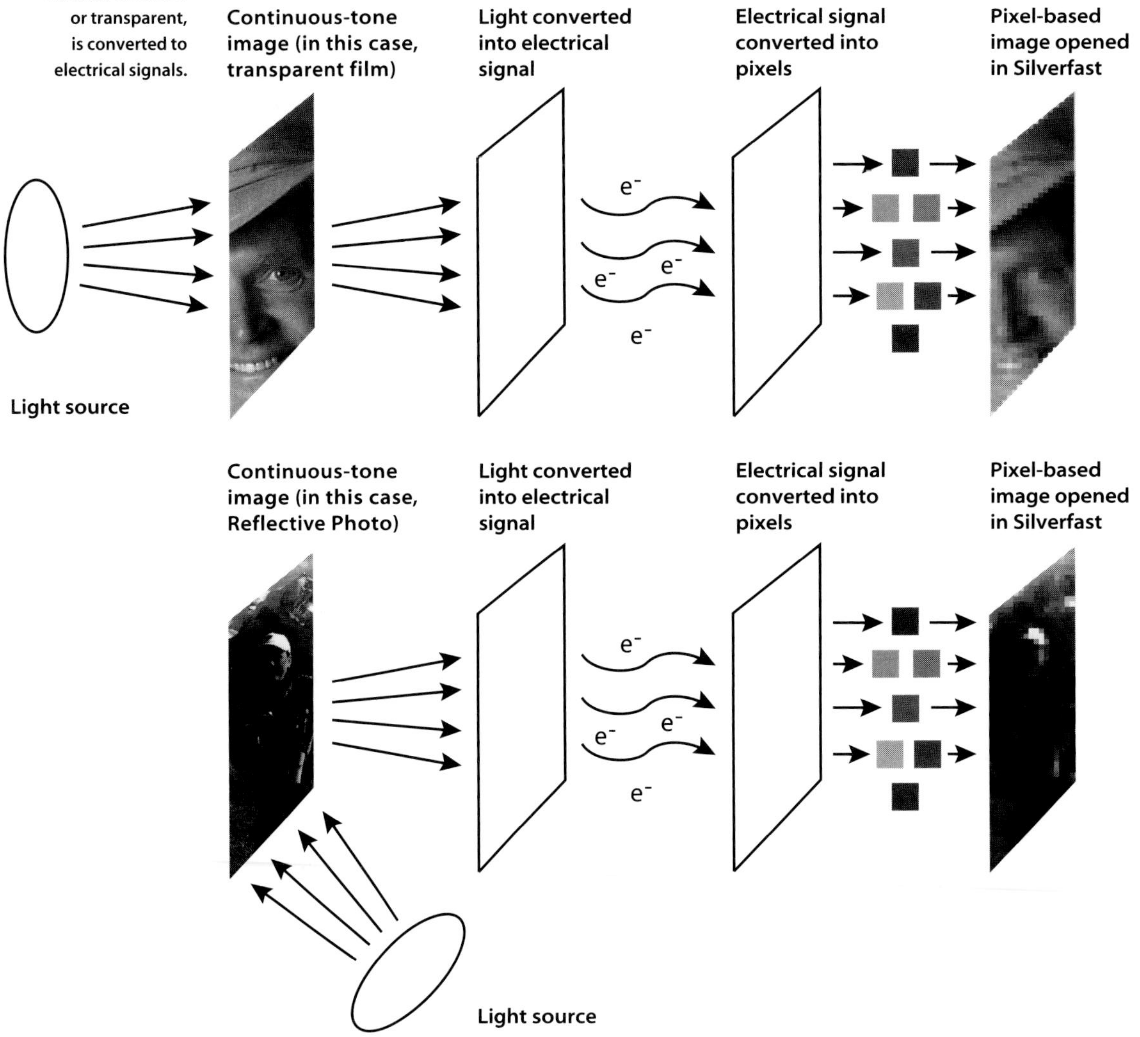

Continuous-tone image (in this case, transparent film)

Light converted into electrical signal

Electrical signal converted into pixels

Pixel-based image opened in Silverfast

Light source

Continuous-tone image (in this case, Reflective Photo)

Light converted into electrical signal

Electrical signal converted into pixels

Pixel-based image opened in Silverfast

Light source

Although this basic premise applies to all scanners, there are many types of scanners available today for a variety of purposes:

Drum	Photo
Flatbed	Sheetfed
Handheld	Book
Slide	Large-format

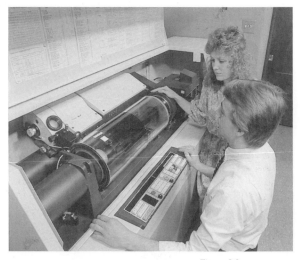

With the exception of the first entry on that list, all of these scanning devices are based on the same technology: the charge coupled device (CCD). However, our list began with *drum scanners* (Figure 2.2); not only were drum scanners the first type of scanner to be sold commercially, they are also the one type of scanner that does not use CCD technology. Instead, drum scanners use an older but highly precise method to analyze light: the photomultiplier tube (PMT).

Figure 2.2

A drum scanner, circa 1980

PMT Scanners

Despite rapid advances in CCD quality over the last decade, drum scanners and their PMT technology are still superior to CCDs in terms of both color quality and resolution. PMT scans are capable of capturing the most faithful rendition of the original artwork's colors, which can be very important for items with a wide gamut (especially slides or artwork that might contain fluorescent pigments, such as oil paintings). Capturing sharp details is also a strength for PMT scanners because their design makes it easy to capture a high-resolution image.

PMT scanners are more commonly known as drum scanners because the artwork is mounted to a glass drum (shaped like a tube, with both ends open) with strips of clear tape. Although the original models held these drums horizontally, newer models (such as the Heidelberg Tango, shown in Figure 2.3) are more likely to hold the drum in a vertical position to minimize the scanner's floor space requirements.

After the original is mounted and the drum is placed onto the scanner, the drum begins to rotate at high speed. The drum scanning process begins when a single, tightly focused beam of white light shines through the transparency, passes through the optics (focusing lenses), and then enters the vacuum tube containing the photomultiplier (see Figure 2.4). In the case of a reflective original, the light source is moved to the other side of the drum. As the scanning process continues, the light source and PMT move in tandem down the length of the tube to examine the entire original.

The small beam of light entering the photomultiplier tube has already passed through or reflected off of the artwork, so the formerly balanced white light is now a beam of colored

light due to the effect of the dyes embedded in the slide, photograph, or painting taped to the drum. Next, this single beam of colored light is split (multiplied) into three beams by a series of mirrors. Each beam passes through a red, green, or blue filter and the qualities of each beam are measured by a highly responsive phosphor sensor; these measurements are then converted into digital information by a sophisticated color computer. The result is a true spectrophotometric analysis of the slide's color content, measuring not just the strength of the red, green, or blue light but the specific spectral wavelengths as well. In addition, the PMT is capable of sensing very minute differences in the relative brightness of areas within the image; this is described as the drum scanner's capability to capture a wide *dynamic range*.

As the scanning process continues, this spectral information is captured thousands of times per second. Each burst of information captured by the PMT becomes one pixel in the resulting digital file; the rapid-fire pace of this data capture as well as the small size of the light beam allow the drum scanner to operate at an extremely high resolution—even the least expensive drum scanners are capable of capturing 2400 pixels per inch, with some models able to scan at 24000 ppi or more!

Figure 2.3

Heidelberg's Tango is an example of a modern vertical drum scanner.

CCD Scanners

Although PMT scanners may win hands down in the competition for quality, CCD scanners have the advantage where it really counts for most consumers: they are more convenient than drum scanners and are far less expensive. Drum scanners range in price from $24,000 to more than $100,000, whereas flatbed scanners can be found for as little as $99 or bundled for free with new computer purchases. In the late 1980s, flatbed scanners (see Figure 2.5) were seen as only suitable for high-contrast image capture, such as reading bar codes or digitizing line drawings. Today, technological and manufacturing improvements allow even inexpensive flatbed scanners to produce excellent results.

Figure 2.4

The components of a PMT scanning system

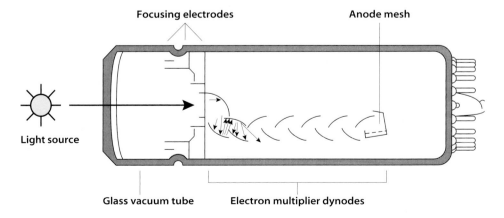

Focusing electrodes   Anode mesh

Light source

Glass vacuum tube   Electron multiplier dynodes

Figure 2.5

A flatbed scanner, circa 1990

Flatbed scanners are the most widely distributed embodiment of CCD technology, but nearly everything else in use today for capturing images is also a CCD scanner. Slide scanners, the input mechanism on your fax machine, even the supermarket's checkout sensor that reads the bar code on your ice cream carton all utilize a charged coupled device. CCDs (Figure 2.6) are actually light-sensitive integrated circuits built on silicon chips. Rectangular two-dimensional (2D) CCDs are commonly used in digital cameras, but most scanners use a long, thin one-dimensional (1D) chip featuring thousands of light receptors arranged in a single row. This chip is accompanied by a long, thin light source that illuminates the artwork being scanned. Inexpensive scanners use a simple fluorescent tube, while more sophisticated devices employ red, green, and blue LEDs (light emitting diodes) that provide a more consistently balanced white light.

Each light-sensitive point on a CCD chip is called a photosite, and light falling on that photosite produces an electrical charge. Compared to the analytic capabilities of the PMT tube, CCD chips are relatively unsophisticated—the more light striking the photosite, the greater the voltage of the electrical charge produced. These electrical impulses are sent to an analog-to-digital convertor (ADC) that converts the charges into digital pixel values. This process is also less sensitive to tiny changes in brightness within the scanned image, so the dynamic range of CCD scanners is less than that of PMT drum scanners. Capturing detail is also an area in which CCDs are inferior to PMTs—while PMT scanners can simply focus the beam of light down to a smaller spot to reveal more detail, it's the physical size of the individual photosites on a CCD chip that determines the resolution of the CCD scanner. Smaller photosites allow more pixels to be captured within a single inch of space; increasing the resolution of the scanned image but packing more photosites into each inch increases the manufacturing challenges exponentially.

Common CCD Configurations

Let's examine the physical configuration of a typical CCD flatbed scanner. Flatbed scanners are named after the large, flat sheet of glass that provides a "bed" upon which the artwork is placed for scanning. The photographs to be scanned go face down on the glass because the light source and CCD chip will pass underneath, traveling from one end of the glass to the other. A fluorescent tube is likely to be the source of illumination during the scanning process; this tube is located parallel to the CCD chip. Light captured by the CCD is converted through an ADC (analog-to-digital converter) to create the scanned pixel-based image. All components, the light source, the CCD, and the ADC are located on a moveable carriage that will smoothly transport them across the length of the scanner. Inexpensive flatbed scanners move this carriage through the use of pulleys and a toothed drive belt, while more expensive models employ electronic servos (Figure 2.7). Typically this is accomplished in one pass of the scan bed.

To capture "color" information during the scanning process, our low-cost device uses filters to separate light into Red, Green and Blue channels.

Mid-range scanners retailing for less than $1000 may feature a CCD chip with dyed photosites, with individual elements on the chip permanently filtered red, green, or blue. Graphic arts companies and other buyers willing to pay premium prices have yet another type of

Figure 2.6

Scanner interior

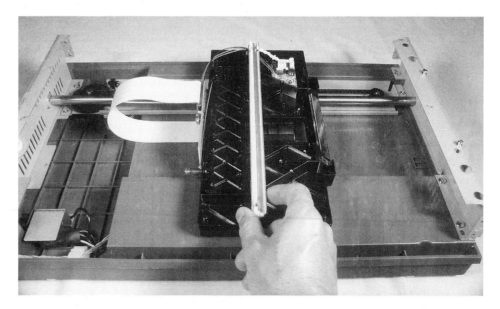

color scanner to choose from: the tri-linear array. In this configuration, three 1D CCD chips are arranged in absolutely parallel position, with each chip devoted to capturing a single color. Technical specifications for tri-linear scanners often list the scanner's resolution with a number 3 followed by the resolution of an individual chip in the array, such as 3×8000. In this way, each color channel in the RGB image uses the full resolution of one chip in the CCD array. Although the cost of tri-linear array scanners was initially very high, improvements in CCD manufacturing processes have reduced the costs of these chips so that tri-linear scanners are now much more affordable.

Understanding Your Scanner's Resolution

We've already touched upon the idea that CCD chips contain tiny light-sensitive surfaces called photosites and that the number of photosites that have been built into each inch of your CCD chip determines your scanner's resolution. As the technology used by CCD manufacturers improves, they are able to make each photosite smaller. As a result, entry-level flatbed scanners have jumped in resolution over the last few years—whereas 300 ppi scanners were once the norm, 1200 ppi devices can now be had for just over $100. Even though scan resolutions are improving, however, it's still important to understand the difference between optical and interpolated resolution, as well as how these figures can be impacted by manufacturing constraints.

Interpolated vs. Optical Resolution

When a manufacturer lists the *optical resolution* of a particular scanner, it is displaying a measure of the true resolution that device is capable of capturing. If only a single number is shown (such as "1200 ppi optical resolution"), it indicates that the scanner captures the same number of pixels per inch in the x-axis direction (across the CCD chip) as it does in the y-axis (the direction of paper or scanner carriage travel). When the statistic is presented as a pair of numbers (such as "optical resolution of 1200×2400 ppi"), the scanner's ADC circuitry will capture data at a rate double the distance between photosites. Although this is a good thing, there's one catch: all bitmap images are required to have *square* pixels! This means you'll have to choose between two options: reducing the y-axis sampling frequency to a rate that matches the photosite spacing (in the case of this example, 1200×1200 ppi), or you can choose to allow the scanner's internal circuitry to interpolate the x-axis resolution up to match the maximum y-axis resolution (2400×2400 ppi in our current example).

Figure 2.7

The components of a flatbed CCD scanner

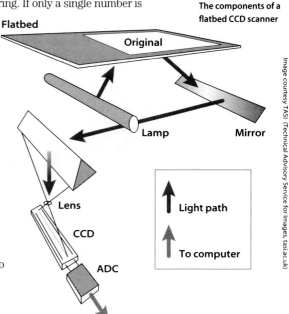

Image courtesy TASI (Technical Advisory Service for Images, tasi.ac.uk)

Interpolation is a process by which a bitmap/pixel-based image containing a specific number of pixels can be changed to incorporate a greater (or smaller) number of pixels while still portraying the same content.

Images can be interpolated upward to increase the total number of pixels; conversely, you might take a scan that was scanned at a resolution appropriate for print reproduction (such as 300 ppi) and interpolate it down to 96 ppi for use on a web page. Another use for interpolation would be to resize an image that was 4 inches wide at 300 ppi so that it would be able to fill a space 8 inches wide yet still maintain a 300 ppi resolution; without interpolation, the resolution would fall to 150 ppi (see Figure 2.8).

The interpolation process creates these new pixels using values that are midway between the existing pixels, which has an effect of smoothing out the image. Unfortunately, this effect is the opposite of what most people have in mind when they think of increasing an image's resolution: they expect that *more pixels* will equal *more detail.* However, because detail in a bitmap image is the result of two very different pixels appearing side by side, the smoothing effect of interpolation may be a disappointment.

So, back to our 1200×2400 ppi example—what to do? In this case, choosing 2400×2400 ppi scanning resolution means that the pixels across the x-axis are interpolated up to match the higher y-axis sample rate. This will allow you to maintain all the detail captured by the CCD as it progresses across the glass, but don't get too excited—because the photosites are only 1/1200′ apart, they can't really resolve detail at a rate of 2400 ppi. As a result, most users would be best served to select 1200×1200 ppi (especially because the 2400×2400 ppi selection would take up four times as much hard drive space).

Now that even bargain-priced CCD scanners sport surprisingly high optical resolution numbers, it's becoming increasingly rare to see a rating for "maximum resolution (interpolated)" in advertisements or technical specification sheets. Just in case you do see such a figure, however, you'll now be armed with the knowledge that these interpolated figures are worthless—after a little bit of software magic, even a fax machine with an optical resolution of 150 ppi could claim 2400 ppi interpolated resolution! Under most circumstances, the interpolated bitmap image would not produce visual results that are any better than the original, uninterpolated pixels presented at the scanner's actual optical resolution. Many manufacturers will list two resolution values, such as 2400×4800. The first, and lower, number should be treated as the true optical or hardware resolution. Later in this book when we will discuss the importance of using the optical resolution when scanning, the lower number, noninterpolated, optical resolution will be the value you should use, rather than the higher (wishful thinking) number.

Figure 2.8

This image was scanned at 300 ppi and then enlarged 400 percent. The close-ups show the resulting image (a) without inter-polation and (b) inter-polated to maintain 300 ppi resolution.

(a)

(b)

The Sweet Spot

There's one more important bit of information to consider when examining the issue of flatbed scanner resolution: the *sweet spot.* Due to the cost and difficulty of manufacturing long CCDs, some inexpensive (and even some moderately priced) scanners contain chips that are not long enough to cover the width of the bed at the rated optical resolution. These devices employ a zoom lens to "zoom back" whenever the entire width of the glass is selected for scanning. As a result, you might scan small photos in the middle of your scanner and obtain the full optical resolution, whereas larger artwork or items placed near the edge of the glass cause the zoom lens to come into play, reducing the resolution (often by as much as 20 percent). That is why it's best to stay in the sweet spot—always place your artwork in the center of the scanner's x-axis (the short direction across the glass).

CHAPTER 3

Up and Running with SilverFast: Quick Start

Perhaps you've just purchased a new scanner that included SilverFast Ai or SE as part of the bundled software, or maybe you've sought out SilverFast Ai because you're unhappy with the capabilities of your current scanning software—whatever the reason, you're about to start using a feature-packed application that makes high-quality desktop scanning a breeze!

SilverFast Ai is a software application that works during the image acquisition (scanning) process, so before we begin, you should make certain that you've got a functioning scanner attached to your computer. If you are currently experiencing hardware or software driver problems that prevent your scanner from working with the software application provided by the manufacturer, your scanner will likely be unable to work under SilverFast. Is your scanner ready to go? Great, let's keep going! Here's what we'll be covering in this hands-on chapter:

- **Checking the system requirements**
- **Verifying Your SilverFast version**
- **Arranging your workspace**
- **Setting up the Scan Control window**
- **Acquiring and saving your first image**
- **Finding even more advanced help**

Checking the System Requirements

Both Apple Macintosh and Windows PC users can enjoy the benefits of SilverFast, but you'll need to make sure your computer meets specific minimum system requirements before installing.

Windows system requirements SilverFast can run on Windows 98, NT4, Me, 2000, and XP. Your computer should also have a minimum of 64 MB of RAM; 128 MB is recommended (minimum RAM requirement for Windows NT4 is 48 MB). You should also have at least 30 MB of available hard drive space in which to install the software.

Apple Macintosh system requirements SilverFast can run on Mac OS 8.6 or later for all compatible scanners (although a 9.0 is recommended). At this point, many (but not all) scanners are also supported under OS X; please check the SilverFast website (www.silverfast.com) for a list of available OS X versions. Classic mode (running OS 9.2 on top of the OS X operating system) is not recommended.

Your computer should also have enough RAM to increase Photoshop's default RAM allocation by at least 10 MB. Only Macintosh computers with PowerPC processors can run SilverFast 6 (68k Macs are not supported). A good rule of thumb is to add three times the size of the scan file you intend to create onto the RAM requirements for the version of Photoshop that you will be using along with SilverFast. This, of course, would be added to the RAM requirements for your operating system. Following would be a typical RAM requirements calculation: OS RAM = 100MB, Photoshop = 64MB, 3 × scan file size (30MB × 3 = 90MB) = Total (100MB + 64MB + 90MB = 254MB RAM). This would be a good minimum amount of RAM to have installed on your scanning computer.

Linux SilverFast cannot run on Linux or other Unix variations.

The ultimate in performance is only possible when enough RAM is available for both SilverFast and the host imaging application (such as Photoshop). Professional users will want to allocate an amount of RAM equivalent to three times the file size of the image being worked on (a 100 MB TIFF would require 300 MB of RAM memory for optimal performance). Don't worry, you can get by with a lot less—you'll just run a little bit slower because Photoshop and SilverFast swap data to and from your hard drive (which is much slower than accessing this data from RAM).

Whether your computer is a PC or a Mac, you'll also need some form of cabling to connect your scanner. SilverFast works with the three most common types of scanner cables: Small Computer System Interface (SCSI), Universal Serial Bus (USB), and FireWire (also known as IEEE 1394).

Some scanners offer a choice of more than one type of connection (such as USB and FireWire), but the version of SilverFast available for your scanner may not be compatible with both of these cabling options. Please verify that your chosen connection method is compatible with SilverFast by checking the Support section of the SilverFast website:

```
http://www.silverfast.com/show/support/en.html
```

The most problematic connection issues involve FireWire support under Windows XP and Mac OS X. If the software supplied by your scanner's manufacturer cannot communicate with your scanner via FireWire, it is also unlikely that SilverFast will be able to establish a FireWire connection.

> Unless otherwise specifically stated in the SilverFast documentation, software supplied by your scanner manufacturer should be installed before you load SilverFast so that all required SCSI, USB, or FireWire drivers are already in place.

There's one more very important requirement you'll need to satisfy before you can install and use SilverFast Ai or SE: you must have already installed an imaging application that can host the SilverFast plug-in. Typically, most users will operate SilverFast as a scanning plug-in for some form of Adobe's ubiquitous Photoshop image editor. Photoshop, Photoshop LE, and Photoshop Elements utilize SilverFast through a Photoshop plug-in in the Import/Export subdirectory, and Adobe PhotoDeluxe users can access SilverFast through a TWAIN module (see the SilverFast installer program for more details).

Verifying Your SilverFast Version

If your SilverFast software came bundled with a new scanner, you'll find a CD-ROM and a manual. The CD-ROM will be marked with a *version number* on the label to indicate which SilverFast application you've received:

SilverFast Ai	The full-featured version, individually customized for a specific model of digital scanners
SilverFast SE	The "lite" version (can be upgraded to Ai)
SilverFast HDR	The stand-alone version of Ai for opening and editing images already saved to disk at color depths up to 48 bits
SilverFast DC	A reduced-price version of HDR that can open only 24-bit images, such as those produced by many consumer level digital cameras
SilverFast PhotoCD	A specialized version of HDR for use with Kodak PhotoCD images
SilverFast DC-PRO	A version of SilverFast that supports the native file formats created by professional-level digital cameras

Applications downloaded from the SilverFast website will be in the form of a compressed archive, which will produce an installer that installs the software listed above as plug-ins for Photoshop and installs the stand-alone versions, as well as a Portable Document Format (PDF) electronic version of the manual.

If you're a SilverFast Ai user, you'll also want to verify that you have the software version specifically developed for your scanner. The scanner model will be noted on the back of the envelope that holds your CD; downloaded software will feature a truncated version of the scanner model number in the name of the compressed archive. Don't try to use SilverFast Ai or SE unless you've obtained the software version that exactly matches your scanner model! SilverFast HDR, DC, and PhotoCD are meant to work with images that have already been saved to disk, so there is only one current version of these programs for each platform (Windows or Macintosh).

Depending on the model of scanner you've purchased, you may also have received several IT8 color management calibration targets; these will be either slides or photographic prints featuring hundreds of small colored squares. If you've downloaded the software, you may order the IT8 targets separately from the SilverFast website. I'll discuss the use of these targets in chapters 5 and 11.

Because SilverFast Ai (and SE) works as a plug-in for an imaging application, you'll also need to have the imaging application installed and configure SilverFast to know where the application's plug-ins folder resides. The majority of people reading this book will be using SilverFast as a scanning plug-in for Adobe Photoshop, Photoshop LE, or Photoshop Elements, so in future references to this scenario, I will talk about "scanning from Photoshop." In addition, all future references to SilverFast software will be to SilverFast Ai unless otherwise noted. (I examine SilverFast HDR, DC, and PhotoCD in Chapter 12; SilverFast SE is so similar to Ai that it isn't covered separately in this book.)

Install and register the software according to the directions found in the SilverFast manual or the `SilverFast_Guide.pdf`. If you encounter difficulty installing or registering the application, consult the Support section of the SilverFast website for further information on technical support options. Once the installation process has been completed, make sure your scanner is connected and powered on; then launch Photoshop. From Photoshop's File menu, choose Import → SilverFast. Complete the registration screen that appears to begin using your SilverFast software.

Make sure to leave your SilverFast CD-ROM in your computer's CD drive bay until the registration process has been completed.

Arranging Your Workspace

What happened to Photoshop? The first time the SilverFast interface appears (Figure 3.1), you may be quite startled—it seems to take over your screen because its multiple windows will largely obscure your view of the image editing program that you had been using only seconds ago. Don't worry; over time, you'll become familiar with every window, button, and menu of this feature-rich application.

When ScanPilot is selected, a small Help Text window pops up to the right of the currently selected tool (such as "Using the Prescan, your images will be quickly shown on the screen"). These Help Text pop-up windows will always appear unless you turn them off (click the Prefs button near the bottom of the ScanPilot, then deselect Help Texts). If you've rearranged your workspace according to the layout in Figure 3.1, however, you'll be able to hide the Help Text window simply by clicking the title bar of the Scan Control window. To make the Help Text reappear, just select the ScanPilot.

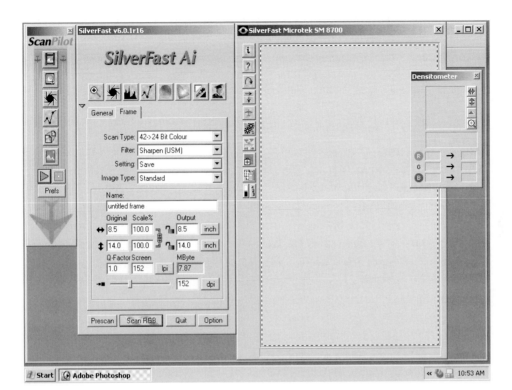

Figure 3.1

**A convenient arrange-
ment of the SilverFast
windows**

Depending on the size and resolution of your monitor, the arrangement of these windows
and dialog boxes (the *workspace*) that you see may be different from the arrangement shown
in the figure. For the greatest ease of use and the maximum resemblance to the familiar
Photoshop workspace, I recommend that you rearrange your windows (resize them and drag
them around by their title bars) until they appear as shown in the figure.

From left to right, let's examine the major components of the SilverFast interface:

ScanPilot window	Presents the major SilverFast tools in the proper sequence for most scanning jobs; allows those functions to automatically be performed in sequence
Scan Control window	"Displays the fields in which you'll input the most commonly used settings, such as scan resolution and enlargement percentage
Prescan window	Shows you what is currently on the glass of the scanner after the Prescan button is clicked
Densitometer window	Displays a measurement of the color values for a specific spot within an image

If your monitor is small or you just want to reduce clutter, you can click the close box in
the upper-right corner of the Densitometer window. Closing this window doesn't eliminate the
densitometer; it just "docks" that window to become another tab in the Scan Control window.
If a circumstance arises that makes you wish the densitometer had its own window again,
just click the Floating button (see Figure 3.2). I'll cover the densitometer in more detail in
Chapter 5.

Now that you've arranged your workspace to your liking, exit the SilverFast program by either clicking the Quit button at the bottom of the Scan Control window or clicking the close box in the upper-right corner of the Scan Control window. This will preserve your workspace in the SilverFast application preferences so that the same arrangement will appear every time you launch SilverFast.

Setting Up the Scan Control Window

Because SilverFast functions as a plug-in for Photoshop, you won't find the commands for opening and saving files located in a menu bar across the top of the screen. Instead, these basic operations and many more can be found in the General tab and the Frame tab within the Scan Control window. In addition, you'll also find the Prescan, Scan, and Quit buttons located across the very bottom of the Scan Control window. (Windows users will also find the Option button in this row, while Macintosh users will find the Option button on the General tab.)

The General Tab

The items on the General tab (Figure 3.3) consist of basic information that pertains not only to your current scan, but also to the scans you'll be making in the future and even some data about your past scans. For some of the settings, I will recommend specific choices, and for others I will only explain the choices, thereby allowing you to either make your own choices or use the default values.

The following items are on the General tab:

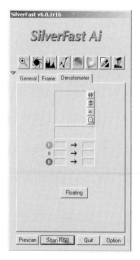

Figure 3.2

Docking the densitometer turns it into a third tab on the Scan Control window.

Device Your scanner name will show up in this list. If you have multiple scanning devices connect to your system, you can choose the scanner you would like to use at this time.

Scan Mode The options here are Normal, Batch Mode, Normal (File), and Batch Mode (File). These options determine whether SilverFast will execute a single scan and then stop (Normal) or acquire every image for which a scan marquee has been created (Batch Mode). Choosing the File variation on these themes means that SilverFast will automatically save the scanned image to disk. This is especially advantageous for batch mode scanning because it precludes the need for an excessive amount of RAM to hold the multiple scans. For your first scan, choose Normal.

Original Here you choose whether the original image you will be scanning is either a reflective or a transparency (positive or negative film).

Pos./Neg. Choose the option that matches the original artwork you're scanning. If Negative is selected, a secondary menu will appear in which you can specify the parameters for the negative. (Chapter 11 covers the scanning of both color and black-and-white negatives.)

Frame-Set This is one of several dialog boxes you'll encounter in SilverFast that allows you to save your chosen parameters for later recall. I'll cover this in more detail in Chapter 10.

The Frame Tab Basics

The General tab contains choices you'll seldom need to alter, but the Frame tab (Figure 3.4) provides quick access to the most important specifications of the scanning process. Because of this important status, the Frame tab is automatically selected every time you launch SilverFast.

Because your version of SilverFast has been customized to reflect the specific hardware capabilities of your scanner, there may be minor differences between the SilverFast interface as depicted in this book and the display that you see on your monitor.

Let's review the critical items found within this portion of the Scan Control window:

Scan Type Choices are 42 -> 24 Bit Color, 24 bit Color, 14 -> 8 Bit Grayscale, 8 Bit Grayscale, 48 Bit HDR Color, and 48 Bit Color. For now, assume that you'll be scanning a color photo and choose 42 -> 24 Bit Color. More details on the various scan types will be discussed in Chapter 4.

Filter These are fine-tuning filters covered more completely in Chapter 8. For now, select Sharpen for a sharp first image.

Setting As with the Frame-Set menu on the General tab, you can use the Setting menu to save all your chosen settings on the Frame tab for easy recall at a later time.

Image Type SilverFast provides preset image corrections in this setting. Select Standard for your first scan (see Figure 3.5).

The bottom half of the Frame tab, shown in Figure 3.6, has specific information relevant to the scan you're working on. Using this portion of the SilverFast interface, you can define the name of the file you're about to scan, note the displayed size of your current prescan marquee, set the amount of enlargement or

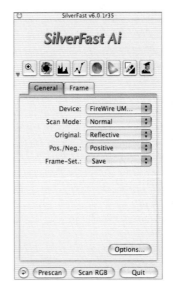

Figure 3.3

The General tab of the Scan Control window

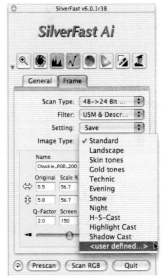

Figure 3.4

The Frame tab of the Scan Control window

Figure 3.5

The Image Type menu

reduction you'd like to use for the current prescan, and determine the resolution of the final hi-res scan.

Let's go through the settings that access these essential bits of information:

Figure 3.6

Close-up of the Frame tab

Effective scan resolution

Name	Enter the name you'd like to apply when this image is saved to disk.
Original	The size of the image defined by your image selection is shown here.
Scale %	Default scale is set to 100%, which is a good choice for your first scan.
Output	Reflects the results of Original × Scale. Leave this at the default for now.
Q-Factor	Quality factor. Leave this set to the default value of 1.0.
Screen	Control of scan resolution via Line Screen values. Ignore this for your first scan.
lpi/lpcm	Clicking this button toggles the display back and forth between lines per inch and lines per centimeter.
MByte	Displays the file size (measured in megabytes) of the scan you're about to make here.
dpi (effective scan resolution)	This data window shows the effective scan resolution. Clicking the button toggles between dots per inch and dots per centimeter. See Chapter 4 for a discussion or the relationship between Q-Factor, scan resolution, and lpi/lpcm. For now just set this value at 300.
Untitled slider (effective scan resolution)	Resolution slider for those who love sliders! Dragging the button on this slider to the left decreases the scan resolution, and dragging it to the right increases the resolution.

Acquiring and Saving Your First Image

OK, that magical time is finally here! You have specified your basic desired settings in the General and Frame tabs of the Scan Control window.

> For the most control over your scanner and SilverFast, set your Option defaults first (see Chapter 4), especially if your goal is to make scans for print reproduction (as opposed to websites and e-mail attachments). These choices will be applied when the scanned image is automatically enhanced and adjusted by SilverFast.

Here's what to do next:

1. Clean the scanner glass and image (see Chapter 4 for more details).

2. Position your (color photo) original. Stay in the "sweet spot" to maximize your scanner's optical resolution, even if this means rotating the artwork 90 degrees (see Chapter 2 for more details on the "sweet spot").

3. Select the image mode you'd like to capture from your scan. The Image Mode setting is found at the top of the Frame tab in the Scan Control window. For scanning color prints or slides, you'll typically want to choose 42 -> 24 Bit Color (or whatever similar option is available).

4. Click the Prescan button to generate an updated view of the full scanner glass in the Prescan window.

5. Adjust the size of the marquee (scan frame) in the Prescan window to avoid high-resolution scanning of unwanted information. This can be accomplished by dragging on the sides or corners of the existing marquee or by inputting numerical values for the horizontal and vertical original size. Once the initial marquee has been set, you can draw additional scan frames by clicking and dragging on the Prescan window. (This is only possible if you begin outside the current scan frame, so the original full-window marquee must be reduced in size before multiple scan frames can be set up.)

6. Click the Camera Shutter icon to apply the current Auto Option defaults.

7. Adjust the results of the Image Auto-Adjust by tweaking the histogram, gradation, and color balance controls. (These controls will be thoroughly covered in our next chapter.)

8. Click the Scan button at the bottom of the Scan Control window to capture the high-resolution scan! Once the scanning process begins, the SilverFast interface will disappear, replaced by a progress bar that indicates the amount of image acquired. Once the scan area has been processed, the progress bar will be gone and the image will open in Photoshop.

So far we have concentrated on what to do. Here are some tips on some pitfalls to avoid. Some of these stress some of the to-do items we have already discussed, but they are worth emphasizing:

• Don't forget to clean your images and your scanner before you begin!

• Don't forget to click the Camera Shutter icon to apply your own customized set of Option defaults.

• If you forget to set your options, don't worry! SilverFast will automatically use its own default set of parameters for the auto-adjustment process—*as long as you click the Shutter icon!*

• Don't scan at too low of a resolution, especially if you plan to print out enlarged copies of an image or take the scan to a print shop. (How to best prepare color scans for the print shop is covered in Chapter 11.)

• Don't place your original in the corner or too close to the sides of the scanner's glass, if you can avoid it (see Chapter 2).

• To avoid burning out the image highlights or plugging up the shadow detail, don't set your highlight offset or your shadow offset to their maximum values (Chapter 4).

• Don't scan at 24-bit RGB mode if your scanner's hardware has an option to scan at a higher color depth and then interpolate down to 24 bits (see the section "The Frame Tab Basics" earlier in this chapter).

Finding Even More Help

Although I have tried to provide a comprehensive guide to using SilverFast, there are inevitably some topics about which you might want more information. In addition, LaserSoft (the maker of SilverFast) is constantly providing upgrades and improvements that you will want to be aware of. So here are some resources you can utilize to obtain more and updated information.

SilverFast includes a question mark icon along the left edge of the Prescan window; clicking this icon will launch the SilverFast Quick Start Guide (`SilverFast Guide.pdf`) in Acrobat Reader. If that document doesn't bring clarity, you might want to consult the lengthy printed manual that came with your software, or download that same manual in PDF format from the SilverFast website. Also, here's where you can find LaserSoft support:

`http://www.silverfast.com/show/support/en.html`

If your question is not specifically concerned with SilverFast but is instead of a more general nature, consider investigating the many resources available on the Internet, including Design Tools Monthly (`www.design-tools.com`) and the Graphic Arts Information Network (`www.gain.org`). Another powerful but often-overlooked option is to enter your topic of concern into an Internet search engine such as Google (`www.google.com`) or Ask Jeeves (`www.ask.com`).

As a final resort, live help is available by calling LaserSoft Imaging at 900-443-4036. Be aware, however, that there is a per-minute charge for this call.

At this point, you should be comfortable with the location and basic operation of SilverFast's Option defaults as well the choices available on the Scan Control window. Now that you're able to start scanning your favorite subjects, the next chapter will focus on how a little more effort spent on the prescan stage of this process can pay handsome dividends.

CHAPTER 4

Automatic Scanning: Working with the Prescan Image

In this chapter, I cover the correct way to set up a scan so that SilverFast does most of the work. "Automatic scanning" is actually somewhat of a misnomer. Using SilverFast's automatic scanning functions involves more than just slapping an image down on your scanner, pushing an "auto" button, and hoping for the best. In order to achieve the results we expect, we must first control the process by carefully configuring the automatic scanning tools. I'll take you through this step-by-step.

In SilverFast, one important key to automatic scanning success is controlling what happens when we activate the auto-adjustment tool, so much of this chapter is devoted to digging into and configuring the options that control this tool. We will also cover, in specific detail, many of the controls such as the General and Frame tabs in the SilverFast Scan Control window, which were introduced in Chapter 3.

The actual scanning process is usually performed in two steps: an initial low-resolution prescan and a second final scan. Adjusting the prescan is critical to creating the best quality scan images. However, before initiating any scan, it's important to first prepare your scanner and images and calibrate your scanner so that your images will be clean and you will achieve consistent results.

The following topics are covered in this chapter:

- Scanner and image preparation
- Calibrating
- Working with the prescan: auto adjustments
- Completing the scan

Scanner and Image Preparation

Before we begin the scanning process, we need to be sure to prepare—and especially clean—the scanner and the image.

Although few of us can afford to perform our scans in the completely dust-free environment of a professional scanning shop, we can and should take reasonable precautions to reduce the amount of dirt and dust in and around our scanners. And any dust or dirt on your image is magnified and enhanced during the image scaling and sharpening process, and at the very least, that will require extra time cleaning up the images after you capture them.

Here are some tips for preparing your scanner and images:

- Place the scanner away from doors and windows. High-traffic areas tend to have lots of dust.

- If the scanner surfaces appear very dirty with lots of visible dust, take a pass over the glass surfaces with a fine hair graphics brush to get rid of the big pieces first.

- Clean your scanner surfaces. Use a lint-free cloth (silk is good) and glass cleaning solution. If you have a flatbed scanner, be sure to clean *both* surfaces, the top and the bottom! Don't spray the cleaning solution directly on the scanner; spray it on the lint-free cloth and then wipe the cloth over the surfaces. If the *underside* of the glass gets dirty, consult your owner's manual or call your scanner manufacturer's technical support hotline to learn how to clean the bottom of the glass.

- Use moisture-free canned air to clean your images.

- Handle your images with cotton gloves instead of bare hands to help prevent skin oils from transferring to the image and attracting dust.

Calibrating

Although *calibration* is one of those big, complicated-sounding words, it is actually an easy concept to understand and implement if you have the proper tools. The goal of calibration is to adjust your scanner so that it performs the same way all the time. Unfortunately, scanners, digital cameras, monitors, and printers vary from device to device and from day to day in terms of how they perform. The result of this variation is inconsistent and unpredictable images. When properly calibrated, your scanner will provide consistent and predicable results.

> If you are interested in achieving the most consistent and predictable results from your scanner, read and use this section. If you are eager to perform a scan now, you may move directly to the later section, "Performing the Prescan."

CALIBRATING MANUALLY

If your version of SilverFast did not arrive with an IT8 target and automatic evaluation and scanner-adjustment software, don't fret; you have some options. You could of course upgrade your SilverFast software to a version that does include the IT8 target and complete calibration and profiling software. You can also achieve basic calibration results performing a manual calibration. For a complete discussion and step-by-step instructions on how to perform a manual calibration using a 10-Step grayscale target, see Appendix A on the CD-ROM included with this book.

Calibration is a three-step process. Step one involves scanning a target that contains areas, known as swatches, that have known values. Step two compares the values that the scanner "sees," or captures, for these swatches with the known values. This evaluation process can be done automatically or manually, depending upon your version of SilverFast. Step three involves adjusting the scanner for any differences between what the scanner captured and the values of the swatches. Once again, the calibration adjustment of the scanner can be performed either automatically or manually depending upon your version of SilverFast.

Automatic Calibration with an IT8 Target

If your version of SilverFast arrived with a multicolored target known as an IT8 target (like the one shown in Figure 4.1; *IT* stands for *international test*), then you have what's required for calibrating your scanner. This IT8 target is a proven industry-standard target that is used for calibration of many scanners and digital cameras. (A color version of this target labeled C7 can be found in the color section.)

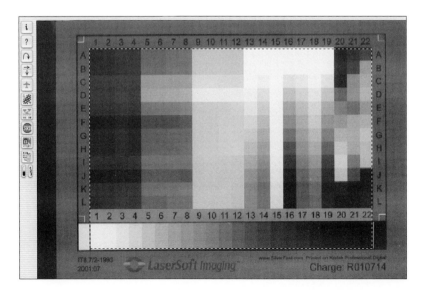

Figure 4.1

An IT8 calibration target is used to achieve consistent and predictable results from your scanner. Note the carefully placed selection area around the swatches, which is used to perform the calibration.

This target consists of 264 color swatches and 22 grayscale swatches, for a grand total of 286! If we were required to measure, compare, and adjust our scanner manually for all 286 swatches, it would be a tedious job indeed, and we might well wonder if it was worth all the effort. Luckily the SilverFast software contains a target file, which contains all of the known swatch values, and a calibration software program that will perform all of the necessary comparison and adjustment chores for us.

Here is how it works:

1. After cleaning the scanner as discussed in the preceding section, place the IT8 target on your scan bed. Make sure the entire target is within the scanner active capture area.

2. Click the Prescan button to initiate a prescan (as discussed in Chapter 3).

3. Enlarge the preview by clicking the Zoom tool ⬚ , located on the left side of the tools palette in the Scan Control window. This will allow you to make a more accurate selection of the swatch area of the target.

4. Draw a selection rectangle around the swatch area like the one shown in Figure 4.1. Start the selection at the upper-left corner of the color swatches (the A1 swatch). Pull the selection rectangle diagonally down toward the lower-right corner of the swatch area. Stop the selection at the lower-right edge of the last labeled grayscale swatch (the #22 swatch). Look carefully at the selection rectangle area, and if necessary, edit the selection rectangle so that it encompasses just the labeled color and grayscale swatches but nothing else.

5. Once you have selected the IT8 target, click the calibration button ⬚ (the third tool up from the bottom in the set of tools on the left side of the window shown in Figure 4.1) to begin the target evaluation process. The IT8 Calibration window (Figure 4.2) appears.

6. Click the Start button in the IT8 Calibration window. An Open dialog appears; use this to find and select a reference file that contains the original swatch data for the IT8 target. The swatch data contained in this file will be compared with the target data just captured from the target by your scanner. It is this comparison that will yield the calibration adjustment for your scanner.

7. Browse to the correct reference file and click Open. To find the correct data file, first look on your target for a six-digit number preceded by either an R (for reflective) or T (for transparency). This number identifies the reference data file with the target you are using to calibrate your scanner. The targets are made in batches, with each batch having its own unique set of values. A typical ID number will look like R020812 and may occur on the target itself or on its protective cover. The reference file may be found in the SilverFast folder, in a folder named IT8 Reference File, or on the CD from which SilverFast was installed. If you cannot find a reference file with a name that matches the name on your target, you can check the IT8 reference file included on this book's companion CD or download one from the SilverFast web site at http://silverfast.com/download/it8calibration-en.html.

8. Click the Activate Calibration check box in the IT8 Calibration window to activate the calibration you have just performed.

9. Click OK in the IT8 Calibration window to finish the calibration process.

> You will notice an Export ICC command on the right side of the IT8 Calibration window. We will use this command in Chapter 11.

How Often Should You Calibrate?

You have now completed the calibration process. Once you've done this a few times, it will become second nature. You may be wondering, "How often should I do this?" A good question! You will want to perform this calibration process at the beginning of every scan session in which you want to create images with consistent, predictable results.

A good example of when you would want to be sure to perform this calibration is when you are scanning a large number of related photographs over several days. In order to guarantee that each day's scan results will match the results from other days, you will want to calibrate at the beginning of each day's scanning session. The calibration procedure will allow you to start each session with the scanner performing the same way.

Target Care

Whether you have and use an IT8 target, my 10-Step grayscale target, or some other, it is important that you handle and care for your targets properly.

Treat your target just like an image. Keep your target in its storage case when not in use, store it in cool, dry, light-free conditions. Handle your target carefully; use cotton gloves and hold it only by the edges. Don't allow your target to be exposed to light for long periods.

If you handle and use your target carefully, it should last you for several years at least. All targets fade and change over time, so you may eventually need to purchase a new target, but improper handling can dramatically accelerate the degradation of any target.

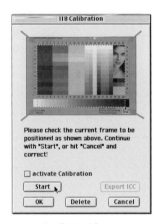

Figure 4.2

The IT8 Calibration window

Working with the Prescan: Auto Adjustments

To get started capturing and adjusting your image, follow these steps to prescan:

1. Place your image squarely on your scanner with the sides of the image parallel to the sides of the scanner. I sometimes use an old-fashioned rule and T-square to help line up images on my flatbed scanner.

2. Launch SilverFast (either the plug-in or stand-alone version). Remember that the advantage of using the plug-in version is that once the scanning is complete, your image will be viewable and editable in your image-editing application. If you are using a plug-in or TWAIN in Photoshop, you will most likely find it in the File → Import submenu.

3. Click the SilverFast Prescan button.

Whenever you scan with SilverFast, you have a choice of making either automatic or manual adjustments to your images during the scanning process. Making automatic adjustments will typically be faster than manual ones, and your results can often be quite satisfactory. This is a good time to reemphasize that automatic adjustments are not entirely automatic.

In SilverFast, the heart of the automatic scanning controls centers on the auto-adjust tool. It can either be used to make a starting adjustment, which can be refined with the use of other SilverFast tools, or it can be used to make all the image adjustments. Although there are some preset values for auto adjustment, if you want to obtain the best results from the use of this tool, you will want to take control of how it adjusts your images.

Automatic adjustments are controlled by the set of preset values and characteristics that we will set in the Options area found in SilverFast's scan window. Once you define the auto options, SilverFast uses its sophisticated built-in automatic intelligence (hence the name *Ai*) to correct your image during the scanning process.

Auto-Adjustment Tools

There are three variations of the auto-adjustment tool: the standard, the calibrated, and the color-managed. Which variation of the tool you are using depends upon how you set up the options in the next section:

Standard auto-adjustment tool This is the basic tool that will be used if you are not using a calibrated or color-managed options setup. With this tool, color cast will be automatically removed from your images unless you change this default adjustment characteristic in the auto-adjustment options.

PHOTOSHOP IS NOT A SCANNING APPLICATION

It is commonly thought that Photoshop is a scanning application. It is not. Photoshop is a painting and image editing application. If you wait until you have your image open in Photoshop to perform most of your image-correction chores, lower-quality images will result. Ask any professional scanner operator where they perform most of their image correction. They will tell you that they do it during the scanning process rather than after the scan in a postscan image editing application.

There are two good reasons for this. The first is image quality. During capture, your scanner has more data to work with than Photoshop will once your image is digitized, so any corrections made during the scan are made with more available data, resulting in a higher-quality final image.

The second reason is speed. If you wait until you are working in Photoshop to perform most of your image corrections, they will take you longer than if you perform image-correction chores during the scan.

Calibrated auto-adjustment tool ▣ This is the tool that will be used if you are using an IT8 calibrated options setup. With this tool, color cast will be automatically retained in your images unless you change this default adjustment characteristic in the auto-adjustment options.

Color-managed auto-adjustment tool ▣ This is the tool that will be used if you are using any color management activated options set up. With this tool, color cast will be automatically retained in your images unless you change this default adjustment characteristic in the auto-adjustment options.

Auto-Adjustment Options

To take full advantage of SilverFast's automatic intelligence and still steer SilverFast in the direction you want it to go, first prepare your scanner and images as outlined previously in this chapter.

Scan Type (Scan Control Window, Frame Tab)

To begin the prescan process, you need to generally define what kind of image you will be capturing in the Scan Type menu on the Frame tab of the Scan Control window. Click the Scan Type pop-up menu. The choices you see will depend both upon the scanner model you have and the version of the SilverFast software you are using, but here is a description of each of the possibilities:

> If you do not have all of these Scan Type choices, either your software or your scanner does not support them. All scanners and versions of SilverFast will provide all the basic choices you will need.

42 -> 24 Bit Color This is a standard choice for scanning color images. This choice will be available to you if you have a scanner that can capture 48 bits of color—three channels with 16 bits of data on each channel (see Chapter 1 for a complete description of bit depth, channels, and shades of gray). If you choose this mode, your scanner will capture and manipulate your image with 48 bits of image data and then deliver the image to you with 24 bits of corrected color. 24 bits is the maximum bit depth that many image editing applications and output devices, especially desktop printers, can recognize and work with.

14 -> 8 Bit Grayscale This will be your standard choice for grayscale images. SilverFast can take advantage of 14 bits of grayscale data, adjust your images, and then deliver a one-channel image with 8 bits of data that will be appropriate for sending to most output devices.

1 Bit Line Art This mode will capture an image with one channel and only 1 bit of data per pixel and is used when you are capturing solid objects such as text and line art.

48 Bit Color In this mode, your scanner and SilverFast will capture, edit, and, unlike the 48 -> 24 Bit Color mode, deliver an image with a full 48 bits of data. You might choose this mode if you are planning to perform extensive image editing on your files after you capture them and you want to have plenty of data to work with or if you will be sending your image to an output device that can accept and process images with 16 bits of data per pixel.

16 Bit Grayscale This mode will deliver an image with one channel and 16 bits of grayscale. Once again, you might choose this mode if you want to edit or output 16 bits of image data.

48 Bit HDR Color Choose this mode if you intend to capture raw, unedited 48-bit data and manipulate it in the SilverFast HDR application. (See Chapter 12 for more information on working with SilverFast HDR.)

16 Bit HDR Grayscale Choose this if you intend to capture raw, unedited 16-bit data and manipulate it in the SilverFast HDR application.

Note that Photoshop provides basic image-editing capabilities for 16-bit grayscale and 48-bit color images. So if you intend on performing extensive editing in Photoshop, you might consider choosing the 16-bit grayscale or 48-bit Scan Type choices.

For this scan exercise, choose the most common Scan Type mode choice for desktop use, the 48 -> 24 Bit Color mode.

Preparing to Set Scan Control Window Options

As we discussed in Chapter 3, setting the auto-adjust tool options controls how your image will be adjusted when you click the tool. Particularly the first time you use the auto-adjust tool, you will want to check and adjust the preset controls that will guide the tool. In the following sections, we will more fully explore adjusting these options.

First, use the selection tool to select just the portion of the image to be captured. It is important that the selection area not extend outside of the image area. Any tools that you use, automatic or manual, will read, display, and adjust the image data inside the selection you choose. If you want to include the white border area of an image in your scan, be sure to adjust the Auto Frame Inset option, which will be described shortly, to remove the border area from the measured and calculated image area.

Click the Option(s) button in the lower-right corner of the Scan Control window. As shown in Chapter 3, this button is at the bottom of the window in Windows (so it can be seen and clicked from either tab), but it's within the General tab in Mac OS. The Defaults window appears, with four tabs: General, Auto, CMS, and Special. Click the CMS tab (Figure 4.3) to show the Color Management setup choices.

Click the Scanner -> Internal pull-down menu. You will see three choices: None, Color Sync (Mac) or ICM (Windows), and Calibration; select Calibration. (Don't worry any more about this for now; Chapter 11 addresses color management in detail.) When you choose Calibration, the color auto-adjustment tool becomes active.

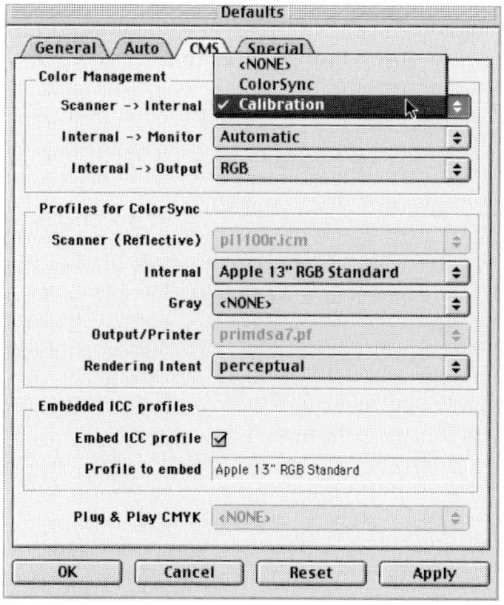

Figure 4.3

The CMS tab of the Defaults window

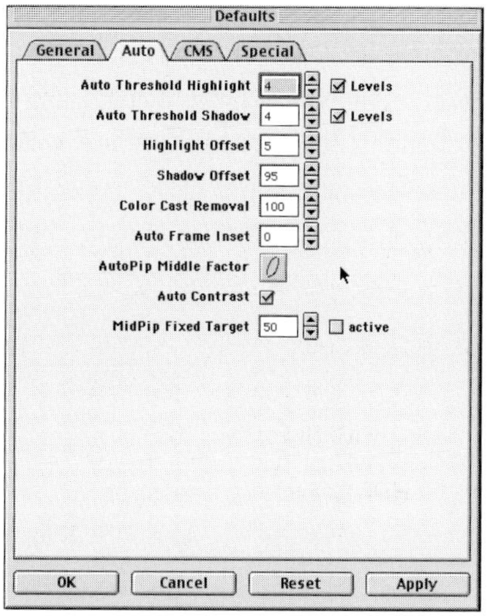

Figure 4.4

The Auto tab of the Defaults window

The other menu choices in the Color Management portion of this window should be set as follows: Internal -> Monitor set to Automatic and Internal -> Output set to RGB.

Now click the Auto tab in the Defaults window (Figure 4.4). You are now prepared to configure how SilverFast will adjust your image when you click the auto-adjust tool. We will work our way from top to bottom to configure the tool.

Auto Thresholds

The Auto Threshold Highlight and Shadow settings are used to help determine which data will be ignored and which data will be utilized by the auto-adjustment tool. The higher the number, the more image data will be ignored at the highlight and shadow ends of the data spectrum. Nearly all images have data that can be ignored. For most continuous tone images, a setting of 3 or 4 will suffice. You might use a higher number in either of two common circumstances:

- Scanning high-contrast artwork such as text or black-and-white line art
- Using a low-quality scanner that routinely captures excess data

This data may show up as long, thin, flat areas at the highlight and shadow ends of your histograms. If you consistently scan the same kinds of images, you may never need to readjust this setting after you set it initially. Set this number at 4 for now; you can always adjust it later.

The Levels Check Boxes

Checking or unchecking the Levels check boxes will determine which values will be used to apply the Auto Threshold Highlight and Shadow settings. If these check boxes are deactivated (the default setting), SilverFast will use a relative measurement, which controls the *number* of pixels that are ignored. If the Levels boxes are checked, SilverFast will use RGB values (0–255) to determine which pixels are ignored. In both cases, larger numbers result in greater numbers of pixels being ignored.

Figure 4.5 shows a comparison of the effects of using the auto-adjustment tool with the Auto Threshold values set to 4 and with the levels check boxes deactivated and activated. Image (a) shows the histogram for the raw uncorrected scan. Image (b) shows the histogram of the image scanned with the levels *deactivated.* Note that the pointer values are 187 for Highlight and 13 for Shadow. Image (c) shows a histogram of the image scanned with the levels *activated;* the pointer values are 203 for Highlight and 3 for Shadow. In this image, the activation of the levels resulted in less impact on the movement of the highlight and shadow points when the image was corrected using the auto-adjustment tool. With some images, the reverse is true.

> If you find the difference between activating and deactivating Levels confusing, you are not alone. The only way to truly understand the difference between the impact of the two methods is to alternately apply the two methods to the same image and view the results in the histogram and images. If you do not want to experiment, use the following rules: For continuous-tone images, leave the Levels check boxes unchecked and adjust the Threshold values to between 2 and 10. For high-contrast images or flat color images (such as line art), activate the Levels and raise the Threshold number until you achieve good visual results on screen.

Highlight Offset and Shadow Offset

To properly set the Highlight Offset and Shadow Offset values, you need to know the highlight and shadow reproduction limit values of the printing device(s) you will be using. Most printing devices cannot print all of the data that can be captured by your scanner. This is particularly true of data in the extreme highlight and shadow portions of an image. These limits are known as the minimum highlight and maximum shadow values. These values vary widely from one device to another, but here is a guide to some common devices:

Let's assign highlight and shadow values as if we were scanning for commercial printing; use 5% and 95%. This will register as 242 and 12 in the histogram and densitometer. (See in Chapter 1 for a discussion of the 0%–100% and 0–255 grayscale value scales.)

There are two types of image highlights: diffuse, which contain detail, and specular, which do not. If your image has a pure white specular highlight, such as a reflection of glass, that you want to maintain with no detail, you will want to set your highlight offset to 0. Often I have to resort to some manual tweaking of my highlight with the curve tool, which we will cover in the next section.

DEVICE	HIGHLIGHT	SHADOW
Commercial press	3%–5%	95%
Desktop printer	8%–10%	90%
Newspaper press	17%–20%	80%

Color Cast Removal

By default, Color Cast Removal is set at 100-percent removal of color cast, which is fine for most images. However, if you will be scanning images that have strong color casts that you might want to preserve, such as sunsets, you will want to set this at 0 percent. If you want to remove some but not all of a color cast, you may use intermediate values between 1 percent and 100 percent.

When you have the CMS options set to calibration, the auto-adjustment tool will not remove any color cast because the tool assumes a calibrated setup will be neutral. This can be overridden, as you will see.

To see the impact of either leaving or removing color cast, you can use the auto-adjustment tool histograms. We will make a manual adjustment to the automatic setting in the next chapter.

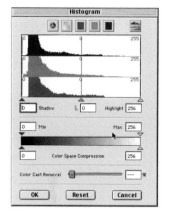

(a) Raw image

Auto Frame Inset

The Auto Frame Inset adjustment is used to adjust the area within your selected area that will be used for the measurement, evaluation, and display of data in Silver-Fast. This would be used, for instance, if you were scanning an image with a white border and you wanted to capture the border but did not want to have the white border register in the histogram or be used by the auto-adjustment tool. The values represent the percentage of reduction of the selection area that will occur (10 percent is the default). If you use this setting to control how much of your selection area is used, you will need to experiment with how much your selection area is reduced to make sure that enough area is removed to avoid the white border or other unwanted image area.

Be careful not to eliminate any important portion of your image, such as a critical highlight or shadow area that may be near the edge of your image.

I typically set this Auto Frame Inset setting to 0 and control my selection area directly with my selection tool. If I want to have a border on my image, I will often add it in Photoshop.

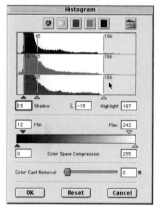

(b) With levels deactivated

AutoPip (Middle Factor)

Set the AutoPip Middle Factor to adjust the overall brightness of your scan. The AutoPip (auto pipette) setting adjusts how much overall lightening or darkening will be applied to your image. This adjustment should not affect the highlight and shadow values we set in step 8 but will affect all of the values in between. The values assigned here will control the application of a gradient adjustment curve to your scans when you use the auto-adjustment tool. The defaults are set at –30 (for lightening) and +30 (for darkening). When you use the auto-adjustment tool, SilverFast evaluates your image and decides whether it thinks your image is a low-key image

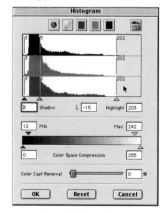

(c) With levels activated

Figure 4.5

Comparison of the histograms

(too dark) or a high-key image (too light). It will then apply either a lightening (negative number) or darkening (positive number) curve to your image. How much you need to adjust an image really depends upon your image.

To view the gradation curve results of a particular AutoPip setting, click the Gradation Curves tool after you have assigned an AutoPip setting in the Defaults window.

> Be aware that when you use the auto-adjustment tool, your image will nearly always be lightened or darkened. If you are working with an image that, for creative reasons, you want to be particularly high or low key, you may want to disable or severely restrict the impact of the adjustments made through the AutoPip values by dramatically lowering its numbers.

Auto Contrast

Depending upon your scanner and version of SilverFast, you may find an Auto Contrast check box. If you check this box, the contrast in your image will be automatically enhanced. If the contrast in your images is too high, deactivate this check box. When this check box is activated, a slight *S*-shaped curve is applied to your images. To view the difference, click the Gradation Curves tool both before and after you have activated the Auto Contrast option setting. See Figure 4.6 for a comparison of the Gradation Curves tool with and without the Auto Contrast option.

> I typically have the Auto Contrast option active. But I also often tweak my contrast by making further manual adjustments to the Gradation Curves tool. We will cover this adjustment in the next section on manual adjustments.

MidPip Fixed Target

The final options setting, MidPip Fixed Target, is not available with all versions of SilverFast, nor will it work with all scanners. If you have this option, for now leave it on its default settings; we will address this tool in Chapter 7.

Applying the Auto-Adjustment Tool

Once you have fully configured your auto-adjustment tool options, you are ready to apply the automatic image adjustments. Simply click the auto-adjustment tool 🌀 in the SilverFast Scan Control window. Your image will be instantly corrected.

> If you are curious and want to learn more about what kind of adjustments are made during this auto-adjustment process, look at the various tools, such as the histograms and curves, before and after the adjustments are made. SilverFast allows you to readily reset any changes you make so that you can easily go back and forth from raw to adjusted.

Other Frame Tab Settings: Finishing Up

In Chapter 3, there was a general discussion of the Frame tab options. Let's flesh that out a bit more to complete our automatic scan setup. I'll cover these options in the order you need to deal with them. Thus, the Setting or Settings drop-down list and the Name text field are discussed at the end of this section because they're the last things you set before you scan.

Filter Click the Filter option and you will see choices for sharpening (USM), descreening, and GANE controls. These are controls that will help us fine-tune the quality and appearance of our scanned images. Choosing one brings up the corresponding dialog box, where you can determine your preferred settings based on a visual preview. For a complete discussion of these controls, see Chapter 8. For now, set this on Sharpen (USM).

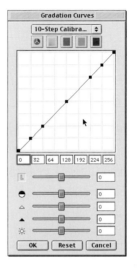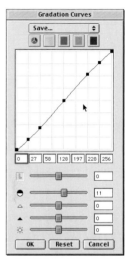

Figure 4.6

The Gradation Curves tool with (left) and without (right) the Auto Contrast option set

Image Type Another fabulous timesaving feature of SilverFast, the Image Type menu, presets the Histogram and Gradation Curves dialog boxes to best suit a wide selection of image types. This menu contains a list of basic image types from which you may choose. Each choice contains a set of adjustment parameters, such as contrast, brightness, highlight, shadow, and color cast handling options that may coincide with certain specific types of images, such as nighttime or snow images. If you have an image that is well defined by one of these preset auto-adjustment configurations, try it.

If you don't find (or aren't satisfied with) an image type that suits your needs, select the User Defined option, which allows you to define your own set of auto-adjustment tool options in the Motive dialog box (Figure 4.7).

If you create a set of your own user-defined settings, they can be a saved as a choice in this list and used again. Because we have already defined our auto-adjustment tool options for our scan, we will leave this Image Type setting at Standard.

Note that when you make a selection from the Image Type menu, the tools in the tool palette change color just as if you had clicked open the auto-adjustment tool. Selecting one of the settings choices applies a predetermined set of adjustments to the tools in the tools palette.

Figure 4.8 shows the Frame tab with the selections we've made so far.

Original This displays the current dimensions of the active prescan marquee.

See the description for the Settings control at the end of this section for a discussion of the difference between saving an image type and saving settings.

Figure 4.7

Defining your own set of options

Scale % With these two data control areas, you can control the final size of your image. The default values here are 100 percent so an image will be automatically scanned at its original size. If you want to scan an image either larger or smaller than its original size, change the scaling percentage to match your needs.

Output values This shows the final output size that results after you have determined the original image area and the scaling percentage. If you do not like working with percentages, you can instead directly input your final image dimensions here. If you directly input values in the Output data fields, you will see that the scaling values will change automatically.

Output buttons Click these to change the output dimension values between inch, centimeters, picas, points, and pixels. Remember that the default values for these displays are set in the General tab of the Scan Control window.

Proportional adjustments As you can see, the previous three settings—Original, Scale, and Output—are all related to one another. By default, the horizontal and vertical dimensions are scaled proportionally (as indicated by the link symbol) when either the Scale or Output values are changed. If you would like to adjust the scaling of an image *without* maintaining the original image proportions, simply click the link symbol. The symbol will appear to be broken, giving you the ability to adjust scaling in either direction independently.

> Be aware that if you scale your images in a nonproportional manner, your image will appear distorted. If you are trying to fit an image into an area of a specific size and shape, you are better advised to scan the image proportionally and crop it rather than to engage in nonproportional scaling. If you scan an image nonproportionally, you'd better mean it!

Locked output If you prefer to make only dimension changes with the Output data fields, you can lock out the ability to edit the Scale data fields by clicking the locks next to the Output data field boxes. Click these locks to lock and unlock them. Either output dimension can be locked separately.

MByte This is a noneditable display that shows what size the file will be, in megabytes, once the scan is complete.

Image resolution The image resolution can be assigned in one of two ways: either directly in the dpi data field or by using the Q-Factor and Screen (line screen) data fields.

> Desktop printers typically require far less image resolution than commercial printing devices do. I always scan for commercial printing, because it is the most demanding, and then downsize and sample my images for other uses.

Q-Factor Q stands for quality. If you choose to set your scan resolution by using the Q-Factor, you will need to know the line screen at which that image will be printed. This is a multiplier that varies within the range of 1.3 to 2. The SilverFast manual recommends a Q value of 1.4 for commercial printing; others (such as most printing companies) recommend a minimum value of 2.0, for guidance. I tend to side with the SilverFast suggestion of Q at approximately 1.4. I use 2.0 for images with lots of high-contrast edges.

Screen This data field only applies to images that will be printed with a halftone dot (also known as AM screening). The value entered here will be automatically multiplied by the Q-Factor value to yield the effective scan resolution. The line screen of devices varies widely. Table 4.1 presents some standard line screens for common printing devices. Most inkjet printers will produce good-quality final images with image resolutions in the 150–200 ppi range. Test your specific printing device to determine the lowest acceptable resolution.

DEVICE	LINES PER INCH
Commercial printing	133–200
Commercial printing: uncoated stock	133–150 (150 most common)
Commercial printing: coated stock	150–200 (175 most common)
Newspaper printing	85–110 (85 most common)
Desktop laser printers	50–110

Table 4.1

Common Print Device Line Screens

If you will be sending your images to a service bureau or printing company for output, call and get their image resolution suggestions before you scan.

Lpi/lpcm button Clicking this button toggles the display back and forth between lines per inch and lines per centimeter.

Resolution field (effective image resolution) This displays the result of multiplying the Q-Factor value by the Screen value. For situations in which your scan will not be screened into halftone dots, try these recommendations—for on-screen display, set a Q-Factor of 1.0 and a screen of 96 lpi; for inkjet printer output, set a Q-Factor of 1.0 and a screen of 150 lpi.

If you prefer not to use the Q-Factor and line screen, you can simply input the resolution figure directly into this data field. For instance, instead of assigning a Q-Factor of 2.0 and an lpi of 150, you could simply type 300 into this data field.

Dpi/dpcm button Clicking this button toggles between dots per inch and dots per centimeter.

Untitled slider (effective scan resolution) Dragging this slider to the left decreases the scan resolution, and dragging it to the right increases the resolution. This is yet another alternative fashion for assigning resolution.

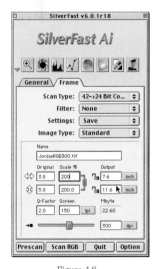

Figure 4.8

Scan Control window settings

EFFECTIVE SCAN RESOLUTION

The figure representing the effective scan resolution is not displayed anywhere, but keep it in mind. There is a difference between the effective scan resolution and effective image resolution. Although the effective image resolution data field displays the final resolution of your image, even this does not tell the entire story of what is going on during the scan. The actual resolution at which your scanner will capture your image is not only a function of the effective image resolution, it's also affected by any scaling that you may assign to the scanning process. If you ask a scanner to scale an image up, it must scan that image at a higher resolution to deliver the image at a larger size at the same resolution. That increase in scan or input resolution will be directly proportional to the amount of scaling required.

For instance, in this example we are assigning an input or effective image resolution of 300 ppi (dpi). We are also scaling the image 200 percent. In order for the scanner to deliver the final image to us at 300 ppi at twice the dimensions, the scanner must actually scan the image at 2 (scaling factor) × 300 ppi = 600 ppi.

In Chapter 1, I mentioned that if you scan an image using a resolution that is greater than its optical resolution, the scanning software would be forced to interpolate your image, thereby lowering its quality. To prevent this, you should make sure that the effective scan resolution never exceeds the optical resolution of the scanner. This means of course that there is a practical limit to the amount of scaling that you can have your scanner apply without using interpolation.

Avoid scanning at resolutions that exceed the optical resolution of your scanner. To determine how much you can scale an image without interpolation, use this formula: optical resolution ÷ effective image resolution = maximum scaling factor. For example, 1200 ppi ÷ 300 ppi = 4. This means you could scale your image 400 percent and still have an effective image resolution of 300 ppi without involving any interpolation.

Untitled lock icon (the Pixel Lock) Clicking this icon toggles between locked and unlocked. When locked, this feature allows you to adjust the resolution (dpi), lpi, or Q-Factor without changing the resulting file size. (In other words, the resulting scanned image will be protected from changing the number of pixels; the pixels will be captured at a different resolution or physical size.)

Settings Once you have set all of your options and configured the tools, you may want to save all these settings as a file for reloading and using on other images. Click the Setting or Settings menu button and select the Save choice. A small window appears in which you can name and save these settings for later recall and use.

Creating and saving a group of settings using the Settings menu is similar to saving a user defined image type. The difference is that when you define an Image Type choice, you have access to only a limited set of controls. When you save settings, you are saving a more complete set of settings.

Name The last thing to do before clicking the scan button is to name the image you are about to create. I prefer to use a four-part naming system when naming an image:

- A logical name, such as Jordan (my niece's name)
- A color space, such as RGB
- A resolution, such as 300 ppi
- A lowercase three-character suffix indicating the file format, such as `.tif`

So the name I would apply to this image would be `JordanRGB300.tif`. I often change the names of my files later, often with a shorter name, but I give my initial files complete names to make them easier to find, organize, and manage.

As discussed in Chapter 3, if you've chosen the Normal (File) or Batch Mode (File) option under the Process Mode menu on the General tab, enter the name you'd like to apply when this image is saved to disk. If your Process Mode choice was Normal or Batch Mode, the

Figure 4.9

A raw prescan and the final scan. Note the improved brightness, contrast, and color saturation of the final scan. Color versions of these images labeled C12 and C13 can be seen in the color section. A copy of the raw image named JordanRAWRGB.tif can be found on the CD.

name you enter here will be shown in the title bar of the image when it is passed to Photoshop; you will have another chance to rename the file when you choose Save from Photoshop's File menu.

> When using files for various purposes, such as for printing or for use on the Web, always make copies of the original scanned image. I have one rule I never violate: I always work with copies of my original images, never on the original scanned image. I save an archive copy of the original scan so that I can always return to that unaltered image.

Completing the Scan

Now, finally we get to click the scan button to complete our scan. Click the Scan RGB button along the bottom of the Scan Control window to initiate the final high-resolution scan. All the adjustments we have set in this chapter will be applied to your image and delivered to you as a finished scanned image. If you are using a Photoshop plug-in or TWAIN, when the scan is complete your image will be open, viewable, and editable in Photoshop. If you are using the stand-alone SilverFast application, your image will be saved to disk. Figure 4.9 shows the initial raw preview and the results of the application of the auto-adjustment tool settings in the final scan.

The Scan Pilot

SilverFast provides a step-by-step scanning guide, called the Scan Pilot, which will lead you through the entire scanning workflow we have just completed. The Scan Pilot is an automated, and customizable, and graphical step-by-step guide through the scanning process. See the beginning of chapter 10, PowerUser Tips, for an overview of the Scan Pilot.

In the next chapter, I will discuss how you can either fine-tune the automatic adjustments we have made here or control the entire scanning process manually.

CHAPTER 5

Manual Scanning: Working with the Prescan Image

In Chapter 4, we discussed the details of capturing and adjusting a low-resolution preview scan image and of setting up the options for the auto-adjustment tool and other prescan setups, such as image type, naming conventions, resolution, scaling, and file format. For many if not all of your images, you may be satisfied with the image results you obtain by using the knowledge and techniques in Chapter 4.

In this chapter, you will learn how to use the manual scanning tools to either set up the scan entirely manually or to tweak the results that would be obtained from using the auto-adjustment tool alone.

The following topics are covered in this chapter:

- **The general defaults options**

- **SilverFast scanning tools**

- **Image information tools**

- **Image corrections and tools**

The General Defaults Options

In Chapter 4, we set the options for the auto-adjustment tool. Here I walk you through setting the general defaults options, several of which have a direct effect on how our manual tools function. To access these options, click the General tab of the Scan Control window, then click the Options button in the lower-right corner. Finally, click the General tab in the Defaults window. The Defaults window with the General tab is shown in Figure 5.1.

The general defaults options determined under the General tab include settings for a mixture of many different areas. Here's a line-by-line rundown:

Colormodel With the Colormodel option, you can determine whether you will adjust the amount of red, green, and blue in your image or the amount of cyan, magenta, and yellow when manipulating the Histogram or Gradation Curve tools. (The Histogram is analogous to Photoshop's Levels, and of course the Gradation Curves are similar to Curves in Photoshop.) RGB is the factory default for this option, but you can also toggle between RGB or CMY within the Histogram and Gradation Curves dialog boxes. This setting does not alter the scan mode, which will by default be RGB; it alters only the display in the editing tools. It is generally best to leave this set on RGB unless you are more comfortable with or want to check on the specific CMY values.

Units Of Measure This determines the units that will be used in the dimension displays in the Scan Control window. Most U.S. users will be happiest with the default choice of inches, but photographers and web designers may prefer to see their sizes shown as a pixel count (such as 640×480). I leave this set on inches.

Densitometer Radius This option determines the number of pixels that will be sampled when measuring RGB or CMY values with the densitometer. The default allows the densitometer to display a reading that averages the value of a 4-pixel grid (2×2); select 1 if you need to know the exact value of a single pixel or 3 if you would like the broadest average sample. I choose 2 Pixel here.

Default Setting With this menu choice, a previously created setting, such as Landscape Slide Frame shown here, can be assigned as the default settings. These settings are created in the Frame tab of the Scan Control window. Saving settings is discussed more fully in Chapter 10. I select SilverFast Defaults here.

Option Parameter The Option Parameter setting allows you to save the various Option settings for all the Option tabs as a single parameter file. Clicking the Save menu item will display a box containing an automatically generated name; if desired, you can replace this with a name that is more personalized, such as Catalog Scan shown here. Once created, a set of parameters can be recalled and used at any time.

Interpolation SilverFast Standard provides faster results and will be acceptable for most users, but Anti Aliased produces the smoothest results. (Interpolation is discussed in detail in Chapter 2.)

High Resolution Prescan With this option, you can set a higher default prescan resolution, which will allow you to zoom in on a prescan image for more accurate selections and readings. Selecting higher numbers will increase the initial prescan time but often saves time by improving accuracy and by eliminating rescanning every time you would like to zoom in on an image. I typically set a 2x default to provide me a moderate amount of zooming without creating unnecessarily long prescan times.

Scratch Disk Particularly if you are performing multiple scans such as batch scans, you will want to have a large enough volume to hold all the files during the scanning process. I like to assign the same scratch disk that I use for Photoshop, which is a large free hard-drive partition.

Gamma-Gradation Changes in this value affect the midtone brightness of the image. Most desktop scanners will work best with a value of 1.80, but if you feel that all your scans tend to be too dark, increase the number to brighten the image. Conversely, lowering the number will darken the image (the minimum gamma value is 1.0, but you should never reduce it to that extent). See the manual calibration directions in Appendix A on this book's CD-ROM for instruction on using this setting to calibrate your scanner.

For HDR (High Dynamic Range) Output If this box is checked, the same gamma value chosen in the previous menu will be applied to 48-bit color scans and 16-bit grayscale scans. Because 48- and 16-bit scans may not reproduce in the same way as normal 24-bit color and 8-bit grayscale scans, you should test this option with your particular reproduction system (printer, RIP, and publishing applications) to determine what the proper HDR gamma value should be. If you are performing a manually calibrated scan (see Appendix A on the CD) and want to deliver a calibrated scan for HDR processing, check this box.

Q-Factor The Q-Factor number will be multiplied by the halftone line screen (lpi) figure entered in the Scan Control window's Frame tab. The default value is 1, but the traditional graphic arts formula (as discussed in Chapter 1) specifies a value of 2. This number can always be adjusted in the Scan Control window, but the value set here will be used as the initial default value.

Reopen SF After Scan When used as a Photoshop plug-in, SilverFast automatically quits after the scan is completed, leaving your image open in Photoshop. If you would prefer to leave SilverFast running (for making several scans from different originals), check this box. I typically leave this unchecked because that matches the way I work. I typically view my image(s) after each scan.

Realtime Correction In this mode, color corrections are instantly applied to the Realtime Correction ☑ on-screen rendition while the adjustment sliders are moving; with this box unchecked, the changes will not update on your monitor until the mouse button is released. If your computer is not very powerful, deselecting this box may speed up performance. I typically have this turned on.

Mask Edge Size This number determines the amount of feathering along the Mask Edge Size 0.00 edge of the current selection. The default value of 0 produces a crisp edge, which is how I will set it here.

SilverFast Scanning Tools

Final image quality is not just a function of *what* you do, it's also a function of *when* you do it. For instance, as we will discuss in Chapter 8, most images need to be sharpened through the application of the Unsharp Mask tool. But if sharpening is applied too early in the work-flow process, it can actually lead to a degradation of image quality. SilverFast is designed around this concept of using a sound step-by-step workflow. I will cover a variety of tools in this chapter, in the order in which they should be used on an image. We will begin by taking a quick look at the tools you have in SilverFast for gathering information about your image. I will then use the remainder of the chapter to discuss how to properly use these tools to adjust and fine-tune your images.

SilverFast has a variety of tools that can be used to control how you adjust your images: pre-scan, image area selection, magnification and auto-adjustment tools (all of which we discussed extensively in Chapter 4). You will now add to your list of image adjustment weapons and learn to use the Histogram, Gradation Curves, and Color Balance tools (all of which appear on the

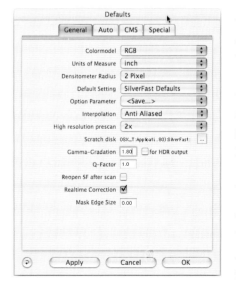

Figure 5.1

The General tab of the Defaults window

Scan Pilot). Along the way, you will also learn to use the densitometer and tools that help you measure image values and make highlight and shadow adjustments. Other tools, such as the Selective Color and Unsharp Mask tools, warrant special attention, so we will tackle them in later chapters.

All of the tools mentioned here can be found in the horizontal tools palette in the Scan Control window or in the vertical tools palette along the left side of the preview window. All of the new tools covered in this chapter are located on the horizontal tools palette, shown in Figure 5.2.

Following is a list of the tools we will be using and brief description of their use:

Zoom tool Used to magnify the prescanned image for closer inspection of the entire image or a portion of the image.

Auto-Adjustment tool Used to make a variety of adjustments to an image (see Chapter 4 for a complete description of setting up this tool).

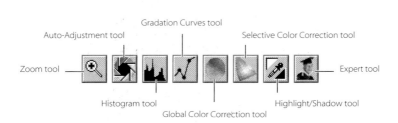

Figure 5.2

Horizontal tool palette names and uses

Zoom tool

Auto-Adjustment tool

Gradation Curves tool

Selective Color Correction tool

Expert tool

Histogram tool

Global Color Correction tool

Highlight/Shadow tool

Histogram tool Used to view the pixel data in an image as well as make adjustments to how that pixel data is distributed, specifically for setting highlights and shadows.

Gradation Curves tool An input/output tool used to control and adjust the brightness and contrast of an image, as well as make adjustments to how colors are distributed in an image.

Global Color Correction tool Used to adjust the global color adjustment to an image.

Selective Color Adjustment tool Used to make color adjustments to selective portions of an image (this tool is not covered in this chapter but will be addressed in Chapter 6).

Highlight/Shadow/MidPip tool The highlight (upper white triangle) and shadow (lower dark triangle) are used to set highlight and shadow points. These can be used instead of or along with the Histogram tool. The MidPip (click the pipette itself) is used for neutralization of any tonal range area (see Chapter 6).

Expert tool Used to precisely control the distribution of color values in any portion of an image. This tool is so powerful it warrants its own chapter, Chapter 7.

These tools are used roughly in the order in which they appear in the tool palette, although as you will see, the Zoom tool can and will be used in many circumstances. The Highlight/Shadow tool is often used early in the scan setup process along with the Histogram tool.

The Zoom Tool

There are several reasons you will want to enlarge your image with the Zoom tool :

- To make sure that you accurately place the selection rectangle
- If you intend to make manual adjustments to your scan controls
- If you want to take a closer look at the detail of your preview image

If your prescan image is too small to be easily seen, you can click the Zoom tool to magnify the image. If you select an area first, the zoomed area will be controlled by your selection. If you have not preset the Zoom tool to allow the prescan to capture enough data to magnify the image enough, another prescan will be performed when you click the Zoom tool. This can be annoying and time consuming, so if you have not done so already, now would be a good time to reconfigure this tool so that the prescan is performed at a high enough resolution to allow enough magnification when you zoom in without the need to initiate another prescan.

The Zoom tool's capability to enlarge an image without having to affect a new prescan is controlled by adjusting the resolution of the initial prescan in the general defaults options. Refer to the section "The General Defaults Options" earlier in this chapter. The multiplier you choose will control the amount of magnification you can achieve without having to perform a new prescan. The more magnification you need, the higher you should set the prescan multiplier.

> I recommend a setting of 2x for the Zoom tool multiplier. Higher settings will allow you to enlarge your preview to greater magnifications but will also require longer prescan times. Don't set higher multiplier values than you really need.

SilverFast offers both a whole-image zoom and a partial-area zoom. To enlarge the entire image, simply click the Zoom tool one or more times depending upon the x value set in the Zoom tool options. To zoom in on a specific area, first select the area on which you would like to zoom and then click the Zoom tool. Note that in SilverFast, you will click the Zoom tool rather than the image to effect a zoom.

Image Information Tools

If you are going to manipulate your image adjustments manually, it is important that you understand what you are manipulating and that you be able to track the adjustments you make. There are two key types of data display in SilverFast: the densitometer and the histogram. The densitometer displays data numerically, and the histogram displays data graphically. Both are useful tools. They are often used together to display as well as adjust image data.

The Densitometer

The densitometer (Figure 5.3)—often called an "info" tool in applications such as Photoshop and in other scanning programs—displays your image's pixel data numerically.

Figure 5.3

Densitometer display (here, in RGB mode)

Click to change mode

But what do all those numbers mean? The densitometer shows grayscale and related color values of the pixels in an image measured and displayed on one of two scales. The most common, and default, value in SilverFast is the 0–255 scale, which expresses the grayscale values of a pixel (or group of pixels) on a scale where 0 is pure black and 255 is pure white. The other scale commonly used is a 0–100 scale, where percentages are used to express the grayscale and color values of pixels. If you remember our discussion in Chapter 4, scanners can capture only grayscale data, which is converted into color when the image is output on a monitor or printer. Even if your scanner is capturing images in 16-bit mode (which will capture 65,536 shades of gray), the densitometer in SilverFast will display these shades of gray/color on a scale of 0–255.

Often the densitometer will display two sets of values. They represent before and after adjustment measurements of the grayscale/color values of the image area being measured.

The left value is the previous, pre-adjustment value(s), and the right set of values is always the current, or post-adjustment, value(s).

The densitometer can be stored and used either as a tab choice in the Scan Control window or as a floating palette. To float the densitometer palette from its tabbed location, simply click the Float button.

Measurement Modes

The densitometer in SilverFast can measure the pixel values of your image in several ways. It can record the values in the modes listed in Table 5.1.

To navigate from one display mode to another, click the right-pointing arrows located between the previous and current value windows.

> Always check the scale you are working with when you use a densitometer or info tool. Values in different scales are sometimes directly and sometimes inversely proportional to each other. For instance, in the binary scale, 255 equals white and 0 equals black, but in the percentage scale, 0 equals white and 100 equals black.

Densitometer Radius Check

One final detail we need to check is the sampling radius of the densitometer. The SilverFast densitometer can be set to measure single pixels or sample a range of pixels. Typically, you will want to set the densitometer to measure the average of a range of pixels rather than just one pixel because individual pixels may provide spurious values.

To set the radius of the densitometer, click the Option or Options button located in the lower-right corner of the Scan Control window. The Defaults window options will appear (you can see these back in Figure 5.1).

Click the General tab and then click the Densitometer Radius drop-down menu. Choose either 2 Pixel or 3 Pixel radius. Use 2 Pixel if the size of the smallest areas you will be measuring is small (up to 10 pixels across) or 3 Pixel radius if it is larger (more than 10 pixels across). If you ever set the radius value to 1 (as I do when working with black-and-white line art images), be sure to change the radius back to 2 Pixel or 3 Pixel before working with contone images.

ABBREVIATION	MODE
CMY	Cyan, magenta, yellow
CMYK	Cyan, magenta, yellow, black (*K* stands for *black*)
HSL	Hue, saturation, lightness
K	Grayscale (*K* stands for *black*)
Lab	Luminescence, a channel, b channel (CIELab color standard)
LCH	Luminescence, chroma, hue
RGB	Red, green, blue

Table 5.1

Densitometer Color Modes

The Histogram

First let me state that histograms are our friends. Why? Because histograms show where and how much data we have in our images. And if you learn to interpret them correctly, they can be one of your most valuable guides to how to adjust images. First let's get more familiar with what a histogram shows.

The first thing you need to know about histograms is that they show us only image data that is inside of the selection rectangle. This is why I have made such a big deal about zooming in on the preview image—to make sure the selection rectangle does not extend beyond the actual image area. You do not want any extraneous data being displayed in your histograms. The same rule applies here.

To access, read, and interpret a histogram, first draw a selection rectangle around the entire image, but just inside the edge of the image, being careful not to include any non-image area (use your Zoom tool for exact placement). Then click the Histogram tool ![]; the Histogram window will appear (Figure 5.4).

There are three possible ways to view the histogram:

Standard histogram mode This histogram view shows a one-part histogram, which shows mainly the luminance values of the image; no color data is shown. This is the only histogram you will see when you perform a grayscale prescan.

Combined histogram This view shows all three color channels—Red, Green, and Blue—superimposed one on top of the other. This is a useful display if you would like to compare the data from all three channels to see how they overlap and/or adjust all three channels at the same time.

Separated histogram This view shows all three histograms displayed separately. Here you can clearly see and manipulate the histogram data for each color. This is the mode in which we will work most of the time.

You can switch from one view to the other by clicking the histogram mode button in the upper-right corner of the Histogram window.

The histogram first and foremost shows us where the image data is in the image, how much data there is in various portions of the grayscale spectrum, and also where there is no data. This last bit of information, knowing where there is no data, is just as important as knowing where there is data.

The histogram itself shows a series of peaks and valleys distributed across the grayscale spectrum for white (left side) to black (right side). Anywhere there is a data peak in the histogram, there is data in the image as well. The height of the data peaks indicate how much data there is in a particular portion of the grayscale spectrum. Typically, as you will see, flat areas in the histogram, which represent areas of little or no image data, should be avoided and removed prior to scanning. In addition, you will see that in RGB color images, the key to removing and/or controlling color casts is to adjust the start and finish of the significant image data in the individual RGB histograms.

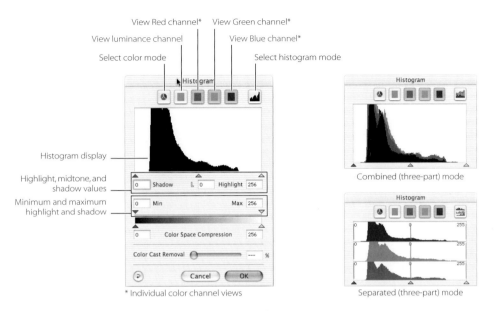

View luminance channel
Select color mode
View Red channel*
View Green channel*
View Blue channel*
Select histogram mode

Histogram display
Highlight, midtone, and shadow values
Minimum and maximum highlight and shadow

Shadow   0   L   0   Highlight   256
Min   0   Max   256
Color Space Compression   0   256
Color Cast Removal   ---   %

Cancel   OK

* Individual color channel views

Combined (three-part) mode

Separated (three-part) mode

Figure 5.4

Histogram displays and components

I show examples of how to use the histogram in various sections later in this chapter, especially "Using Histograms for Easier Highlights and Shadow Corrections" and "Using Histograms to Correct Color Cast."

The Show Lightest And Darkest Points Tool

When you are engaged in manual image adjustments, and particularly if you are tweaking an auto-adjustment correction you have already made, there are two important points of reference you would like to know. What are and where are the lightest and darkest points in your image? Then you will want to evaluate the relative importance of these data points to your corrections. It is particularly important to know these two points of data if you have made an auto-adjustment tool correction, because this correction uses the lightest and darkest points of your image to evaluate and correct your image.

> Sometimes when your lightest and darkest points are not in significant areas of your image and/or they are very much lighter or darker than other areas of your image, adjustments made using these areas as reference points (as is done when the auto-adjustment tool is used) result in less than optimum results, and sometimes the results are just plain awful.

There is a tool created specifically for identifying these points on your images. It is called, amazingly enough, the Show Lightest And Darkest Points tool ▯. (Please note that, although their names may sound similar and they can be used in conjunction with each other, the Show Lightest And Darkest Points tool is not the same as the Highlight/ Shadow tool.)

To find the lightest point in your image, click the white/upper half of the tool. A small red target circle will appear (see the upper-left corner of Figure 5.5). You can also find this spot by holding down the Shift key plus the Command or Ctrl key.

To find the darkest point in your image, click the black/lower half of the tool, or hold down just the Command or Ctrl key. In Figure 5.5, a target circle appears near the middle-left edge.

Image Corrections and Tools

Now that you have learned how to access information about your images, you're ready to begin making evaluations and corrections. We will use the tools such as the histogram and the densitometer as well as some new tools such as the Gradation Curves and Global Color Correction tools to help make manual adjustments for setting the following:

- Highlights and shadows
- Color cast adjustments
- Brightness and contrast
- Global and restricted color adjustments

Often the only adjustment that is necessary when using SilverFast to scan your images is to click the auto-adjustment tool, as we did in Chapter 4. There are times, however, when you want to either manually tweak the adjustments made by the auto-adjustment tool or perhaps even take manual control of the process entirely. We will examine several common approaches to manual tweaking and control of your image capture.

Setting Highlights and Shadows

There are several ways to set highlights and shadows. The two most common tools are the Highlight/Shadow tool and the Histogram tool. These tools can often be used together. Let's start with the Highlight/Shadow tool. I will continue to use the Jordan image so you can compare these processes and results.

Figure 5.5

The Show Lightest And Darkest Points tool

Lightest point

Darkest point

Evaluating an Image

When I use the Highlight/Shadow tool, I like to first start by determining the lightest and darkest points in my image to see if they coincide with important content areas of my image.

As you know from our previous determination, the lightest point in the Jordan image is in the upper-left corner (as was shown in Figure 5.5). This is not a significant content point in the image. If I use the auto-adjustment tool to make a correction, this lightest point will be assigned the highlight value of 5% set in the options resets and the highlight values of another portion of the image will probably be darker than 5%. A much more significant area in this image for highlight values would be the lightest area of the white jersey. Because that area isn't the lightest portion of the image, its value is likely to be darker than 5%.

Viewing Auto-Adjustment Tool Results

When we return to and measure the Jordan image's highlight value, which we corrected in Chapter 4, we will see that the highlight values in the lightest area of the jersey are darker than 5%.

Here I place the cursor over the lightest portion of the jersey, the collar. When the results are viewed in the densitometer, you see that the highlight values are 228, 226, and 224. These values are in the range of 11% (228) to 13% (224) highlight values, significantly darker than the 5% (242) we want (see Figure 5.6). Other images with similar highlights can be similarly evaluated.

Using the Highlight/Shadow Tool

This is where the Highlight/Shadow tool is the best tool to use because I can assign the preset 5% highlight value to any specific area in the image. To assign and check a 5% highlight value to the white jersey, I do the following:

1. Zoom in on the image by clicking the Zoom tool.

2. Click the highlight (top) portion of the Highlight/Shadow tool to activate 🔲.

3. Click the lightest portion of the jersey collar.

4. Without moving the cursor, read the values that now register in the densitometer. As you can see in Figure 5.7, all the values for the collar now read 242, or 5%.

Figure 5.6

Using the densitometer to measure initial highlight value (original image)

Figure 5.7

Densitometer reading after using the Highlight tool to set a lighter highlight value

Now I will perform the same function in a significant shadow region by doing the following:

1. Measure the RGB values of the image in a significant shadow detail area such as the shadow area in the tree just up and to the right of Jordan's head.

2. Measure the RGB values with the densitometer. They read 36, 35, 33.

3. Select the Shadow tool by clicking on the shadow (bottom) portion of the Highlight/Shadow tool 🔲.

4. Click in the shadow area of the tree I just measured.

Now view the densitometer reading again (see Figure 5.8). Note that the values have changed from 36, 35, 33 to 12, 12, 12.

> Manually setting the highlight and shadow has not only changed the values but also made them all equal, which results in the removal of color cast. If you want to make a manual adjustment to highlights and/or shadows without removing the color cast, just hold down the Shift key when you click the highlight or shadow area with the tool.

Now compare the manually highlight-corrected image in Figure 5.7 with the manually highlight- and shadow-corrected image in Figure 5.8. You can see once again that the image has improved.

When all three images are lined up—the raw scan, the auto- corrected image, and the manually tweaked image, as in Figure 5.9—you can easily see the improvement progression. Each step improves the highlight and shadow appearance as well as the overall brightness and contrast of the image. The color section of this book presents color versions of these three images.

Figure 5.8

Original image with initial shadow values (left); image after using the Highlight/Shadow tool to adjust the shadow value down, with corrected shadow values (right)

Using Auto and Manual Adjustments Together

Now visually compare Figure 5.7 with Figure 5.8. As you can see, the highlight is a brighter white. The lightest point in the image will now be lighter than 5% (242) and may be pushed to 0 (commonly known as "blowing out," showing no detail when printed). But this may be acceptable because we have directed attention and adjustments to the most significant light portion of the image. If a small unimportant area in the upper portion of the image is too light, it is a small price to pay for an improved image overall.

As you saw, the result of the automatic adjustment to this Jordan image in Chapter 4 was certainly an improvement over the raw scan, but manual adjustments allow you to further improve an image by fine-focusing and -tuning the adjustments in the highlights and shadows on the more important parts of the image. A good approach and workflow is to apply the automatic adjustments to an image, followed, as I did here, with an image evaluation and, if necessary, a manual tweak of the automatic adjustment.

Using Histograms for Easier Highlights and Shadow Corrections

Histograms may also be manually adjusted to correct an image. The advantage that a histogram has is that you can actually see the data while you make your adjustments. The following is an example of how I would use the histogram to adjust an image.

I begin by selecting the prescanned image area I want to scan. I am careful to exclude any unwanted areas, and especially any area outside of the image. Remember that any area inside of the selection rectangle will be included in the histogram display and will be factored into any auto-adjustments you may make.

Figure 5.9

Progressive image improvement

Raw scan

Auto-corrected image

Manually corrected image

I typically enlarge the image by clicking the Zoom tool. This will allow you to view and measure key areas of your preview image more easily.

USING THE SINGLE-CHANNEL HISTOGRAM

Here I'll use an autumn landscape photo (Figure 5.10), which has two specific characteristics of note: there is no neutral highlight for me to use in setting my highlight and shadow values, but there is a sunlight flare in the upper-left corner.

Weird lighting circumstances like this can often dramatically lower the contrast of an image, as it has here, and create some unusual challenges for scanning the image. Images such as this, which have odd lighting circumstances and no highlight neutrals, often benefit from a bit of manual handling (or, as I sometimes call it, "manhandling").

1. Click the Histogram tool. The Histogram window appears.

2. Click the Histogram Mode Selection button until the single-channel view appears, as in the first image of Figure 5.11. We will use the single-channel histogram to set our basic highlight and shadows. You will notice that there are some small thin flat data lines on both ends of the histogram. Our first adjustment will be to remove these flat ends.

Figure 5.10

Autumn image, raw

3. Move the highlight triangle inward so that it is positioned just at the beginning of the significant data in the image, as in the image on the right in Figure 5.11.

4. Now perform the same function on the shadow end, moving the shadow slider triangle inward until it just touches the beginning of the significant shadow data.

Now I will adjust the highlight minimum and shadow maximum values. Normally with an auto-adjustment tool correction, the minimum and maximums would be set to 242 (5%) and 12 (95%). For this image, we'll retain the shadow maximum at 12 (95%) to protect our shadow detail. I will, however, set the highlight minimum at 255 (0%) because there really is no highlight value to protect and reducing the highlight minimum to 242 compresses the image's tonal range unnecessarily.

Here I tab through to the maximum value and set it at 12 (95%). Tab to the minimum and set it at 255 (0%).

The advantage of using a histogram, particularly with images that have odd characteristics that may beg for some uncommon manipulation, such as our autumn landscape image, is that the histograms allow you to see the data rather than just rely on numbers. And for those of us who are visually oriented, a little visual assistance is very welcome! This manual setting of the highlight and shadow, which compresses the tonal range slightly, gets me set for the remainder of my adjustments coming up next.

> If you use a manual histogram highlight and shadow adjustment on an image that has a nice diffuse highlight, use the densitometer along with the histogram to check your highlight value to be sure it is right at 242 (5%) or another value you may prefer. SilverFast updates the image and its RGB values on the fly as you make your adjustments, allowing you this kind of interactivity and control.

This is probably a good place to mention that when scanning a grayscale continuous-tone image, a single-channel histogram is all that you will have to evaluate and manipulate. All of the same principles apply; there is just less data and fewer channels to worry about.

Removing and Retaining Color Casts

Perhaps the single most common challenge we have when working with color images is dealing with color cast. Color cast is the presence or absence of too much of one color or not enough of another. In SilverFast, one of the most effective tools we have for both evaluating and correcting color casts is once again the Histogram tool.

Using Histograms to Correct Color Cast

Using the histogram, as you have seen, is a good way to look at how pixel data is distributed in an image. In the previous highlight and shadow adjustment exercise, I used the simplest, single-channel histogram adjustment to accomplish tone compression by setting our highlight

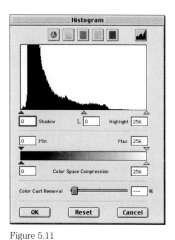
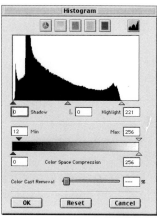

Figure 5.11

A single-channel histogram (left) and a manually corrected histogram (right); note the changes in highlight and minimum shadow values.

Figure 5.12

Separated multipart histogram

and shadow points. Moving forward, we'll take advantage of even more information and adjustment controls that are available to us in the individual histograms. I'll continue to evaluate and adjust the autumn photograph.

To begin the color cast evaluation and adjustment process, I need more information than is available in the single-channel histogram. I need to activate a multipart histogram.

Here I click the Histogram tool, and then click the Histogram Mode button until I see a separated multipart histogram, as in Figure 5.12. Each data channel—Red, Green, and Blue—is separated into its own channel.

This histogram is the multipart version of the single channel I adjusted in the previous example (Figure 5.11). You will notice that the three histograms are slightly offset from one another. As we discussed in Chapter 4, this means that this image has a color cast.

If you examine the histogram highlight and shadow triangle points closely, you will see that the triangles have been moved from their initial positions. This occurred during the single channel highlight and shadow adjustment that I applied above to remove the flat ends of the histogram. The removal of the flat data areas affected primarily the Red channel for the highlight data and the Blue channel for the shadow data. The data in the Green channel exists between the extremes of the data found in the Red and the Blue channels and was therefore little altered. This offsetting of individual channel histograms is a common circumstance when an image exhibits a color cast.

Removing or Saving the Color Cast

At this point, because I have determined that this image does indeed have a color cast, I need to decide whether or not to keep the color cast. As discussed earlier, weird lighting conditions, such as this backlit sun-flared lighting, can often introduce data that can flatten an image. In this case, there is no particular lighting effect I am interested in preserving, so I will remove the color cast.

To do this, I simply slide the color cast slider located in the bottom of the histogram so that the value reads 100%. As I perform this slide, I closely watch the highlight and shadow triangle point locations and values. An example of this change is Figure 5.13; color versions of this image are in the color section.

The shadow starting point value for all channels is 3, and the highlight starting point for all channels is 213. Once the color cast correction slider is moved to 100%, the shadow values become Red = 6, Green = 7, and Blue = 3. The highlight values become Red = 212, Green = 213, and Blue = 202.

Now view the change in the image itself. You will see that that removing the color cast from this image has two major impacts:

- The color saturation in the image improves.
- The overall contrast of the image improves.

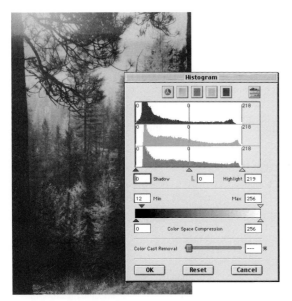
Original image

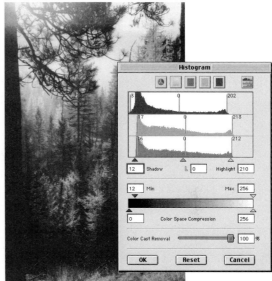
After removing color cast

Figure 5.13

Removing a color cast

If you prefer to remove only a portion of the color cast, the color cast removal slider tool will easily allow you to remove as little or as much as you like!

You will note that the differences here are more subtle than in the Jordan image correction performed earlier. But while these changes are less obvious, they are nonetheless important. And as your skill level in scanning increases so will your demands for image quality. Small changes will become increasingly important. SilverFast provides you with all the tools you need even for the most demanding observers.

Other Color Cast Removal Techniques

You have just seen how you can use the Histogram tool for color cast removal. But there are numerous ways to accomplish the same task in SilverFast. Color cast can be automatically removed through the use of the auto-adjustment tool when the auto-adjustment tool is configured to do so. Earlier in this chapter you saw how to remove color cast when setting highlight and shadow points using the Highlight/Shadow tool with the Shift key. You can even use the Gradation Curves tool and your densitometer. And there are other methods as well. But I suggest that you use the Histogram tool, at least at first, because it is easy to use, visual, and can be applied progressively. SilverFast's color cast removal Histogram tool is about the most intuitive and easy-to-use color cast correction tool you will find anywhere.

Be sure that you really do want to remove the color cast from your image. Evaluation of your image and its histograms is a good way to make this choice.

If you work in calibrated mode and use the auto-adjustment tool to correct your images, even if you set the tools to automatically remove color cast 100 percent in the options, Silver-Fast will not automatically remove the color cast. You must perform the color cast correction as I have done here (or using other color cast correction methods).

Not all color casts are undesirable. Remember that some images, such as sunsets, depend upon the presence of a color cast for their key image characteristics.

Controlling Brightness and Contrast

Once we have set our highlights and shadows and retained or removed our color casts, we need to examine the overall brightness and contrast of our images. The tool we use for controlling brightness and contrast is a curve tool, known as the Gradation Curves tool in Silver-Fast. With this tool, we concentrate on controlling the distribution of the grayscale values that exist between the highlight and shadow values we have already set in our images. I will continue adjusting the autumn image on which we have already set highlights and shadows and removed color cast.

Brightness Control with the Gradation Curves Tool

To adjust brightness, click the Gradation Curves tool icon. You will notice that this tool is basically a curve tool. The curve controls how the grayscale values are distributed between the highlight and shadow points we have already set.

A curve tool is less intuitive than a histogram tool because there is no data actually displayed. But use this tool for a while and you will become more comfortable with it.

As a starting point, let me explain that a curve tool is basically an input/output control where input values (from highlight to shadow) are along the horizontal bottom edge and output values (also from highlight to shadow) are along the vertical side edge. When we start, the curve is straight, so input and output values are equal. Once we start moving the curve, the input and output values will be different. Enough explanation; let's use the tool and you'll see.

You will notice that there are control points along the path. These allow us to control various portions of the curve, and therefore the image, independently of other areas of the curve and image.

Also in this window is a sequence of curve adjustment tools that can be used to adjust the position and shape of the curve, and therefore the distribution of the data values in your image. These curve control tools are labeled in Figure 5.14.

Figure 5.14

The Gradation Curves tool

Save Settings menu

Color channel mode selector buttons

Gradation curve

Midtone adjustment— linear (N) or logarithmic (L)

Contrast control

Highlight area control

Shadow area control

Brightness control (see note!)

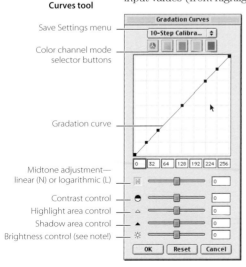

Following is a list of these curve adjustment tools and a brief description of their function:

Save Settings menu Allows you to save and load for later use any gradation curves you create.

Color channel mode selector Used to select whether you will be working on a composite channel or individual channels and in RGB or CMYK mode.

Midtone adjustment tool Used to adjust the overall brightness of an image. There are two basic curves, a linear and a logarithmic curve. (See Chapter 6 for more on this tool.)

Contrast control Used to adjust the overall shape of the curve and therefore the contrast of the image.

Highlight control Used to isolate adjustments in the highlight portion of an image.

Shadow control Used to isolate adjustment in the shadow portion of an image.

Brightness control Used to change the position of the highlight or shadow points in an image—but don't use it!

> The brightness control is a very dangerous tool because it alters the highlight or shadow points that have been already set. I avoid the use of this tool on most images. I suggest that you use the midtone adjustment tool to control overall brightness in your image.

These adjustments can be allied to either all channels at once or to individual channels by selecting your channel choices from the channel buttons at the top of the Gradation Curves window.

> Any gradation adjustment curve you create can be saved and loaded for use at another time. Just click the drop-down list at the top of the Gradation Curves window.

Adjusting Brightness

For all the following adjustments, make sure that the color mode selector is set to edit in RGB color space and that you will be adjusting all three color channels together with a single curve. These are the default settings.

To brighten an image, adjust the set points along the curve path so that the curve arches upward. To darken, adjust the set points along the curve path so that the curve arches downward. It is easy to move the entire curve up or down by adjusting the midtone slide. Or you can manually adjust the entire curve at once by holding down the Command or Ctrl key while you drag the midtone point. If required, the individual points along the curve can be fine-tuned after the initial overall adjustment.

In this image I want to lighten the midtones just a bit, so I will set the midtone tool to –5 (see Figure 5.15).

When you use the midtone adjustment tool, you have a choice between a linear and a logarithmic curve. The logarithmic curve (Figure 5.16) affects a larger adjustment in the shadow region than the linear curve does. Compare the shadow regions (circled) between the linear curve and logarithmic curve.

Adjusting Contrast

Adjusting the overall contrast of an image involves adjusting the overall shape of the curve. An S-shaped curve, flattened in the highlight and shadow regions, will increase the overall contrast of the image, whereas a reverse S-shaped curve, flattened in the midtone, will lower the overall contrast of the image. You will find that most images, including the autumn image, will benefit from a little increase in contrast.

To increase the contrast of this image, I move the contrast slider until it registers about +10. An S-shaped curve will appear, with the result being an overall increase in image contrast (see Figure 5.17).

If you now switch on the linear and logarithmic midtone curves, you will see a significant difference in the shadow adjustment.

Fine-Tuning Highlights and Shadows

If we want to fine-tune the highlight and shadow areas, we can move on to the next tools in the sequence, the highlight and shadow sliders in the Gradient Curves window:

- I move the slider in either direction to lighten or darken only the highlight portion of this image. Lighten the highlight area a bit with a +5 value.

- I fine-tune the shadow by darkening it slightly, make a similar adjustment to the next tool down, the shadow adjustment tool, with a value of –2.

The result of this fine-tuning is to increase the contrast of the image a bit more by being able to adjust the highlight and shadow regions separately and with different amounts. The values I have chosen here for my contrast adjustments suit my purposes for this image. Your image may vary depending upon your choices (see Figure 5.18).

The Brightness Tool: The Evil One!

Avoid the use of this tool if you want to protect the highlight and shadow points you have so carefully set. Unlike the other tools used in this contrast control exercise, this tool does not leave the highlight and shadow points alone. If you want to increase or decrease the overall brightness or contrast of an image while protecting your highlight and shadow points, *do not* use this tool. Use the midtone adjustment tool I discussed earlier.

Curve tools are better choices for most people's "brightness" adjustment needs.

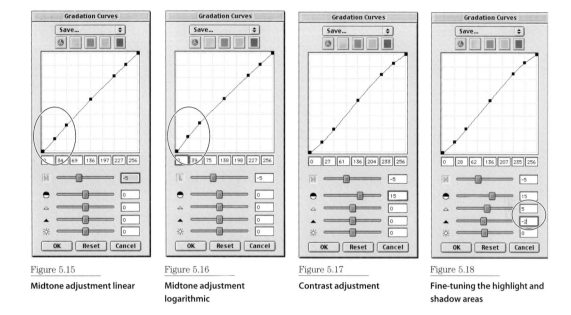

Figure 5.15

Midtone adjustment linear

Figure 5.16

Midtone adjustment logarithmic

Figure 5.17

Contrast adjustment

Figure 5.18

Fine-tuning the highlight and shadow areas

Use the brightness tool only if you intend to make dramatic adjustments to your highlight or shadow areas. Move the slider for this tool and you will see that the end value moves when the tool is adjusted. When would you use this tool? You might use it to adjust images that have flat color areas that you would like to have all the same values in the highlight or shadow. Otherwise you will typically want to avoid the use of this tool.

Figure 5.19 shows the final results of my image adjustments compared with the raw unadjusted image The final image has all the adjustment applied to it: tone compression (highlight and shadow adjustments), color cast correction, and final brightness and contrast adjustments. In the grayscale versions of this image, you can see the improved brightness and contrast of the final image. Again, color versions of these images can be found in the color section. When you view the color versions, note the improved color saturation of the final image.

Changing Your Scan's Color Balance

Sometimes you may want to change the overall color look of your image or part of your image. This of course can be performed in an image-editing application such as Photoshop. But remember that any changes made after the scan, particularly if they are significant changes, typically result in the removal of image data and the reduction of image quality. So if you know that you would like to change the color look of your entire image or of a certain tonal range portion of your image, it will be best to do so during the scan. You will want to complete the setup for a typical scan prior to making adjustments with the Global Color Correction tool.

Figure 5.19

Image progression

Original image   Final image

Adjusting with the Global Color Correction Tool

The Global Color Correction tool [icon], which when selected activates the Global Color Correction window, is located to the right of the Gradation Curves tool in the Scan Control window.

First perform a prescan and set up your prescan image with all the regular adjustments, including highlight and shadow points, color cast removal, and brightness and contrast. Now you are ready to make any color balance adjustments you might like to. I will use a photograph of a pink rose for this exercise.

I activate the color balance tool by clicking its icon; the Global Color Correction window (Figure 5.20) appears. (Its official title is the Global Color Correction dialog, but this type of correction is better known as "color balance.")

You will notice that there are three distinct parts to the color balance window:

- The top portion controls and displays the portion of the image that will be affected by the color balance adjustments.

- The middle portion contains a color circle.

- The bottom portion contains sliders, which are used to actually effect the color balance changes.

The curve window in the upper-left corner displays the changes that will be applied to the gradation curves, including which portion of the tonal range will be affected.

One of the keys to a successful color balance adjustment is not to overdo it by making too many adjustments or too much of an adjustment. You can only push color values so far before your image begins to lose details.

In SilverFast's color balance tool, we can apply color balance changes to the entire image or to various portions of the tonal range. Let's begin, because using the tool is the best way to understand how it works.

Global Color Balance Adjustment across the Entire Tonal Range

Click the three-dot icon (tonal range controls) arranged in a triangle underneath the curve display in the upper-left corner. This will activate the entire tonal range for color balance adjustment. The three-dot icon will turn from yellow to green when selected, and all three of the individual tonal range dots will turn red as well.

> Because you're not working with the same picture I have, your curves and numbers and values will differ. Adapt these instructions to your own hands-on work. See the rose images in the color section to follow along with my adjustments.

Notice that there is a small black-outlined square in the middle of the color circle, which we will call the color data point. As we make our adjustments, this small black-outlined square will move around inside the circle, indicating the direction in which we are moving our color balance.

We can affect movement of this square, and therefore our color balance, in three ways:

- Drag the color data point around directly.
- Click the color spots that surround the color circle.
- Move the sliders.

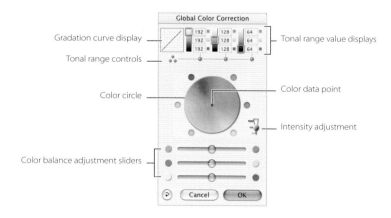

Gradation curve display

Tonal range controls

Color circle

Color balance adjustment sliders

Tonal range value displays

Color data point

Intensity adjustment

Figure 5.20

The Global Color Correction window

Try all three. For a simple demonstration of how this tool works, move the three-position intensity slider to the top (highest) position. Then move the top color slider (the one with red on the right end and cyan on the left end) all the way to the right. Note that four changes occur simultaneously:

- The color data point in the color circle moves toward the red edge of the color circle.

- The numbers in the top part of the window change to reflect the new color balance adjustment.

- The small gradation curve window displays the curve adjustments (across the entire tonal range) that are being made to accomplish the color balance adjustment.

- The view of the image changes in the preview window.

Figure 5.21

Color balance adjustment changes in the color balance window when the top slider is pulled to the far right with high intensity applied to the entire tonal range

See the starting and ending color balance windows in Figure 5.21 to view the change that occurred when I made the color adjustment. Color versions of the initial rose and the red color-balanced rose can be seen in the color section.

Color Balance Adjustment Applied Just to the Highlight

Return to the color balance adjustment window with the same settings from the global change made in the preceding section. In the upper part of the window (Figure 5.22), click the dot beneath the first column of numbers that is immediately to the right of the curve window. This will activate (make red) only the highlight area to receive the color balance adjustments.

Notice in the Gradation Curves window that the curves bulge out only in the highlight area of the curve, indicating that adjustments are being made just to the first 25 percent of the tonal range.

> Color balance adjustments can be made directly through the Gradation Curves tool. In fact, the color balance tool uses that tool to make its adjustments. But the color balance tool provides a very intuitive and visual way to decide on your color balance changes.

Viewing and Tweaking the Color Curves

Once you have made your color balance adjustments, you can view, and if needed, edit the color curves. Let's view and edit the color curves from the global color balance adjustment made earlier.

I will start with the color balance adjustment made in Figure 5.21, which is repeated in Figure 5.23a:

1. Apply the color balance adjustments as we did in the global color balance adjustment earlier.

2. Click the Gradation Curves tool icon in the tool palette to bring up the gradation tool.

   Notice that the changes we made in the color balance adjustment tool show up here in the Gradation Curves window. In fact, you can see that the color balance tool is a visual and intuitive way to manipulate the color curves in the Gradation Curves window.

   In this master curve window (Figure 5.23b), you can see the master, red, and green curves which have been moved as a result of the adjustments made in the color balance window. However, only the master (black) curve is editable.

   You will notice that the red curve is flattened out along the top of the curve graph. This type of flattening will result in a loss of detail on the red channel. This curve can and should be edited to prevent this loss of detail.

3. Click the Red channel button at the top of the master channel window. The Red channel now appears on its own, and it is editable (Figure 5.23c).

4. Click and drag the upper points along the flattened upper end of the curve so that the curve is no longer flattened but shows a more gradual transition like the curve in Figure 5.23d.

5. Apply this same curve smoothing edit to the curve in the highlight-only red curve.

Image Results

The results of the color balance adjustments can be easily seen when we compare the Red channels and histograms of the original rose scan (see Figure 5.24) with the Red channel images and histograms from the whole tonal range and highlight-only adjusted image.

Note how the Red channel histogram for the whole tonal range adjustment shows increased data across the whole tonal range and how the entire Red channel image is lighter as a result. In contrast, the highlight-only adjusted image shows data gain primarily in the highlight end of its histogram, and only the lighter outer edges of its rose are lighter in the Red channel image than the original image. Full-color versions of these images can be found in the color section.

Figure 5.22

Red curve window showing highlight-only adjustment

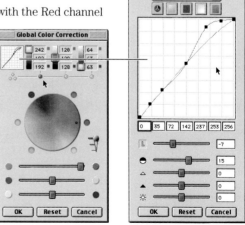

a) Color balance window

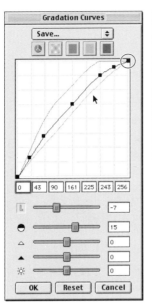

b) Master Gradation Curves window

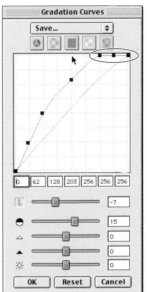

c) Red channel window

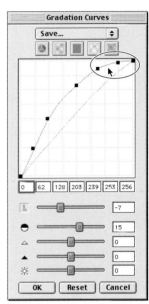

d) Edited Red channel window

Curve Editing Shortcuts

When editing a curve in SilverFast, there are a couple of keyboard shortcuts that can make the process easier and faster. Following are a couple of helpful ones:

- Hold down the Command or Ctrl key when you drag a curve control point and the entire curve will adjust smoothly.

- Hold down the Option or Alt key and click a control to alternately activate and deactivate the point as you click it.

> Much can be learned about editing color by viewing and studying the color curves in the Gradation Curves windows after color balance adjustments are made with the color balance tool.

With the tools and skills you have learned in this chapter, you are well on your way to creating consistently good scans. In the next few chapters, we will explore some of the finer points of image adjustments.

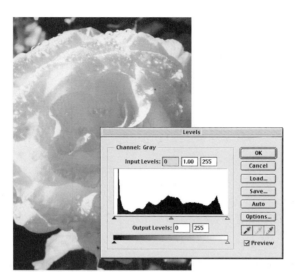

Original unadjusted

Figure 5.24

Effects of whole tonal range and highlight-only color balance adjustments

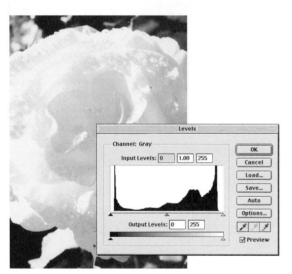

Whole tonal range unadjusted

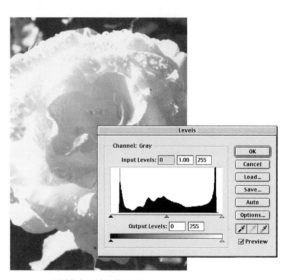

Highlight-only adjusted

CHAPTER 6

Fine-Tuning the Color in Your Scans

We've discussed the details of capturing and adjusting a low-resolution preview with the auto-adjustment tool (Chapter 4) and with manual adjustments (Chapter 5). In this chapter, we dig a little deeper into some of the tools and techniques for fine-tuning your color and discuss some alternative methods of making adjustments.

The following topics are covered in this chapter:

- Setting and using densitometer points
- Color correction with curves
- Color correction using the powerful MidPip tool
- Selective color-based corrections
- Making your own selections through masking
- Color restoration made easy

Setting and Using Densitometer Points

It is often useful to measure, monitor, and adjust grayscale values and the values of specific color—such as neutrals (grays) and "memory colors" (such as facial skin tones)—within an image. This can easily be done in SilverFast through the use of densitometer points. SilverFast allows for the setting and editing of up to four densitometer, or "fixed-pipette," points (known as fixed-PIP points). Each point can be set to measure in a different color mode if you prefer.

Color by Numbers

The human eye is notoriously inept at making quantitative color judgments. And our evaluation of color changes with time of day, surrounding colors, how we feel, lighting conditions, even what we had for lunch!

When we were kids we used to create pictures by filling in the color-by-numbers spaces. We can, and often should, take advantage of this same concept when we adjust colors in our scanned images. Using numeric values to adjust our colors frees us from the uncertainty that exists when we make color judgments strictly by eye. One of the most effective ways to evaluate and monitor numerous values in your images is to use densitometer/fixed-pipette points. Here is how you can use fixed-PIP points to evaluate and adjust the color in your images.

Figure 6.1

Set four fixed-pipette locations in this image.

As always, perform a clean prescan first. For this exercise, let's use a picture of another of my nieces, Lindsay Faye. (An uncorrected copy of this image can be found on the CD.) This image has several points we can use to monitor and adjust numerically. Also, zoom in on your image; working with an enlarged image is usually a good idea because a bigger image allows you to place your PIP points more accurately. This (and other color images) is shown in the color signature and can be used for reference, but cannot really be used for scanning purposes as it is screened there. However, I have selected my scan images to be representative of what you will find in many images. You can find similar measurement points in your own images.

Choosing and Setting Fixed-PIP Points

I typically look for two kinds of areas in an image to measure, monitor, and adjust: I look for neutral areas first and then any key memory color areas. Memory colors are important areas of our images that need to "look" right. Key memory color areas include facial skin tones, green grass, blue skies, and red stop signs. In this image of Lindsay, there are several neutral areas we can use, including the white areas of her dress and hat, the white snow on the barn roof, and the wicker chair in which she is sitting. The key memory color area in this image is Lindsay's skin.

> If you remember our discussion of color theory basics in Chapter 1, all color values in a digital image are controlled by the underlying grayscale values of the pixels. We can take good advantage of this concept by looking for and adjusting neutral/gray areas in our images. If we find and make our neutrals neutral, the remainders of the colors in our images should fall into place as well. Working with neutrals is one of the cornerstones of color capture, correction, and editing.

To set a pipette point, simply hold down your Shift key and click the areas you would like to monitor. Place four PIP points at the following locations, as shown in Figure 6.1:

1. The bright white spot on the hat

2. In the snow on the roof of the barn

3. On the wicker chair

4. On Lindsay's forehead

PIP points 1–3 are neutral points, and point 4 is a skin tone memory color.

Once the PIP points are placed, fixed-pipette symbols will be placed over each spot on which you click. In addition, an individual densitometer window will appear for monitoring each point (Figure 6.2).

Figure 6.2

Initial PIP densitometer readings

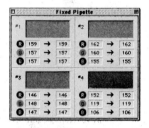

Reading the Raw Measurements and the Histogram

Once we have set our four fixed-PIP points, we can evaluate the values and start correcting our image, monitoring the densitometer reading as we go. The initial densitometer readings are as follows:

PIP	Location	R	G	B
1	White hat	159	157	157
2	Snow on barn roof	162	160	155
3	Chair arm	146	148	147
4	Skin tones	152	119	106

Figure 6.3

Initial histogram of raw image

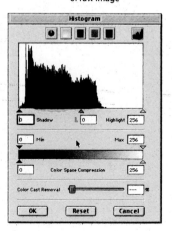

Click the Histogram tool and then click the mode button in the upper-left corner of the Histogram window until the single-channel black data histogram is visible (Figure 6.3).

When we analyze highlight neutrals, we are looking for two things: our highlight values should be equal (that is, neutral or gray), and our diffuse highlight should be about 242. As we can see by looking at the PIP densitometer numbers in the white hat and the snow on the barn, our white highlights are neither neutral nor light enough. For instance, we would like to see our white hat values, which are currently 159, 157, 157, to be closer to 242, 242, 242. A look at our initial histogram shows why our highlight readings are so dark. The highlight triangle is set way out to the right of the significant data, as shown in Figure 6.3.

Making Initial Image Adjustments and Tracking Numbers

We will use our histogram to adjust our image and we will use our PIP densitometer reading to guide our adjustments.

Click the auto-adjustment tool to initiate the adjustment and then view the PIP densitometer points (Figure 6.4). Note that PIP densitometer values for point #1 now read 201, 200, 200. The #2 point now reads 205, 202, 197. This is an improvement. All the numbers are now closer to our target highlight value of 242.

Because the image has improved, we may be inclined to accept the auto-adjustment. But our densitometer reading informs us that we can do better:

1. Activate the single-channel histogram we used earlier. Note that the highlight triangle has moved significantly to the left as a result of our auto-adjustment tool use.

2. While watching the #1 and #2 PIP densitometer readings, move the highlight triangle slider farther to the left until one of the three (red, green, or blue) values reaches 242.

3. Note the position of the highlight triangle and the new PIP densitometer values (Figure 6.5).

Our readings at point #2 are now 243, 242, 239. These values are very close to the neutral highlight targets values of 242, 242, 242.

Fine-Tuning Histogram Values

To fine-tune our highlight values, we will now go to the three-part histogram:

1. Activate the three-part RGB histogram by clicking the Histogram tool and clicking the histogram mode selection button in the upper-right corner of the window. The dialog now presents us with histograms for all channels (Figure 6.6) so that we can edit them separately. Our current #1 PIP densitometer values are R = 243, G = 242, and B = 239.

Figure 6.4

Readings after auto-adjustment

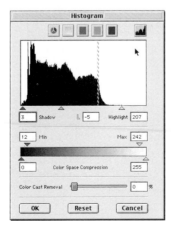
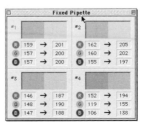

2. While watching the #1 densitometer values, move the Red channel highlighter until the R densitometer value is 242.

3. Now, while again watching the #1 densitometer values, move the Green channel highlight slider until G equals 242 in the densitometer.

Your final histogram and densitometer readings are shown in Figure 6.6.

Evaluating Skin Tone

Once we have the highlight adjusted, we can have a quick look at the skin tones. Unlike neutral values, skin tones are never equal (as long as we are working with live bodies). Also, unlike white highlights, which have specific target values such as 5%, skin tones will have a wide range of tonal values depending upon whether we are viewing and measuring the values in a highlight, midtone, or shadow region.

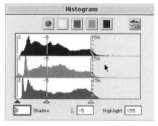

Figure 6.5

Readings after manual adjustment

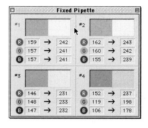

What we do know about skin tones is that they should fall in a range of RGB ratios. Now, whole books and careers have been based upon evaluating and adjusting skin tones, but we don't have time for all that here, so I would like to provide some simple guidelines to get you started.

Nearly all people have skin tones values in which red is greater than green and green is greater than blue. This is easy to remember because that is the order in which most of us refer to those colors: RGB. So just remember RGB (R > G > B).

Now, to get a bit more numerical about it, these RGB ratios typically fall in the range of 5/4/3 to 5/3/2. For skin that you think should be a bit more red, like the skin of a red-haired Irishman, you might look for a ratio of 5/3/2, which places more emphasis on the red values. If your image is of a Polynesian surfer, who will naturally have more green in their skin, then a 5/4/3 ratio might be more appropriate.

Measure the skin tone of Lindsay. Look at the densitometer reading for point # 4 in Figure 6.6. We see that Lindsay's skin tones measure a perfectly human R = 237, G = 201, B = 182, with R > G > B.

Now compare the original image with your final corrected image, shown in Figure 6.7 and also in the color section. Notice how the final image is much brighter and has better contrast and that the highlights are bright white and neutral. And

Figure 6.6

A three-part histogram

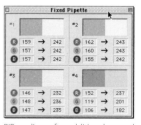

After additional manual corrections

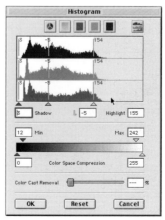

After initial auto-correction

PIP readings after additional manual corrections

because we guided our adjustment based upon numbers rather than just visual cues, we can have confidence that the corrections we have made are good ones.

If you actually calculate the ratios here, you will determine that they are 5/4/1.7. This deviates slightly form our 5/3/2 target but is acceptable, because 5/3/2 is a general target value, not an absolute. If you care to fine-tune to these values, you can make adjustments to the individual channels (of the color values you would like to change) of the Gradation Curve tool. (See Chapter 4 and the next section in this chapter for specific instruction on use of the Gradation Curve tool.)

Color Correction with Curves

For making highlight and shadow value adjustments, nothing beats the histogram; it's visually easy to adjust and intuitive. But for adjusting the values between the highlight and shadow, we need a different tool, one that gives us more subtle control of the entire range of grayscale values from the highlight to the shadow. That tool is the curve tool, or in the lexicon of SilverFast, the Gradation Curve tool .

Figure 6.7

Comparison of the Lindsay photo (left, original image; right, the final corrected version)

Unlike the histogram, which allows you only one point of control (the midtone slider) for adjusting all the grayscale values, the curve tool, which offers a line rather than a single tri-angle slider point, gives us virtually unlimited ability to control the distribution of our intermediate grayscale values. It is worth mentioning that because we cannot actually see any image data in a curve window, we nearly always use the densitometer measurement values to help guide us when we work with curves. To see how a curve tool is used and fits into a workflow, use the following example. For this example, scan an image of a barn and some autumn trees in which there is no true white highlight. (An uncorrected image of this barn can be found on the CD.) Perform a clean prescan, then follow along through the subsequent sections.

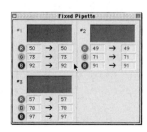

Figure 6.8

Raw barn image with location of fixed-PIP points

Evaluating an Image

The first three characteristics you may notice about this image are as follows:

- It is rather flat looking (low contrast).

- The colors are not well saturated.

- There is no true diffuse highlight.

In cases like this, we must depend upon image help and information from our tools. As we learned from previous exercises, we look for neutrals to measure and then we view and evaluate our histogram to look for clues about color cast and where to set our highlights and shadows.

When we look for a neutral in this image, about the best we can find is the weathered wood on the side of the barn. Although this wood may not be perfectly neutral, it's close enough for us to measure while we look for any obvious color cast. Besides, it's all we have!

Place several fixed-PIP points around the barn to measure and monitor the RGB values, as in Figure 6.8.

Read the RGB values and you will notice that the wood is nowhere near neutral. There is a strong presence of blue, and red is weak. For example, the PIP #1 values are R = 50, G = 73, B = 92, as shown in Figure 6.9.

Figure 6.9

Initial fixed-PIP densitometer readings

Activate the three-part histogram by choosing the Histogram tool and selecting the three-part histogram mode as we have done before.

When we view this histogram (Figure 6.10), we see two obvious clues to this image. We see that both the highlight and shadow ends of the histogram need to be compressed. Also, due to the offset nature of the histograms, we can see that this image probably has a color cast.

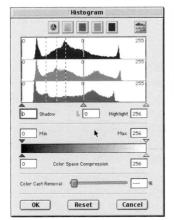

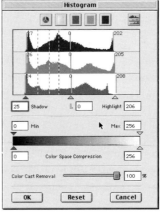

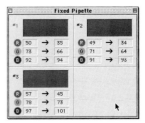

Figure 6.10

Initial histogram needing tone compression and color cast correction

Figure 6.11

After applying tone compression and color cast correction

Figure 6.12

Fixed-PIP densitometer values after histogram correction

First Histogram Corrections

We begin our image correction by working in the three-part histogram, compressing the highlight and shadow points separately on each channel to improve the contrast of the image and remove the color cast from the highlight and shadow regions. The corrected settings are shown in Figure 6.11. (See Chapter 4 for more information on these topics.)

Now remeasure the three fixed-PIP points. Note that the RGB values are closer to neutral but not quite there yet. In PIP # 1, R = 35, G = 66, B = 94 (see Figure 6.12).

The highlights and shadows have been neutralized, but the midtones clearly are not. This is where the Gradation Curve tool will be most useful, working on midtones.

Click the Gradation Curve tool . The Gradation Curves dialog appears. Initially, it is a straight line (see Figure 6.13).

The Adjustment Plan

Our plan is to use the closest object we have to a presumed neutral, the weathered gray side of the barn, to guide our adjustment to neutrals. We will make the barn a neutral gray. If we manipulate this first black (master) curve, we will be editing all three colors at once. We need instead to manipulate the color channels separately.

Because all of the RGB values are different, we will use the middle values—which in this case are the green values 66, 64, and 73 for the three fixed-PIPs—as our numeric targets. This means that we will adjust the red and blue curves.

Click the red square at the top of the window. A new window with an editable red curve appears.

Keeping your eye on the three fixed-PIP densitometer readings, pull the middle of the red curve up until the red values are approximately equal to the green values on all three readings. They will rarely all be equal in a circumstance like this, but get as close as you can to something like Figure 6.14. Experiment with changing the arc of the curve to get the best results. You may notice that I have moved the midpoint of the curve toward the shadow end as well as up. This is the type of subtle adjustment and control that a curve adjustment affords us. A simple movement of a histogram midtone slider would not.

> Hold down the Command/Ctrl key when you click and drag the middle point and the entire line will move smoothly. If you do not hold down the key, only the dragged point will move.

View the RGB values in the updated fixed-PIP densitometer. Notice how the red values, while not exactly equal to the green values, are close.

Now perform the same adjustment using the blue curve. Activate that curve by clicking the blue square at the top of the window. Pull the blue curve down until its values on all three fixed-PIP densitometers are as close to the red and green values as possible (as shown in Figure 6.15).

Color Correction Using the Powerful MidPip Tool

One of the most powerful, and easy-to-use, color correction tools provided by SilverFast is the MidPip (middle pipette) tool, located between the highlight and shadow point tools. The

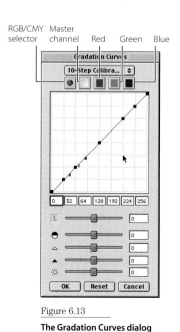

Figure 6.13

The Gradation Curves dialog

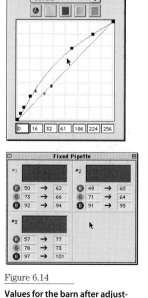

Figure 6.14

Values for the barn after adjusting the red curve

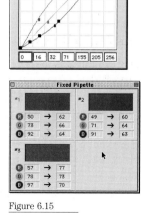

Figure 6.15

Values for the barn after adjusting the blue curve

MidPip tool was designed specifically to help us quickly and easily color-correct images by allowing us to neutralize up to four different areas in an image. This is particularly useful for images having color cast that varies from one portion of the image to another.

In this exercise, I use the MidPip tool to color-correct the original autumn barn images by neutralizing the barn, which showed a complex color cast (review Figure 6.12):

1. Perform an initial preview scan.

2. Adjust the image with the auto-adjustment tool.

3. Select the MidPip tool by clicking in the pipette tool symbol between the highlight and shadow point tools 🖉 .

4. Click on the left side of the front of the barn (see Figure 6.16).

5. Select the MidPip tool again and click in the middle of the front of the barn.

6. Select the MidPip tool a third time and click on the right side of the front of the barn.

7. Now double-click the MidPip tool. This will activate the MidPip data window.

The MidPip data window shows both the initial (source) and corrected (destination) data for each point. For instance, point number 1 has R/G/B source data values of 85/101/122. The destination data values are 76/76/76, thereby making that point and surrounding area neutral. Similarly, the other two points have been neutralized. (Uncorrected and corrected versions of this barn image labeled C20 and C21 can be seen in the color section.)

Tweaking the MidPip

If you prefer to work with CMY values rather than RGB, simply click the color space selector button 🔘 in the MidPip data window to change the displayed values back and forth from RGB to CMY.

To alter the color balance from neutral, click any of the MidPip data window fields and type in whatever value you prefer. For instance, I added a bit of a red color cast to the area around point number 1 by adjusting the red value up from 76 to 80, which is evident in Figure 6.16.

You can easily navigate through the MidPip data window by simply tabbing to move forward or Shift+tabbing to reverse direction.

ADJUSTING OVERALL IMAGE CONTRAST

When you have completed your color cast correction, whether you use the curve or the Mid-Pip method, you may want to adjust the overall contrast of the image while leaving the corrected color balance unchanged. The Gradation Curve tool is typically the best tool to utilize for this type of adjustment. Here I would use the Gradation Curve tool to increase the overall contrast of the barn image. This should be accomplished using the master curve only so that no alteration of the color balance of the image will occur.

Selective Color-Based Corrections

You might also find it useful to be able to adjust the color values of a specific color rather than a tonal range in an image. This is what the Selective Color Correction tool allows us to do. To demonstrate how this Selective Color Correction tool works, we will use a sunset image. (An uncorrected copy of this image can be found on the CD.)

Perform a clean prescan and apply the basic histogram and curve adjustments discussed in previous chapters.

Here I click the Selective Color Correction tool ![tool] in the SilverFast tools. The Selective Color Correction window appears (Figure 6.17).

Selecting the Color Matrix Set and Color to Adjust

SilverFast offers two color matrix sets: a standard 6-color set (labeled CM6 in the window) and a 12-color set (labeled CM12). Which you choose depends upon how tightly focused or restrictive you want your selective color adjustments to be. The standard 6-color set includes the basic red, green, blue, cyan, magenta, and yellow. The 12-color set further divides the original 6 colors into 6 more categories. We will use the standard 6-color set for this exercise.

Click the color in the image you would like to adjust—in my case, the portion of the orange area in the clouds. That color will be placed at the center of the color circle. The colors around the edge of the circle are called the contaminating colors and can be added to or subtracted from the color at the center of the circle. The color in the top horizontal set of color matrix boxes that is closest to the color you selected will be activated in the horizontal boxes of the color matrix set. In this case, it is the red box at the far left.

Figure 6.16

The MidPip tool

Figure 6.17

The Selective Color Correction window

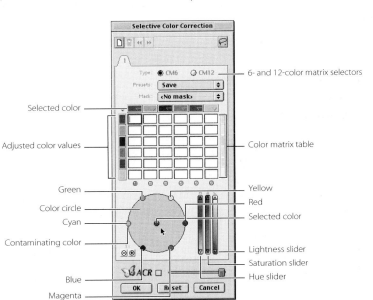

If you use the 12-color set, you must scroll back and forth through the colors, as all 12 will not fit in the visible window space.

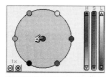
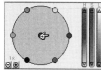
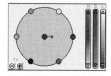
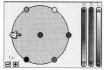

Manually Adjusting Color

The surrounding contaminating colors can be either added to or subtracted from the selected color at the center of the circle. This addition and subtraction can be accomplished either manually or by the numbers. Let's try the graphical approach first.

First move the cursor over the central spot that displays the selected color. A hand will appear with a + sign in it.

Now click and drag to the right toward the red contaminating color.

A stick with a ball on the end will be drawn out toward the red contaminating color. The farther you move the hand, the longer the stick becomes and the more red will be added to the original color.

Alternatively, colors can be subtracted from the central color. Click and drag from the cyan contaminating color spot toward the selected central color spot. A hand with a negative sign will be displayed as you drag the stick ball symbol toward the central selected color, indicating a removal of cyan.

Color Matrix: Adjusting by the Numbers

Color addition and subtraction can also be accomplished numerically by making changes to the color matrix table. The best way to see how this works is to make a manual adjustment and view the changes to the color matrix table. The top row includes the starting colors, and the vertical set of colors includes the contaminant colors. The selected color occurs at the far-left side of the horizontal set of colors (see Figure 6.18).

Here I make the same manual addition of red we made earlier to the central selected color but view the changes to the color matrix table. The table will reflect numerically the manual adjustments you make in the color circle. (In the example shown in Figure 6.18, the color matrix box for the starting and red colors increased by 8.) To adjust another color, simply click the color in the preview scanned image. The new initial color will appear in the center of the circle, and the nearest starting color will be activated in the top row of colors in the matrix table.

Make the same manual subtraction of cyan we made earlier from the central selected color but view the changes to the color matrix table. Note that the color matrix box for the starting and cyan colors decreased by 8. If you end up changing the initially selected color to another basic hue, the new hue will be shown in the color circle and activated in the top row of colors in the color matrix table.

Adjusting Saturation

In addition to manually adjusting the color ball sticks in the color circle or adjusting the numeric values in the color matrix, you have the option of manipulating the slider to the right of the color circle. This slider allows you to control hue (H), saturation (S) and brightness/lightness (L).

Click and drag the saturation slider to increase saturation. Note that when the saturation slider is moved, both the ball sticks and the color matrix are modified (Figure 6.19). Color versions of the original and red-enhanced sunset images can be seen in color-section images C22 and C23.

Adding Colors to the Adjustment

After you have defined your initial color by clicking the color you want to adjust in the preview image, you can add other colors. In this example of a sunset image, we might want to add yellows to our initial red-orange color selection prior to adjusting the saturation. In this way, surrounding yellows in additions to the reds and oranges will be affected by the saturation enhancement

Hold down the Shift key and click the small radio button underneath the color matrix data boxes below the yellow color. The button will change to green. Now both the first column and the next to last column will be active, as indicated by the green radio buttons, and affected by any changes you might make.

Adjust the saturation slider to increase saturation. You will see that the matrix values underneath both the red-orange and the yellow columns will be changed, as shown in Figure 6.20. A color version of this red- and yellow-enhanced sunset can be seen as C24 in the color section.

See the color section to examine the results of changes made on a raw scan of this image with basic scan adjustments and selective color adjustments. To see the differences between enhancing just the reds and enhancing both reds and yellows, look carefully at the edges of the sunset colors, where the yellows dominate.

Preset Adjustments

SilverFast has a whole set of preset adjustments if you don't want to make your own adjustments. Just click and hold on any of the starting colors along the horizontal set of boxes and a menu of choices will appear.

Figure 6.18

Color matrix addition and subtraction results

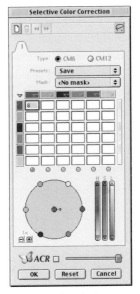
Adding the selected color

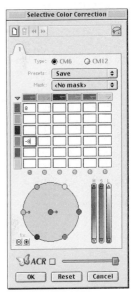
Subtracting a contaminating color

Figure 6.19

Saturation adjustment in HSL sliders

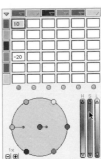

If you have several sets of corrections you would like to keep track of and apply, it's easy to do. You can save multiple sets of selective color correction values in tabs (Figure 6.21).

Click the document icon in the upper-left corner of the Selective Color Correction window. A new tab will appear, in which you can create and save another set of selective color correction parameters. Each of these tabs can then be saved for loading and use on another day.

Making Your Own Selections Through Masking

So far we have controlled the editing adjustments of our images by selecting their tonal and color ranges. There are times when even this isn't enough. If you just want to adjust one small area of the image and tonal and color range selections don't do the trick, masking will make it possible.

Masking involves making a physical selection of a specific area of an image. Prior to making any color adjustments, we make our selections and adjustments using the tool we just used, the Selective Color Correction tool. The masking capability is an extension of this tool's capabilities. For this exercise, I work with an image that has one flower, a Hawaii sunset image with a bougainvillea in the foreground. The original and corrected versions of this image can be found on the CD. Here is how it works:

1. Perform a clean preview scan and apply basic histogram and curve corrections to the image.

2. Zoom in on the area of the image from which you would like to make a mask.

3. Activate the Selective Color Correction tool [icon].

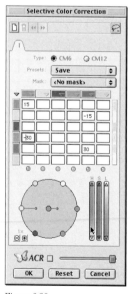

Figure 6.20

Matrix changes to multiple colors

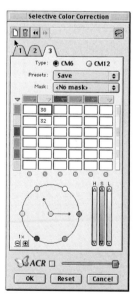

Figure 6.21

Tabs for multiple sets of correction values

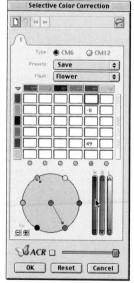

Figure 6.22

Adjusting within the flower mask

4. Click the Mask drop-down menu and select New Mask.

5. With the lasso tool that appears, draw a mask around the area you want to color-adjust. I have drawn a careful mask here, but if the surrounding areas do not have any similar colors to the colors in the area you want to adjust, you don't have to be too careful with your mask drawing.

   You have your choice of three kinds of masking tools: a lasso (the default), a polygon tool, and a brush accessed through the masking tool menu at the upper-right corner of the window. The use of any of these tools results in the creation of a selected area on the image.

6. When you are finished drawing the mask, a small window appears asking you to name it; give your mask a helpful name. Once named, this mask will appear in the same Save menu and can be loaded at any time.

Any mask you create can be edited with the use of the Shift key and the Command or Ctrl key. Hold down the Shift key to add to a selection and the Command/Ctrl key to subtract from the selection. Masks can also be inverted, deleted, saved, and loaded under the Mask drop-down menu.

7. Click the color inside of the mask that you would like to adjust. Here, I clicked the flower petals.

8. Adjust the settings in the Selective Color Correction window. Here I have decreased the saturation and lightened the selected color range. In Figure 6.22, the flower mask is visible in the Mask menu.

9. Click OK and finish the scan as you would normally. See Figure 6.23 for a comparison of a scan done with and without the mask correction applied.

ADJUST NOW OR ADJUST LATER?

These same types of mask-based adjustments can, of course, be made in a postscanning image editing application such as Photoshop. However, there are three advantages to performing the correction here:

- It's faster to perform the function here; once the scan is complete, you are finished.

- If you perform this image correction after the scan, you will likely be reducing the quality of the image. Remember that any adjustments made in Photoshop will typically be made with less image and often result in the loss of more image data, therefore lowering image quality.

- The Selective Color tools in SilverFast are more intuitive and easier to use than many image editing application tools, so you are more likely to achieve the result you want.

Color Restoration Made Easy

We are often challenged with having to scan images that have, through time and abuse, been significantly faded. Although it is certainly possible to use SilverFast's wide range of image correction tools in concert to help correct these images, it would certainly be a challenge. Newer versions of SilverFast (6.0+) have a tool specifically designed to handle this challenge. It is called the Adaptive Color Restoration, or ACR, tool. ACR has been added as a component to the Selective Color Correction window. It is an easy one-button solution:

1. Select the area of the faded prescanned image you would like to correct.

2. Activate the Selective Color Correction tool .

3. Click the ACR check box located at the bottom of the window.

4. Now move the slider until you achieve the results you like.

It's a good idea to take a look at an ACR corrected image with your densitometer and perhaps fine-tune it with your histogram and curve tools.

My experience is that sometimes this ACR adjustment works very well and all I need to do is fine-tune the results. On some images, however, I actually get better results performing the standard scanning steps used in Chapters 4 through 6.

Figure 6.23

Correcting a masked area: left, without the mask, and right, with it. Color versions of these two images can be found in the color section as C25 and C26.

Figure 6.24

Comparison of fading (left) and correcting (right)

Images that have *not* experienced strong color cast shifts during fading respond well to the ACR adjustment. Images with strong color casts, such as the one in Figure 6.24, will probably be best corrected using the auto-adjustment tool followed by manual fine-tuning to restore neutrals and memory colors, as we have performed previously in this chapter. Figure 6.24 shows a faded image that I corrected using SilverFast's auto-adjustment tool, histogram, and gradation curves (color versions of these images are shown in the color section). So, try the ACR on the faded image. If you do not like the results, use the conventional method as I have done here. In either case, SilverFast provides a set of tools to help you get the job done. Try your hand at correcting this image and compare your results with mine. Original and corrected versions of the image "Tina" can be found on the CD. Printed color versions can be seen in the color section as C8 and C9.

24-bit RGB color (three-channel) image

32-bit CMYK color (four-channel) image

▲**Figure C1** RGB and CMYK color channels. The number of channels and their content determine the color mode of the image. (Chapter 1)

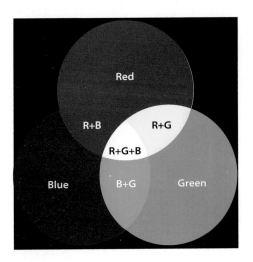

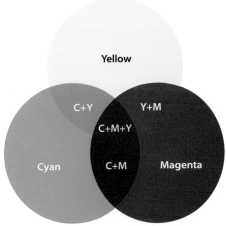

◀**Figure C2** RGB color circles. Various percentages of red, green, and blue are added together to make a wide range of colors. (Chapter 1)

▶**Figure C3** CMY color circles. Various percentages of cyan, magenta, and yellow added together subtract light to create new colors. (Chapter 1)

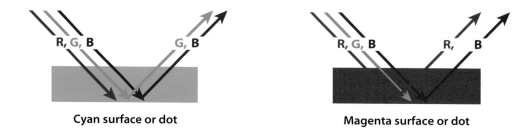

Cyan surface or dot   Magenta surface or dot

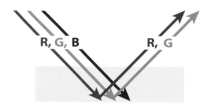

Yellow surface or dot

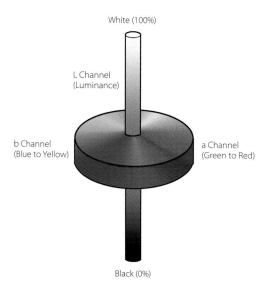

▲**Figure C4** CMYK subtractive color process used in printing. Transmitted (RGB) light is selectively absorbed by various combinations of the three process colors (C, M, and Y). The color(s) we see on a printed piece comes from the light that is transmitted and reflected rather than absorbed by the process colors. (Chapter 1)

▼**Figure C5** In Lab mode, all the grayscale values are placed on one channel. (Chapter 1)

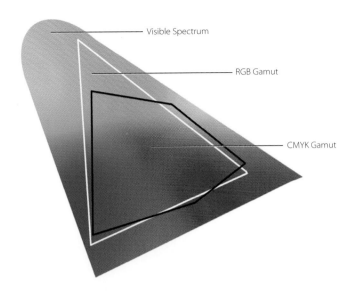

Visible Spectrum

RGB Gamut

CMYK Gamut

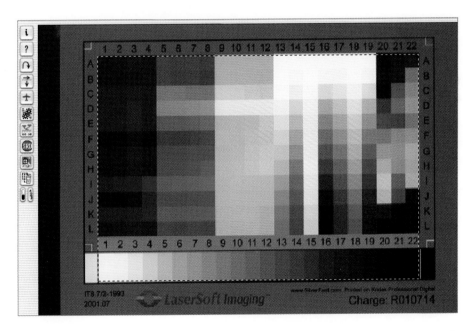

▲**Figure C6** A schematic comparison of the gamut of visible, RGB, and CMYK colors. (Chapter 11)
▼**Figure C7** IT8 target. This multicolored and grayscale target is used to calibrate your scanner and to create color profiles of your scanner that are used in the color management process. Note the selection rectangle carefully placed around the swatches. (Chapter 4 and Appendix A)

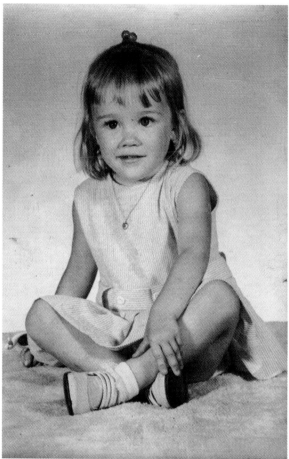

◀**Figure C8** Tina uncorrected. This image is on the CD. Try your hand at correcting it and compare your efforts with mine in C9. (Chapter 6)
▶**Figure C9** Tina corrected. (Chapter 6)

◀**Figure C10** Autumn image uncorrected. Note the overall flatness and poor color saturation. (Chapter 5)
▶**Figure C11** Autumn image final. (Chapter 5)

▲**Figure C12** Uncorrected image of Jordan. Note the low brightness, contrast, and poor color saturation. (Chapter 5)
▼**Figure C13** Auto-corrected image of Jordan. Note the improvement over the raw image. (Chapter 5)
▶**Figure C14** Manually corrected image of Jordan. Compare with the raw and auto-corrected images and note the further improvement of brightness, contrast, color saturation, and image detail. (Chapter 5)

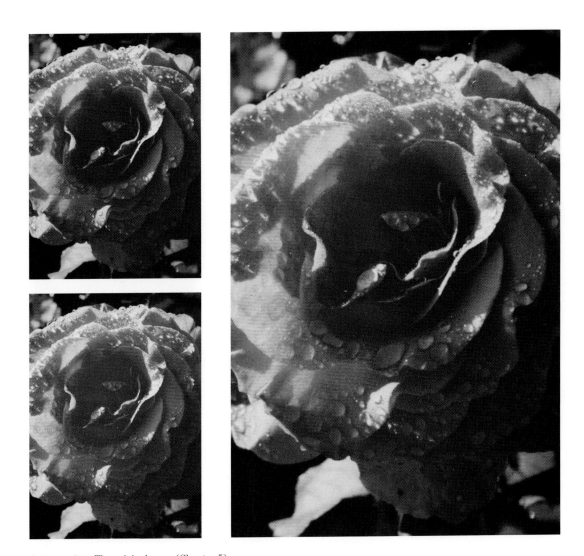

▲**Figure C15** The original rose. (Chapter 5)
▼**Figure C16** The entire rose is now redder. (Chapter 5)
▶**Figure C17** Highlight of rose is redder. Note that unlike in C16, where the entire rose is redder, in this image just the highlight regions of the rose are redder. (Chapter 5)

◄**Figure C18** Lindsay uncorrected. Note the low contrast, dull colors, and "dirty" white highlights in this image. (Chapter 6)
►**Figure C19** Lindsay corrected. Note the improved contrast, the "popping" colors, and the "clean" white highlights in this image. (Chapter 6)

◄**Figure C20** Barn uncorrected. Note the flat smoky appearance to this image. Also note the poor color saturation in the grass and trees, as well as the obvious blue cast to the barn wood. (Chapter 6)

▶**Figure C21** Barn corrected. Note the much improved contrast. See how the colors pop in this image, the grass is greener, the trees have more saturated colors, and the barn wood now looks more like true weathered (neutral gray) wood. (Chapter 6)

▲**Figure C22** Sunset uncorrected. (Chapter 6)

▲**Figure C23** Sunset with red enhanced. (Chapter 6)

▲**Figure C24** Sunset with red and yellow enhanced. (Chapter 6)

◀**Figure C25** Hawaiian flower. Note the initial saturation of the bougainvillea. (Chapter 6)
▶**Figure C26** Hawaiian flower after masked adjustment. Note the enhanced saturation of the bougainvillea. (Chapter 6)

◄**Figure C27** Scan of a printed (screened) logo. Note the obvious reproduction of the printed halftone dot pattern. (Chapter 8)

►**Figure C28** Descreened logo. Note the smoothing of the original printed halftone dot pattern. (Chapter 8)

◄**Figure C29** Grainy image. Note the obvious pattern in the background of this image. (Chapter 8)

►**Figure C30** GANE-adjusted image. Note the removal of the pattern from the background of this image. (Chapter 8)

▲ **Figure C31** Tori and company with lots of dust and scratches. (Chapter 8)
▼ **Figure C32** Tori and company with dust and scratches removed through the use of SDR. (Chapter 8)

▲ **Figure C33** Uncorrected 48-bit image used in the HDR exercise. (Chapter 12)
▼ **Figure C34** Corrected 48-bit image for comparison (Chapter 12)

◀**Figure C35** The Apple logo. Scan this logo and then compare your results with this image. (Chapter 9)

▶**Figure C36** Apple logo prescan image. This is an example of how the logo would look in a prescan preview. (Chapter 9)

◀**Figure C37** Apple logo after an auto adjustment. This shows how the logo might look in an auto adjustment of the preview image. This is certainly an improvement, but some manual tweaking can result in some significant improvements. (Chapter 9)

▶**Figure C38** Apple logo intermediate adjustment. This shows the result of manually tweaking the image after auto adjustment. (Chapter 9)

▲ **Figure C39** Starting gladiolus image for the color-to-grayscale conversion in HDR using SC2G capability of the Selective Color tool. (Chapter 12)

CHAPTER 7

Getting Control with the Expert Dialog

For those of you who hate numbers and can't imagine why you would need more control over your images than you would have with the features already discussed in the first six chapters, you are welcome to skip this one and move on to Chapter 8. But for those of you who revel in the ultimate control of your scans, and for whom numbers are not a mystery but a key to more control, read on.

The Expert Dialog in SilverFast is here to give those of us who want it complete numeric control of our scans. This kind of control is most useful when you are trying to hit certain target values in your images and/or you want the most consistency you can obtain from one scan to another. For instance, performing color correction adjustments by the numbers will provide more dependable, predictable, and consistent results than making adjustments based upon the view of an image on a monitor.

The following topics are covered in this chapter:

- **Where do all those numbers come from?**

- **Editing the Expert Dialog**

- **Saving changes**

Where Do All Those Numbers Come From?

Before you can hope to understand how to adjust all the values in the Expert Dialog, you need to first understand where they come from and what they control. I always find it useful to break down seemingly complex items into smaller, more manageable parts. Once I understand each part, the whole is not nearly so intimidating.

The core of the Expert Dialog (Figure 7.1) contains four columns of data divided into four, and in some cases five, sections. These columns display numerically all of the RGB, CMY, or grayscale data that has been assigned by the adjustment of all of the other preferences and tools utilized by SilverFast. In addition, there is a curves window to supply a graphical display of the data (this can be closed if you prefer). And finally, there is a button that is used to switch between RGB and CMY mode ⊘, and a button for exporting data to a text file ▤. In truth the Expert Dialog has far fewer options than many other tools, such as the Selected Color Correction window, which often has several layers of tabs or settings.

It is perhaps useful to think about this expert window as a table filled with a database of all the adjustment values for the image. In the following sections you will learn where these values come from and what they control. If you have read through Chapters 4, 5, and 6, all of these values will be familiar to you. Once we break the window down into sections, it will be far less intimidating and confusing and ultimately more useful to you. I'll use Figure 7.1 to discuss the basic organization of the columns and the two data display scales. Later figures will show all the relationships between the data field values and the options and adjustment tools to which they relate.

The Columns

The four columns show image data either in terms of 0%–100% grayscale or 0–255 shades of gray (which in turn control output color values to your monitor or printer). When we select RGB as the display mode, the first three columns display RGB values on a scale of 0–255 because they are the units we typically use when we work in RGB mode (the window on the left in Figure 7.1).

When we select CMY as the display mode, the first three columns will display CMY values on a scale of 0%–100% because they are the units we typically use when we work in CMY mode (the window on the right in Figure 7.1).

To clearly see the difference, look at the two rows of Range-Max and Range-Min data. This data is set at 242 and 12 in RGB mode but registers as 5% and 95% when viewed in CMY mode. These are identical values, just calculated on two different scales: 5% CMY = 242 RGB, and 95% CMY = 12 RGB. (Remember that the 0–255 scale is based upon the minimum 256 shades of gray we work with in computer-based publishing.)

The reason high and low values are not equal on the two scales is that the two scales are the opposite, or inverse, of each other. White to black in RGB is 255–0, whereas white to black in CMY or grayscale mode is 0–100. So RGB 255 (white) equals CMY 0%, and RGB 0 equals 100% CMY.

The value conversion math works like this, using the inverse, decimal version of each percentage (for example, 5% requires multiplying by 0.95):

- To calculate 5% highlight value: 0.95 × 255 = 242
- To calculate 95% shadow value: 0.05 × 255 = 12

The far right column, labeled Gr, always shows grayscale data and is displayed either on a 0–255 scale or the 0%–100% grayscale scale, depending upon which mode is selected. This column is most commonly referred to when we are working with grayscale contone images.

The Graph, or Curves Display

The graph at the top of the expert window displays the data from the image data fields graphically as curves. This curve view window can be either displayed or closed by clicking the small arrow next to the upper-left corner of the display.

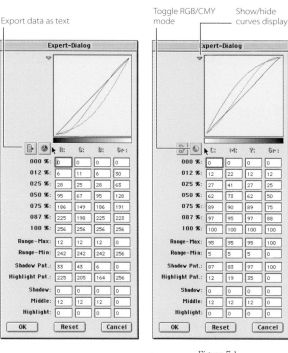

Export data as text

Toggle RGB/CMY mode

Show/hide curves display

Figure 7.1

The Expert Dialog; RGB (left) and CMY (right)

The curves will display either RGB or CMY data depending upon which mode is selected (this graph will display one gray for grayscale-only images). The two curves in Figure 7.1 display equal data values but in the two different color modes. You will note that the curves curve *down* for the RGB data and they curve *up* for the CMY data. This disparity is once again due to the inversion of the 0–100 and 0–255 scale. SilverFast has elected to deal with this disparity by reversing the directions of the grayscale value scales when it displays data. Note that the gradients at the bottom of each graph trend in opposite directions. When displaying in RGB mode, the highlight values are on the right end and the shadow values are on the left end. When displaying in CMY mode, the opposite holds true; shadow values are on the right end and the highlight values are on the left end. As a result of the inversion of the gradients, the curves are inverted as well.

You will notice that this inversion of the graphical display of data is consistent throughout SilverFast's windows and dialog boxes. This inversion is done so the numeric data is displayed consistently. The high and low values for both RGB and CMY will always be on the same side.

As we move forward to discuss the data sections of the Expert Dialog, I am going to take my own advice and work in one color space, RGB. It will be easy to understand and less confusing…so off we go!

REVERSED CURVES

The inversion of data can be very confusing if you are somewhat familiar with either the RGB or CMY world and you have to learn what the values mean *and* a new color space. But it's often particularly confusing for newcomers to the world of color who are both unfamiliar with color spaces and struggling to learn what the various values mean.

My suggestion is to initially work predominantly in one color space or the other. Develop a real proficiency in understanding and manipulating one set of data. Then with one color space firmly under your belt, it will make it much easier to learn the other. I suggest that you begin in RGB, because it is a more flexible color space and it is the natural color space of your scanner, your monitor, and the World Wide Web. After you are comfortable with RGB values, then tackle CMY and CMYK. As you may have already noted, I've used RGB exclusively up to this point. In Chapter 11 we will delve deeper into CMY and CMYK.

This confusing inversion of RGB and CMY values is *not* my fault, and I beg you to not hold me responsible!

The Data Sections

All versions of SilverFast have at least four sections of data. More recent versions (5.0+) have a fifth as well. We will cover all five sections here:

The gradient data The image data controlled by the gradient curves is shown in the top seven rows of data fields labeled with the percentages (Figure 7.2). The values in these data fields exactly match the values set on the seven points of the three (red, green, and blue) curves in the Gradation Curves dialog box.

Tone compression data The two data fields labeled Range-Max and Range-Min contain the data values that reflect the setting assigned in the tone compression slider in the Histogram dialog box (Figure 7.3). As we discussed in Chapter 4, this tone compression value is initially set in the Auto tab of the Defaults window but can be later reset in the Histogram tool or here in the Expert Dialog.

Shadow and highlight points These data fields reflect the highlight and shadow point values for the three (RGB) channels shown in the three channel histograms found in the Histogram window (Figure 7.4). These values of course may have been determined through the use of the auto-adjustment tool or the highlight and shadow point tools, or they may be the result of a manual adjustment of these values. But in any case, the current values are shown here.

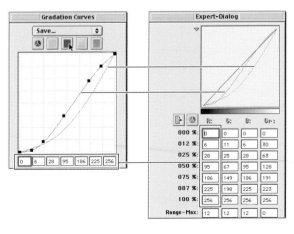

Figure 7.2

The curves points and percentage data matches the values in the Gradation Curves dialog. (Here, only the red curve is shown.)

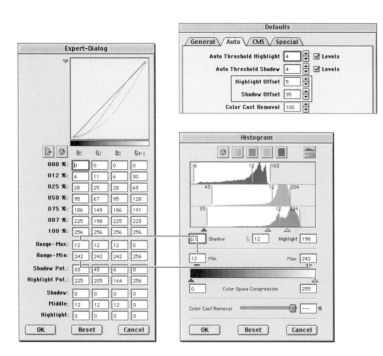

Figure 7.3

Min and Max settings originally come from the Defaults window but change in tandem with the values in the Histogram dialog.

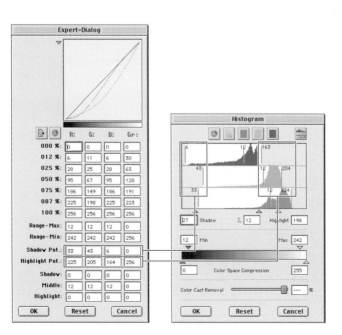

Figure 7.4

Highlight and shadow points match the values in the Histogram dialog.

In some cases, the values shown in the histogram graphs and those in the Expert fields may vary by 1 unit, just as the highlight values do in Figure 7.4. This divergence is due to a slight variation in the averaging function used in displaying the grayscale values in the histogram and the expert data fields and is not significant. I have found that the Expert data fields are the most accurate.

Shadow, middle, and highlight These three data fields again reflect the values set in the histogram. The middle tone data is controlled by the midtone values set in the histogram (see Figure 7.5). The Highlight and Shadow settings, typically 0, here initially reflect any compression applied to the gradient data at the highlight and shadow ends of the curves. The Highlight and Shadow settings here refer specifically to any compressions applied to those set in the histogram HL and SH points. Because none was applied, the values are 0.

MidPip values The fifth and final set of values shows the values set for the image controlled by the MidPip tool. These data rows will show the data as it was set when the MidPip tool was applied. If the MidPip tool was not used, these values would be 0 (see Figure 7.6).

Some versions of the SilverFast Expert Dialog may not show the MidPip values; it was omitted due to space limitations.

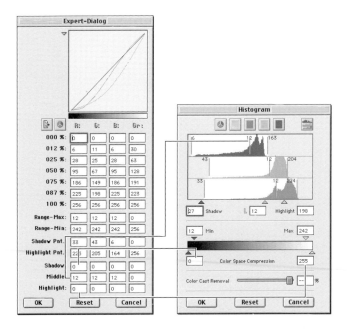

Figure 7.5

Highlight, midtone, and shadow values match those in the Histogram dialog.

Editing the Expert Dialog

The Expert Dialog shows all of the image data for the image as it is currently adjusted. You can control any of the values for the image here directly rather than going back to the other tools, such as the Gradation Curve tools, the histogram, the Highlight and Shadow settings, or the MidPip tools. Following are some examples of how the Expert Dialog can be used to quickly and accurately adjust some image values.

Adjusting the Ramps

In the Expert Dialog, it is easy to control the values in a spe-cific portion of the tonal range. For instance, you may want to make sure that the values for the image in the quartertone are all equal—that this portion of the image is neutral gray. In the gradient portion of the expert window, we see that the quartertone (25%) values for the Red, Green, and Blue channels are 28, 25, and 28, respectively. Changing the green value to 28 can easily neutralize the quartertone.

Figure 7.6

The sometimes-absent MidPip dialog.

MidPip	R:	G:	B:	Gr:
MidPip 1 Src.:	163	171	190	0
MidPip 1 Dest.:	191	191	191	0
MidPip 2 Src.:	151	166	188	0
MidPip 2 Dest.:	184	184	184	0
MidPip 3 Src.:	112	122	147	0
MidPip 3 Dest.:	139	139	139	0
MidPip 4 Src.:	228	226	227	0
MidPip 4 Dest.:	249	249	249	0

Cancel OK

012 %	6	11	6	30
025 %	28	25	28	28
050 %	95	67	95	128

012 %	6	11	6	30
025 %	28	28	28	28
050 %	95	67	95	128

The fast way to change all the values on a row is to press the Option or Alt key and click the value you want. Then all the values on that row will be changed to the value you select.

Compressing the Image Data

If you wanted to compress the image data from the current 242 (5%) and 12 (95%), which is a good tonal compression for commercial printing, to a 204 (20%) and 48 (80%), which is good for outputting the image to newspaper print, you can quickly adjust the Range-Max and Range-Min values.

| Range-Max: | 12 | 12 | 12 | 0 |
| Range-Min: | 242 | 242 | 242 | 256 |

| Range-Max: | 48 | 48 | 48 | 48 |
| Range-Min: | 204 | 204 | 204 | 204 |

Any of these values can be adjusted using the original tools such as the Histogram tool, the Gradation Curve tool, the White Point Black Point, or MidPip tools. The advantage of using the Expert Dialog is that you have access to all the data at one time and can quickly change any of it in one window. If you venture into this world of numeric control, you might just find that you like it because of its easy access to all the image data and the efficiency it provides in adjusting the data.

One tip for getting comfortable with the Expert Dialog is to make some changes in one of the tools, such as the Gradation Curve tool, and then view the change that this adjustment affected in the expert window. Conversely, also make changes in the expert window and go view the impact the change has on the individual tools.

Saving Changes

If you get into the habit of making changes through the Expert Dialog, you may also want to start saving sets of data for use in the future. For instance, you may be scanning a large number of images for placement in a catalog. You might make initial adjustments using the histogram, Gradation Curve, and MidPip tools and then fine-tune some of the settings in the Expert Dialog. Once you have a set of settings you like and would like to be able to apply them to any image you might scan for that catalog, you can save your current data set and access it at any time.

Exporting Data to a Text File

Once you have your expert window complete with the data set you want, you can export this data as a text file. To export data from this window, click the Export button. A Save

Figure 7.7

Browse to the folder to which you want to export your data.

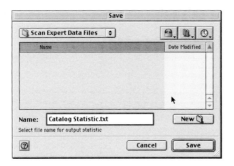

window (Figure 7.7) will appear. Name the file in a manner that will help you identify it later. Here the data file is identified as the `Catalog Statistic.txt` file.

You may want to save this data file in a common scanning data file and as an archive with the jobs on which you use it. This same data will then be retrievable no matter when you need to use it again.

Saving Settings

Just to remind you, the adjusted setup values can also be saved as a Settings choice in the Frame tab of the SilverFast Scan Control window. Saving the scan setup values in this way allows you easy access to the setup, but it does not allow you to actually view the data without going to the Expert Dialog.

CHAPTER 8

Sharpen, Smooth, and Remove

In Chapters 4–7, we discussed all of the fundamental tools and techniques you need to know in order to properly capture an image. In this chapter, we will begin to cover some of the related specialty topics. Here, we will cover three of the most common special image problems you are likely to encounter: soft or out-of-focus images, the challenges of scanning printed images, and how to deal with noise and grain in your images. SilverFast has tools specifically designed to deal with these challenges.

The following topics are covered in this chapter:

- **What is sharpening, and why and when do we need it?**

- **Controlling unsharp mask in SilverFast**

- **The challenge of capturing printed images: descreening**

- **Grain and noise reduction: GANE**

- **Removing pesky dust and scratches with SRD**

What Is Sharpening, and Why and When Do We Need It?

Sharpening is how we control the focus in our digital images. Increasing or decreasing the contrast between adjacent pixels along high-contrast edges controls sharpness. When we apply a sharpening filter to an image, we increase the contrast between pixels along edges. Figure 8.1 shows the difference between a sharpened and an unsharpened edge. Notice how the contrast along the black and white edge increases in the sharpened edge. You will also note that the sharpening of the high-contrast black and white edge not only shows an increase in contrast but the area of sharpening is narrowed as well.

It is this combination of enhancing contrast and narrowing of high-contrast edges that makes this image appear more in focus, or sharper to the human eye (Figure 8.2).

Figure 8.1

Unsharpened images (top): note the low-contrast, smooth edges. Sharpened versions (bottom): note the higher-contrast, more abrupt edges.

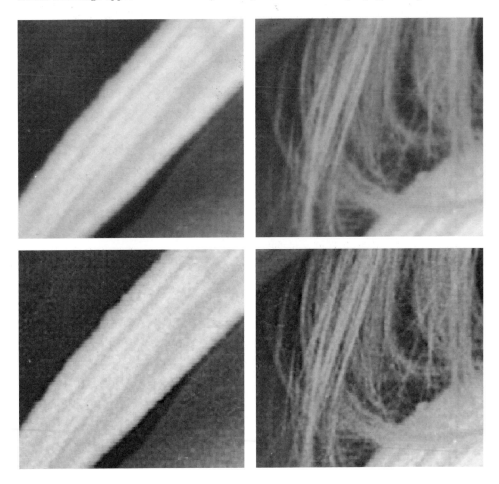

 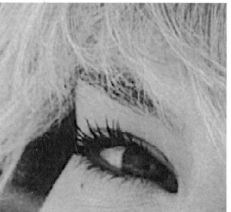

Figure 8.2

(left) Unsharpened and (right) sharpened images

Nearly every image we scan requires some sharpening, and for one very simple reason. Every image captured by a scanner tends to be softened during the scanning process. Because a scanner does not capture all of the available image data but rather samples an image and averages the values, it tends to slightly lower contrast along high-contrast edges and smooth out the image. In order to return the original focus or sharpness, we need to apply sharpening to the image. This scan-related smoothing of an image is more apparent in some images than in others. Images that tend to have more high-contrast edges and more detail, such as product shots, will tend to show more softening and smoothing than an image with fewer high-contrast edges and less detail, such as portraits. So the amount of sharpening we apply to an image is largely dependent upon the content of the image.

Controlling Unsharp Mask in SilverFast

The tool of choice for applying sharpening in the scanning and image editing world is called the unsharp mask. This tool gets its strange name from the way in which sharpening was once controlled. We used sandwiches of focused (sharp) and unfocused (unsharp) film to control sharpening. A good unsharp mask tool allows us to control how much sharpening will be applied to an image, both in terms of the amount of increase in edge contrast and where that sharpening will be applied. It is the masking characteristics of a good unsharp mask that allow us to control where the sharpening will be applied.

There are three levels of unsharp mask controls in SilverFast: an automatic mode, a manual mode, and an expert mode. We will cover each in turn.

Auto Unsharp Mask

The automatic unsharp mask (USM) feature of SilverFast may be the only USM you need to use most of the time. It is a sophisticated tool that automatically adjusts both the amount and the distribution of USM.

To activate and apply the auto USM feature, click the Filter menu in the Scan Control window. Among the options you will find three that pertain to automatic USM preset selections. The three choices you have here are Auto Sharpen (the default choice), Less Auto Sharpen, and More Auto Sharpen. (Note that some versions of SilverFast will show only a Sharpen (USM) choice in this menu.) Now drag down to select the choice that best suits your image. Shown here is the Auto Sharpen default setting.

In general, images with more detail will benefit from the application of more unsharp mask. Here are some examples of images for which you might choose one of these three USM preset choices:

Soft portrait image	Less Auto Sharpen
Standard landscape or people picture	Auto Sharpen
Product shot with many details including logos	More Auto Sharpen

With a little practice, you will gain more confidence in making this choice.

Manual Unsharp Mask

SilverFast gives you access to a bit more control than the three standard Auto Sharpen (USM) Unsharp choices provide. To access and manually control unsharp masking, do the following:

1. In the Scan Control window, click the Filter menu, as we did earlier, and select the menu choice Sharpen (USM). The Sharpen (USM) window appears, with unsharpened and sharpened panels for previewing various sharpening settings (see Figure 8.3).

2. Click the Prescan button. Adjusting the x factor next to the Prescan button can control the amount of preview enlargement that occurs. The default is 2x and the maximum is 8x.

Figure 8.3

Default (left) and custom (right) USM settings

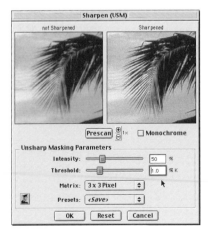
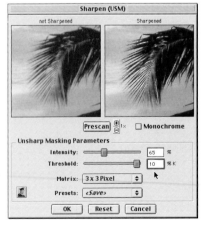

3. Click the portion of the image you would like to use for determining the sharpness controls. (I have clicked the ends of the palm tree branches.) This will provide you with an enlarged, high-resolution preview of that critical area of the image. Having a high-resolution preview of the critical sharpening area will allow you to actually see the impact the USM will have on the final pixels rather than guessing at the final results from the effects you see on a low-resolution preview scan.

4. Compare the unsharpened and the sharpened views. In the figure, note that the palm branches are much sharper on the right USM side.

The default settings are as follows:

Setting	Default
Intensity	50
Threshold	1
Matrix	3 x 3 Pixel

If we are going to manually alter the USM, we must clearly understand what each setting controls. The Intensity value determines the percentage increase in contrast enhancement and therefore the strength of the USM. The Threshold value determines the difference in grayscale values that must exist between two pixels before the USM can be applied. Threshold effectively controls the area of the image that will be affected by the USM. And finally, the Matrix determines the width or radius of the area around an area of high-contrast pixels that will be affected by the USM. Controlling all three of these variables is critical for obtaining the best results.

Adjusting the Manual USM Values

The values you choose will depend on the specific results you want. Let's look at a good example of how we might significantly change the default values to suit a specific image we want.

In this photo of the palm tree against the sunset sky, I want the palm leaves to be sharp but I do not want much sharpening in the sky. In fact, I want the sky to be very soft. The softness in the sky will match not only the feel I want for the sky but also, by contrast, further emphasize any sharpness I might add to the palm leaves. In Figure 8.3, you can view the impact the default setting will have on the images. The palm tree will be sharpened but not quite enough for my liking and the sky will be sharpened too much and therefore look grainy. Here are the adjustments made to obtain the sharpening result I seek:

Intensity I set this to 65. This will slightly enhance the sharpening of the palm trees.

Threshold I set this to 10 (its maximum value). This will effectively prevent the USM from being applied to the sky.

Matrix I left this at 3 x 3 Pixel. In deference to the small ends of the palm leaves, I did not want any larger area than the minimum to be affected by the USM.

Figure 8.4

**Adjusting expert USM
values: before (left)
and after (right)**

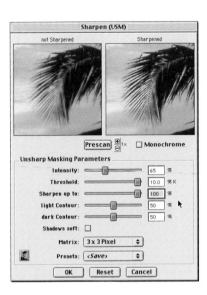 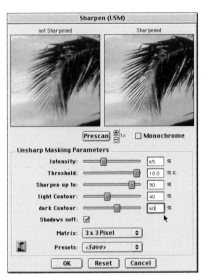

The results of my custom settings are to nicely sharpen the palm leaves while leaving the sky a soft, dreamy texture (see the result in Figure 8.3).

> Although many images benefit from the application of a moderate amount of USM to just about the entire image, it should be noted that scanners will typically soften higher-contrast edges of an image more than lower-contrast areas. So when USM is applied to an image, more emphasis should be placed on applying USM to the higher-contrast edges (such as the palm leaves in this example) while protecting the lower-contrast areas (such as the sunset sky) with the Threshold setting. Too much USM applied to low-contrast areas in an image can create unwanted texture and/or graininess.

Expert USM Controls

If you are a real USM control freak (and some images really do demand this kind of attention), you get even further into USM nitty-gritty by invoking the expert USM controls.

Click the Filter drop-down and choose Sharpen (USM). In the Sharpen (USM) dialog, click the Expert button ![expert button] and four additional controls appear: Sharpen Up To, Light Contour, Dark Contour, and a Shadows Soft check box (Figure 8.4). Let's continue with the palm sunset image to see how we might fine-tune the USM adjustments using the expert controls.

First, note that the Intensity, Threshold, and Matrix values that were set in the manual USM dialog are carried through to the Sharpen USM Expert dialog. Here are the additional controls:

Sharpen Up To This is a handy way of using a grayscale limit value as a masking tool. I will set this value at 90%. The result is that any pixels with grayscale values over 90% will not be affected by USM. This will prevent any graininess from being created in the shadow regions by the application of USM.

Light Contour and Dark Contour These sliders allow us to emphasize either the darker or the lighter pixels along an edge. Typically we would want these both to be 50%. In this case, I would like to emphasize the dark edges of the palm over the light edges of the sky behind so I will tweak this setting so that the dark contour is edged up to 60% while the white contour is lowered to 40%. This creates a little bit shaper edge on the palm leaves. (Note that these two numbers will typically add up to 100%.)

Shadows Soft If you check this box, SilverFast will endeavor to keep dark shadow regions of the image soft, or unsharpened. This will prevent shadow areas from developing USM-related graininess. This button is a more generic version of Sharpen Up To and applies specifically to the shadow regions of an image, whereas Sharpen Up To can applied to the entire grayscale ramp of values. I will turn this check box on.

Compare the sharpened images in Figure 8.5. Note how the palm leaves in the sharpened image stand out with better contrast against the sky than do the palm leaves in the unsharpened image. Equally important is that fact that neither the sky nor the shadows show any graininess from inappropriate application of USM.

Figure 8.5

Unsharpened image (left) and sharpened image (right)

Some Sharpening Cautions

Applying USM can greatly benefit an image, but applying it in the wrong way or at the wrong time can either negate the effect of USM or actually do the image harm. Following are a few tips about using sharpening on your images:

- *Use only high-quality sharpening tools.* Use only sharpening tools that allow you to control the amount of sharpening and where the sharpening will occur. General sharpening tools have a tendency to add unwanted graininess to low-contrast areas of your images.

- *Do not oversharpen.* A little bit of sharpening goes a long way. Remember that sharpening is an edge contrast enhancement tool and too much sharpening or contrast enhancement can create high-contrast halos along your edges. It is better to slightly under- rather than oversharpen.

- *Scan clean.* As far as the scanner and the USM adjustments are concerned, dust and scratches in your images are nothing but high-contrast edges. Sharpening will only further emphasize the dust and scratches on your images, making them more apparent. So, be sure the image and the scanner are cleaned beforehand.

- *Sharpen at the end.* If you plan to resize, resample, and/or apply lots of edits to your images after you scan, wait until all of your dimensional and editing chores are through before sharpening your images. Sharpening reduces the grayscale content of your images (by raising contrast on edges), which may reduce the quality of your editing results. Plus, sizing, sampling, and editing tend to remove the effect of sharpening, so apply sharpening at the end.

- *Save an unsharpened archive image.* If I intend to use my image multiple times and for multiple purposes, I will save an unsharpened image (complete with all its grayscale values) to which I can return, make a copy, edit, and apply USM when I am finished. This way I always have a fresh image with which to begin any project.

- *Reduce or eliminate sharpening of an image to be used on the Web.* Low-resolution images require less sharpening than high-resolution images. So I apply about one half the amount of sharpening on Web images and sometimes none at all. Further, lossy compression schemes such as JPEG, which are often applied to Web images, can easily create posterized high-contrast edges. And because sharpening tends to enhance edge contrast, it promotes posterization in a compressed image, thereby rendering any sharpening enhancements moot.

The Challenge of Scanning Printed Images: Descreening

Scanning previously printed images presents a special problem, and a problem that is not immediately apparent to the human eye. Printed images, unlike photographs, are made up of patterns of halftone dots, commonly known as screen patterns. Although these screen patterns are not usually visible to the unaided human eye, they are easily visible to the scanner, which can recognize the dots and reproduce their screen pattern in the image. If we do not remove it, it gets worse when we reprint the captured halftone dot pattern. Reprinted screen patterns usually result in the production of an even more obvious pattern know as a moiré pattern. SilverFast provides us with a set of descreening tools to help eliminate these screen patterns before they can do too much damage.

Descreening is basically a smoothing process whereby patterns of hard-edged dots, or other pattern elements, are blended with their backgrounds. The amount and type of blurring used should vary with the severity and spacing of the dot pattern. Although descreening is most typically used when scanning printed images, descreening can also be useful for removing patterns of any kind that develop during scanning. Any image that contains repetitive elements, such as fabric patterns, may create a pattern during scanning. Descreening is a useful tool for removing any such pattern.

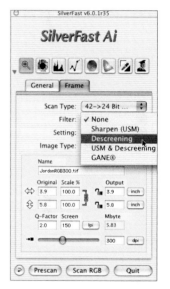

The Descreening Process

SilverFast has a very effective and easy-to-use descreening tool. Here are the steps to take to apply descreening in SilverFast:

1. Complete a clean prescan.

2. Perform all of your standard adjustments to the prescanned image.

3. In the Scan Control window, click the Filter menu and select Descreening.

   The Descreening control window (Figure 8.6) appears with non-descreened and descreened panels for previewing various settings.

4. Click the Prescan button Prescan ⊕ 1× .

5. Click the portion of the image you would like to use for determining the descreening controls. I have clicked the orange stripes on the right side of the SilverFast logo.

6. Zoom in on the preview until the pattern is very clearly visible in the non-descreened (left) side of the preview windows.

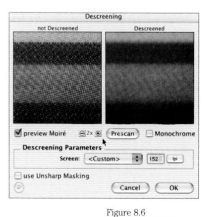

Figure 8.6

The Descreening dialog

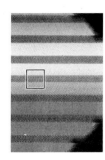

Adjusting the x factor next to the Prescan button can control the amount of preview enlargement that occurs. I have set the zoom at 2x here; the maximum is 8x.

Increasing the x setting will provide you with an enlarged, high-resolution preview of that critical area of the image. Having a high-resolution preview of the critical sharpening area will allow you to actually see the impact the descreening will have on the final pixels rather than guessing at the final results from the effects you see on a low-resolution preview scan.

Compare the non-descreened and the descreened views. Note the obvious halftone dot pattern in the non-descreened side and its absence from the descreened side.

To effect the best results, we need to match the descreening process to the pattern in the image. If the screen pattern is the result of scanning a halftone dot pattern, then we will want to match the descreening to the original halftone dot pattern. We do this in the Descreening Parameters area:

1. Click the Screen drop-down menu (Figure 8.7) and note that there are three default choices and a <Custom> choice. The default settings are as follows:

   - Newspaper (85 lpi)

   - Magazine (133 lpi)

   - Art Print (175 lpi)

2. Select one of the default choices, or if you know the actual screen angle of the printed piece, you may enter this value as a Custom choice.

3. You may change line screen values shown in the Custom choice by clicking the small button just to the right of the data field.

The closer you can be to original screen frequency of the original printed piece, the better the descreening job SilverFast will perform.

If you perform much of this type of descreening work, you will probably want to invest in a line screen counter. These are plastic sheets that you can lay over a printed piece to determine its line screen.

Keep track of the visual impact of your choices in the Descreening window. You can move your view around (if you are zoomed in) by holding down the Shift key and clicking and dragging. Both preview windows will update in real time as you move around the image.

If you change lpi/lpcm values, your right (descreened) preview may go blank. To update the descreened preview, hold down the Option/Alt key and click the update button (the Prescan button becomes the Update button when you depress the Option/Alt key).

Descreening Followed by USM

Because it blends the patterns with their background, the descreening process will soften your image. As a result, it is often advisable to follow up a descreening process with its alter ego, the unsharp mask. SilverFast has made this follow-up process convenient by adding access to the USM controls to the bottom of the Descreening window.

To access USM following your descreening adjustments, follow these steps:

1. Click the check box labeled Use Unsharp Masking.

2. Apply unsharp masking adjustments as discussed earlier in this chapter.

3. Monitor the visual result of the follow-up USM in the right panel (Figure 8.8). Note that this panel is now labeled Descreened And Sharpened.

   It is important to be aware that, because it is an edge contrast enhancement tool, applying USM following a descreening event may restore some of the original dot pattern if there is any residual pattern remaining in the image. So carefully monitor the effect of the follow-up USM.

4. Complete the scan in the normal fashion.

Compare the non-descreened and descreened versions of the SilverFast logos in Figure 8.9.

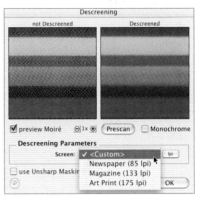

Figure 8.7

Changing the descreening parameters

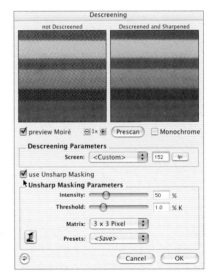

Figure 8.8

Descreening and USM dialog

Figure 8.9

**Non-descreened
(left) and descreened
(right) scans**

Grain and Noise Reduction: GANE

Some scanners, particularly lower-quality scanners, may impart a noisiness or graininess to parts of your image. The shadow region of images is particularly susceptible to noise. Some images, such as those with patterned backgrounds, are prone to creating noisy scans as well. SilverFast includes a technology called GANE, which is an acronym for grain and noise elimination. Here is how you would use it:

1. Complete a clean prescan.

2. Perform all of your standard adjustments to the prescanned image.

3. In the Scan Control window, click the Filter menu and select GANE®.

   The GANE control window (Figure 8.10) appears with panels to preview various GANE settings.

4. Click the Prescan button [Prescan] .

5. Click the portion of the image you would like to use for determining the GANE controls.

6. Zoom in on the preview until the noise or grain is very clearly visible in the Grain & Noise Visible (left) side of the preview windows.

Adjusting the x factor next to the Prescan button can control the amount of preview enlargement that occurs. I have set the zoom to 2x here; the maximum is 8x (see Figure 8.10).

This will provide you with an enlarged and high-resolution preview of that critical area of the image. Having a high-resolution preview of the critical GANE area will allow you to actually see the impact GANE will have on the final pixels rather than guessing at the final results from the effects you see on a low-resolution preview scan.

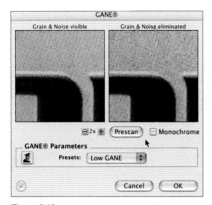

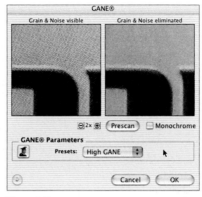

Figure 8.10

The GANE dialog, preview and results with Low Gane setting

Figure 8.11

GANE preset parameters, preview and results with High Gane setting

Compare the Grain & Noise Visible and the Grain & Noise Eliminated views. Note the obvious grain pattern in the Grain & Noise Visible side and its significant reduction in the Grain & Noise Eliminated side.

To effect the best results, we need to match the GANE adjustment to the pattern in the image. To do so, click the GANE Parameters: Presets menu. Note that, in addition to the Custom choice, there are three default choices: Low, Medium, and High. Experiment with the default choices you see. Which one produces the best results? I have selected High GANE here (Figure 8.11).

Expert GANE Controls

Like most of the adjustments in SilverFast, there are expert settings for the GANE adjustment as well. We will use them to fine-tune our results from the application of the High GANE preset adjustment.

Click the Expert button ▮ ; the expert options will appear. The expert version of the GANE dialog box allows us to control the intensity, threshold, and radius of the GANE effect. These adjustments are much like the expert unsharp mask adjustments covered earlier in this chapter, but the results will be the exact opposite. The Intensity setting controls the amount of smoothing that will occur. The Threshold setting controls which portion of the image will be affected, and the Radius setting affects the size or radius of the area to be smoothed.

Adjust the expert values to achieve the visual results you would like. Here are the adjustments I made to the expert dialog to even further improve the removal of graininess. The improvements made with the expert controls will often be subtle; that is the nature of these controls because they are for fine-tuning adjustments. Here, note particularly the improvement of the quality along the edges of the type characters from the High GANE and expert adjustments.

Setting	Initial	Final
Intensity	100	100
Threshold	15	56
Radius	49	59

The comparison of the initial High GANE and final expert GANE can be seen in Figure 8.12. You can see how fine-tuning the Threshold value from 15 to 56 had a significant effect on the smoothness of the application of the GANE effect in the GANE preview windows.

The entire pre- and post-GANE adjustment images can be seen in Figure 8.13. Note that the GANE-adjusted image shows some visible softening as a result of the application of the GANE adjustments. As when we descreen images, it is often useful to follow up any GANE adjustment with the application of some USM.

There are some printed images that respond very well to GANE types of descreening, so I sometimes use the GANE rather than the descreening functions to descreen images.

Removing Pesky Dust and Scratches with SRD

Of course, the best way to mitigate dust and scratches is to prevent them from occurring in the first place by always cleaning your scanner and images and handling your images carefully with cotton gloves. But if your image is challenged with dust and scratches, SilverFast has a terrific tool called SRD 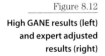 (for "smart removal of defects").

Figure 8.12

High GANE results (left) and expert adjusted results (right)

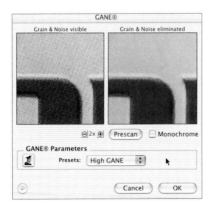
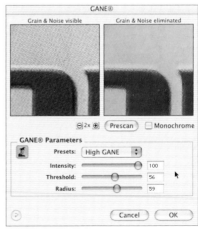

Figure 8.13

Versions before (left) and after (right) GANE adjustment

Here is how to use this powerful tool. For this exercise, I will use a photo of my cousin Tori and some of her friends (from left to right: Tori, Jaz, Mark, and Cal). An uncorrected copy of this image can be found on the CD and corrected using SilverFast's HDR (High Dynamic Range) software.

Perform a standard scan. Then set up your final scan configuration as you would for any scan: select the scan area, apply the auto-adjustment tool and further fine-tune the exposure setting if you want, set the resolution, and most importantly here, set any scaling that you will want to be applied. Then you can activate and use the SRD tool:

1. Click the SRD tool icon ⊞ located near the bottom of the vertical toolbar set on the left side of the preview window. Once selected, this icon automatically morphs into a double-tool icon.

2. Click the second (lower) SRD tool containing the red "first aid" cross. The SRD dialog box and window appear.

3. Click the Preview button in the lower-left corner of the SRD dialog window.

A new preview scan will be performed. The standard preview window will contain an enlarged preview of a portion of the entire image (Figure 8.14). A preview of the entire image will appear at the top of the SRD dialog window. This preview will have an overlaid grid system (red) and a yellow-bordered area labeled Navigator. The yellow-bordered area defines the current enlarged preview image visible in the larger standard preview window.

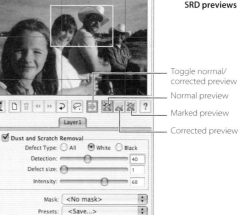

Figure 8.14

SRD dialog with Navigator and standard and SRD previews

Controlling the SRD Preview

The area visible in the standard preview can be changed by either of the following methods:

- Click one of the predefined red SRD grid areas.

- Drag the yellow-bordered SRD preview area.

Here I have dragged the yellow-bordered preview to show mostly Jaz and Mark.

SRD offers three different views of the enlarged preview image: an uncorrected preview, a corrected preview, and a marked preview. For this section, I'll use the marked preview, which marks the areas and relative amounts of correction. Corrected areas are shown in red.

At any time along the way, you can view the impact of your SRD settings by clicking the corrected view preview icon. Or conversely, if you are viewing the corrected image, a quick view of the original uncorrected image can be seen by clicking either the marked icon or the corrected image itself. I recommend comparing the various previews often, and particularly whenever you make a change to any of the SRD settings, and certainly when you are finished.

Using the SRD Dialog

Start the SRD process by checking the Dust And Scratch Removal box in the upper-left corner of the dialog area under the tab labeled Layer 1.

For the Defect Type option, click the All button. (If you just want to remove white or black imperfections, you can click one of those buttons.) The default SRD values (listed in Table 8.1) will be applied to the white imperfections in the image (marked in red in the preview), as shown in Figure 8.15.

Table 8.1

Values for SRD Repair

SETTING	DEFAULT SRD	AUTO SRD	FINE-TUNED SRD
Detection	40	55	65
Defect Size	1	1	3
Intensity	68	57	75

The Detection value controls the sensitivity of the detection tool (higher values equate to higher sensitivity). The Defect Size value determines the size of the imperfections that will be found and altered (larger values find smaller imperfections). Intensity controls the amount of correction that will be applied, with larger values signifying more correction.

Next, click the Auto button along the lower edge of the window. Using these new SRD values, enhanced corrected image portions will be displayed in the preview (as in Figure 8.16).

These auto values can then be further fine-tuned by manually adjusting the SRD values (as I've done in Figure 8.17). To determine these values, closely watch the marked preview to make sure all the dust and scratches are being removed.

Color versions of these images are included in the color section.

Figure 8.15

Marked preview using default values

Protecting Areas with Masks

Detail areas of your image can be protected from the effects of the SRD correction though the use of the masking tools. SilverFast SRD has three masking tools: a lasso, a polygon lasso, and a brush.

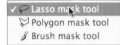

Select the desired mask tool from the tool pop-up. Hold down the Option/Alt key and drag around the area to be protected. To add an area to the SRD corrected area, hold down the Shift key and select again. The area inside this mask will be protected from the SRD corrections.

Figure 8.16

Using auto values

Figure 8.17

Using fine-tuned values

Figure 8.18

Initial image with lotsa dust and scratches (left); final SRD corrected image (right)

Once created, an SRD mask can be inverted, edited, and deleted though the Mask menu in the SRD dialog window. A small dialog box will appear asking you to name the mask. This mask will be added to the Mask list at the bottom of the SRD window.

Figure 8.18 shows the initial dust-filled and scratched image and the final SRD corrected image using the fine-tuned settings applied earlier.

Using the SRD Expert Options

Sometimes images have such a range of dust and scratch sizes and shapes that it is helpful to be able to work on the larger, longer scratches and the smaller dust particles separately. This is where the SRD expert options come in handy; they allow you to isolate the larger and longer scratches.

Click the Expert button ▓ . The SRD dialog will be expanded to include the Longish Scratch Removal pane (see Figure 8.19). This functions much the same way the basic SRD window does. Test various values and preview the results.

> I use this Expert SRD tool primarily on the rare scratches that do not respond well to the basic SRD corrections. Most of the time, the basic SRD is the only tool I need for removing dust and scratches.

Saving SRD Settings and Completing the Scan

If you find a set of settings that you would like to use again, they can be saved and recalled for use at any time in the future through the use of the Presets menu at the bottom of the SRD dialog window.

Once you are through configuring the SRD dialog, click the OK button and complete the scan as you normally would. Just be sure the twin SRD icons are showing in the vertical tool palette on the left side of the main preview window when you complete the scan. These icons indicate that SRD will be active during the scan.

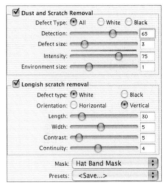

Figure 8.19

Expert options for dust and scratch removal

CHAPTER 9

Seeing the World in Black and White

Line art is defined by its edges, so capturing line art is all about reproducing edges. In Chapter 1 we discussed the concept that your scanner, a digital device, can convert what it captures into only 0s and 1s and therefore really only "sees" in black and white. Color is actually created by output devices. This is a particularly useful concept to employ when we are scanning line art. The scanner sees all line art edges as black and white. So it is particularly useful to be color blind when thinking about scanning line art. With most line art images, I focus on reproducing the black-and-white outlined edges and often add color back in later.

The following topics are covered in this chapter:

- **Pixels and vectors revisited**
- **Simple line art**
- **Detailed or complex line art**
- **Color line art**

Pixels and Vectors Revisited

In Chapter 1 you learned that there are two types of graphic images, pixel (bitmapped) and vector (outline). Scanners create pixel-based images. Pixels are best used to represent highly detailed images, such as continuous tone photographs. Vectors shine when edges—not detail—are the key elements of the image. Vectors are resolution independent, which means that they can be scaled, skewed, and rotated without affecting the resolution or quality of the image. Vectors are also smaller and easier to edit than pixel-based images. But vectors do not show detail well.

It is best to make this pixel versus vector decision before you begin the line art scanning process because this decision will affect how you set up SilverFast to scan the images. Because line art is defined by its edges and vectors are best at representing edges, if I can effectively convert images to vectors, I do so. The key is deciding which image you can take to vectors and which should remain as pixels. The basic decision-making concept is this: If the image is simple, convert it to vectors; if it has lots of small detail, keep it as pixels. The clearly simple and obviously detailed images are easy to distinguish; it is with the in-between ones that you will need experience to decide whether or not you can take your image to vector—all it will take is a little practice.

SilverFast is used to control your scanner to capture the pixel-based line art images. The conversion to vector images will occur using a drawing program such as Adobe Illustrator, Macromedia FreeHand, or CorelDRAW—or better yet, using a dedicated pixel-to-vector application such as Adobe Streamline. How well we set up SilverFast to capture the pixel-based image will determine the quality and ease of conversion in another application.

Figure 9.1 shows two clear representatives of simple and detailed line art. We will scan each type.

The only reason I might not convert a simple line art image to vectors would be if I just can't use vectors on an output device I might be using, such as a non-PostScript printer, or if I need a pixel-based image for use on the Web.

Figure 9.1

Simple and detailed line art

Simple: go to vectors

Detailed: stay as pixels

Simple Line Art

Our intention here is to convert our pixel-based line art image, which the scanner will produce, to a vector-based image. Pay particular attention to two very important setup values for the best results. The first key is to scan using the optical resolution of the scanner because this will minimize interpolation and therefore edge quality degradation. The second key to vector success is to scan the image at 100 percent—no scaling—and wait until you convert the image to vector before applying any scaling. Scanning without scaling will also protect the line art edge from interpolation and quality degradation.

Follow these steps to complete a simple line art scan with a conversion to vectors in mind. In this demonstration, I'm scanning the pumpkin image from Figure 9.1. (This image can be found printed in the color section.) Follow along with your own similar image:

1. Clean the scan bed and the image. Place the line art on the scan bed. If the image has horizontal and/or vertical edges, be sure to place it so that these edges are parallel to the edges of the scan bed.

2. Select 1 Bit Line Art from the Scan Type menu in the Scan Control window. Because this is a very simple line art image, we only need 1 bit of image information to define the edge of the line art. With more detailed images, it is often prudent to capture more data.

3. Click the Prescan button.

4. Draw the scan selection rectangle around just the portion of the preview image that you want to capture. Any extraneous image data just adds to the file size. Remember that white areas also contain pixel data.

5. Set the resolution at the optical, or hardware, resolution of the scanner. The optical resolution of my scanner is 1200 ppi. Although for this image I could use 600 ppi, I choose 1200 ppi for this scan to give me maximum use flexibility with this image (see Figure 9.2).

6. Set the scaling. If you intend to convert your line art image to vectors, your results will be better if you scan your images at 100 percent.

7. Name your image. As I have mentioned, I prefer to label my images with content and characteristic info when I first name them. I named this `PumpkinBW1200.tif`.

8. Click the Scan BW button at the bottom of the Scan Control window. Note that the scan button reflects the choice of the 1-bit, black-and-white Scan Type choice made earlier.

By scanning at 1200 ppi (the scanner's optical resolution) and at 100 percent, I've given myself the maximum flexibility for this image whether I go to vectors or remain with pixels.

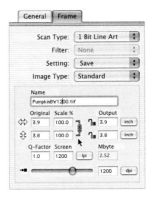

Figure 9.2

**Scan Control
window setup**

RESOLUTION

It is critical to use optical resolution for a scanner when scanning line art, and particularly if you intend to convert to vectors following the scan. Scanning at a nonoptical resolution will result in interpolation of the pixel, which in turn results in a roughening of the edge. This interpolation-based roughening not only lowers the quality of the original pixel-based edge, it also complicates and lowers the quality of the edge when the image is converted into vectors. Rough-edged line art results in many extra and undesirable control points along the vector edges.

If you intend to convert your images to vectors, you could scan a full integer division of the optical resolution of the scanner and still achieve good results. For instance, in this case if we were to scan at 600 ppi instead of 1200 ppi, which would reduce your file size 75 percent, the vector results would be identical. If you intend to use your image as both a pixel-based and vector-based image and/or you are scanning highly detailed line art, err on the safe side and scan at the high optical resolution as we are doing here.

Vector-bound line art images should not be scaled during the scan. Scaling, like nonoptical resolution settings, result in interpolation and edge-quality degradation. Plan to perform all geometrical manipulations such as scaling, skewing, and rotations after the image is converted to a vector and is resolution independent. Your result will be much higher-quality and easier-to-edit images.

If I needed to have a simple line art image at a specific size *and* I intended to keep my image pixel based, then I would scale my image to the desired size during the scale for best results.

Detailed or Complex Line Art

Detailed line art will rarely if ever be converted to vectors because vectors are not the best at rendering detail. So we can make the decision to stay with pixels for detail work and not have to worry so much about making sure our images will be vector ready. Unlike simple line art where edge consistency is the most important item, with detailed or complex line art, capturing and manipulating the detail is our primary concern.

Setup and Prescan

Detailed line art nearly always demands higher resolution to capture the detail that may be lost when scanning at a lower resolution. Lots of detail also means that the scanner may have some difficulty capturing all the data correctly, so it is good to provide your scanner with the capability to capture more than 1 bit per pixel. This time, I'm using the detailed butterfly image from Figure 9.1. Scan the image and follow along:

1. Clean the scan bed and the image. Place the line art on the scan bed. This image does not have specific horizontal and/or vertical edges, so image placement with edges parallel to the edges of the scan bed is less critical than in images with more linear elements.

2. Select 14 -> 8 Bit Grayscale from the Scan Type menu in the Scan Control window. We'll capture in higher bit depth mode to allow the scanner to capture all the detail present.

3. Click the Prescan button.

4. Draw the scan selection rectangle around just the portion of the preview image that you want to capture. Any extraneous image data just adds to the file size. Remember that white areas also contain pixel data.

Histogram Analysis

Because we are capturing an image in grayscale mode, and particularly if our line art image has fine edges and/or tonal variations along its edges, we need to treat this image as a contone image and adjust the distribution of grayscale values. In addition, if our line art image is on a colored or textured background, working with the tonal values in our image will allow us to remove unwanted or unnecessary image data.

Click the Histogram tool ; a single-channel histogram appears (Figure 9.3). This histogram shows two areas where the scan of this butterfly can be improved, both the shadow and the highlight areas. And the highlight area of the histogram provides us with a special opportunity to remove the background from this image.

CAPTURE BIT DEPTH

Even if we ultimately intend to down-sample our image to 1-bit black and white, it is typically best if we capture detailed line art in grayscale (8 bit or higher) mode rather than 1 bit. By capturing our line art in grayscale mode, we allow the scanner to capture all the detail present. This is particularly true with rough- or fuzzy-edged line art, which has some grayscale value to it. The resulting grayscale images can, in an image editing application such as Photoshop, be fined-tuned to look exactly the way you choose in the postscan. You may decide to leave some of your detailed line art as grayscale and convert others to 1-bit black and white depending upon the look that you want.

Figure 9.3

**Initial histogram
and image**

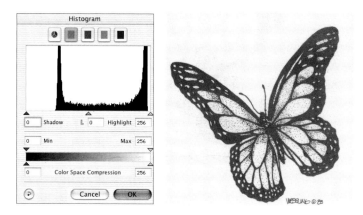

Figure 9.4

**Highlight and shadow
tone compression
in histogram and
image result**

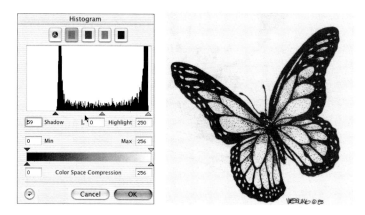

Shadow Adjustment

The initial histogram displays a large flat area to the left of the image data. The shadow point needs to be moved in to where the significant shadow data begins to appear in the histogram.

Move the shadow point in until it just touches the shadow data in the histogram. The Shadow value moves from 0 to about 59 (your specific values may vary slightly from these). You will notice that the contrast of the image will improve with this shadow adjustment.

Highlight Adjustment

The initial histogram (Figure 9.4) shows in the highlight end an obvious flat area, which needs to be removed just as we did in the shadow end.

Move the highlight slider into the beginning of the significant highlight data. The Highlight value is adjusted from 255 to about 250 (your specific values may vary slightly from these). Once again, you will notice that the contrast of the image will improve with this highlight adjustment.

Background Removal

However, there is an additional highlight adjustment we can make. This involves using the scan setting to remove the tinted background from around the image. There is a large spike in the highlight end of the histogram. This spike is the background paper surrounding the image. Sometimes the background values will stand out as separate peaks in the histogram. In this case, the background values are distinguished from the image data by the change in smoothness and the slope of the histogram increase. The portion of the histogram that is very steep and smooth is the background. The lower-sloped, more irregular portion of the histogram represents the image data. Note that your specific histogram may vary from these.

Slide the highlight pointer to the boundary between the background data (smooth and steep) and the image data (irregular and lower slope). When the highlight point is moved in to the boundary between the rough image data and the smooth (background data) portion of the image, the Highlight values change from ~250 to ~236. You will also see a significant increase in the contrast of this image as the background is removed from the image (see Figure 9.5).

Figure 9.5

Background tone compression in histogram and removal of background data from the image

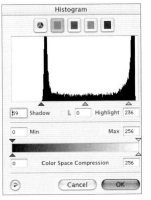

Finishing the Scan

I think you can see from this last example the benefits that can be gained by paying close attention to the data in the histogram. Once you've adjusted the histogram, it's time to finish off the scan:

1. Set the resolution. Once again, we want to use the optical or hardware resolution of the scanner. With some simple images that are scanned in 1 Bit mode and converted to vectors, we can get by with scanning at lower resolution such as 600 ppi. However, for detailed line art, we will always want to scan at the higher full optical resolution, which in this case is 1200 ppi.

   If you select a scaling factor other than 100, SilverFast will automatically instruct your scanner to capture your image at a higher resolution to provide for the scaling while maintaining the image resolution requested. In this case, a 250-percent scale should result in a 250-percent increase in the resolution of the scan (or 1200 ppi × 2.5 = 3000 ppi). You will note in this scan setup that the actual resolution used by the scanner is 4000 ppi, which is the closest optical resolution to 3000 ppi. If your scaling request demands a higher resolution than the optical resolution of the scanner, some interpolation will occur, usually resulting in loss of image and, in the case of line art, edge quality. If you intend to scale your images often, be sure to purchase a scanner that has enough optical resolution to accommodate your scaling demands.

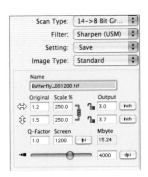

2. Because we will not be converting any highly detailed image to vectors, we want to per-
    form any scaling adjustments during the scan. Apply a 250-percent scale for this image.

> Unless you intend to convert line art images to vectors and perform the scaling in a drawing
> application (as we did with the simple pumpkin image), scaling images during the scan is the
> rule. You'll nearly always achieve better results, and faster workflow, if you allow the scanner
> to scale the image rather than waiting to perform this function later in the postscan. This is
> particularly true if your scanner is capturing images at greater than 8 bits per pixel. So, if you
> intend to leave your images as pixels, perform the scaling during the scan.

3. Name the image. As before, I will label my image with content and characteristic info;
    here it is `ButterflyGS1200.tif`.

4. You can apply sharpening to your detailed line art image during the scan. Particularly if
    you do not plan to perform any postscan image editing in an application such as Photo-
    shop but you would like to sharpen up the edges of your line art, sharpening during the
    scan may be a good choice. See Chapter 8 for details on using the Unsharp Mask filters.

This final scanned image can now be opened in a pixel-based image editing application such
as Photoshop and either converted to black and white though a threshold function or fine-
tuned with sharpening tools to emphasize details. For more information on this type of image
editing tools and techniques, see the resources listed in Appendix B on this book's CD-ROM.

Color Line Art

At the risk of being redundant, I want to emphasize that scanners do not actually "see" in
color. The color is provided by an output device such as a monitor. So when we scan line art,
we know that the scanner will use differences in grayscale value to distinguish different colors.
These differences in grayscale value show up as separate objects on either the same or different channels. Our goal is to always be able to separate the various colors from the background
and each other.

Color in line art is notoriously difficult to capture accurately with a scanner. This is particularly true with colors such as commercially printed spot colors, which have very specific
percentages of ink color mixtures. If you are just trying to capture general color differences,
you can do this with a scanner, but even this can be a challenge, as you will see in the section
"Complex Color Line Art" later in this chapter. If, however, you are trying to scan colored line
art with the goal of ultimately reproducing the original spot or other color, the best approach
is to scan to reproduce the colored components. This allows them to be easily selected and
colors can be assigned to them after in the postscan.

We will go through two different exercises. The first involves a simple color line art scan. We will focus on converting the original colored line art elements to black and white or grayscale for later coloring. In the second exercise, we will work with a much more complex colored line art scan. We will reproduce the image for general color reproduction, selection, separation, and later color assignment.

Simple Color Line Art

Our emphasis here will be on reproducing a colored line art image as a black-and-white or grayscale image whose individual elements can then be selected and assigned specific color values. The biggest challenge we will have with this image is that the background values interfere with separating the logo elements.

Setup and Prescan

Follow along with your own similar image:

1. As usual, clean the scan bed and the image. Place the colored line art on the scan bed. In this case, I'm using a logo scan with red letters (PMS 185) on a gray colored background. This image does have horizontal and/or vertical edges, so I must be careful to place the image so that the edges are parallel to the edges of the scan bed. (A color version of this image can be found in the color section of this book.)

2. For Scan Type, we have three choices here: RGB, grayscale, or 1-bit black and white. Because we are striving to separate the colored line art from the background as black-and-white images, we would be well served to scan in either 1 bit black and white or in grayscale mode. And because the colored logo characters are on a gray background, we will probably find the image easiest to work with if we scan in grayscale mode.

   Click the Scan Type menu and choose 14 -> 8 Bit Grayscale scan mode.

3. Click the Prescan button.

4. Draw the scan selection rectangle around just the portion of the preview image that you want to capture—in this case, I want to capture the UMAX logo.

Histogram Analysis

Because we are capturing an image in grayscale mode, we will utilize the histogram to help define the logo. Click the Histogram tool 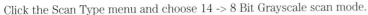; a single channel histogram appears (Figure 9.6).

This histogram shows the image data surrounded by a flat white end on both the highlight and shadow ends. The image histogram data is characterized by tall peaks at the highlight and shadow ends with a range of low amplitude variable data in between. The right (highlight end) peak is the background data, the left (shadow end) data is the logo, and the remainder is the small amount of intermediate grayscale data along the boundary of the logo and scattered throughout the background.

The initial histogram displays large flat areas to the left and right of the image data. Unlike some of the other adjustments we have made, such as moving the highlight and shadow slider to the beginning of the significant data, in this case we will move the shadow toward the center of the histogram data, well inside of the shadow end data.

Move the shadow point in toward the middle of the histogram. The Shadow value moves from 0 to 134, and the contrast of the image improves.

Also move the highlight slider in toward the middle of the histogram data. The Highlight value is adjusted from 255 to 154. Once again, you will notice that the contrast of the image will improve dramatically with this highlight adjustment (Figure 9.7).

> Be aware that the software contains an error. The Highlight value of 256 that is shown in Figure 9.6 should be 255, as is written here.

Finishing the Scan

Having used the Histogram dialog to increase the contrast, we can make the final scan:

1. Once again we want to use the optical, or hardware, resolution of the scanner, especially if we intend to convert this image into vectors. For this image, because it is simple and we intend to convert it to vectors, we can get by with scanning at lower resolution such as 600 ppi, rather than 1200ppi if we were to keep this image as a pixel-based image, as shown in Figure 9.8. (Refer back to the sidebar "Resolution" earlier in this chapter.)

Figure 9.6

Histogram and prescanned image

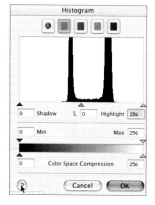

2. Set the scaling. If you intend to convert this image into vectors, set the scaling to 100 percent. If you will be keeping this image as pixels, apply any scaling you might want here. We will apply a 100-percent scale for this image to keep our options open.

3. Name the image. Because I prefer to label my images with content and characteristic info, I will name this `UMAXLogoGS600.tif`.

4. You can apply sharpening to your detailed line art image during the scan. Particularly if you do not plan to perform any postscan image editing in an application such as Photoshop but you would like to sharpen up the edges of your line art, sharpening during the scan may be a good choice. See Chapter 8 for details of using the Unsharp Mask filters.

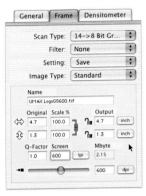

Figure 9.8

Scan Control window setup

In an image editing application such as Photoshop, you can perform many adjustments such as sharpening, converting to 1-bit black and white (typically using a Thresholding function), or assigning color directly to the image. Alternatively, you can now take this image to a vector format and perform your image editing (including color assignment) there. By scanning the image as we have and creating a high-contrast version of the logo elements, we have given ourselves the option to go in either direction.

Complex Color Line Art

Some of the most difficult scans to perform correctly are those of complex colored line art that includes similar colors that are touching. For this exercise, I will scan an Apple logo that has six touching colors, two of which are very similar. (Various color versions of this multi-colored apple graphic in different stages can be found in the color section of this book.)

Setup and Prescan

Follow along with your own similar image:

1. Clean and place the logo image on the scanner as we have in previous exercises.

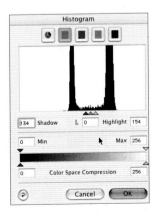

Figure 9.7

Adjusted histogram and adjusted image

2. Once again we have the option of choosing black-and-white 1-bit, grayscale, or RGB. The colors in this logo are so similar that I am nearly forced to use RGB mode. Remember that when you scan in RGB, the scanner will deliver an image with three different grayscale versions of the image. Our goal again is to try to gain separation between the colors so that we may select and work with them in the postscan. Select the 42 -> 24 Bit Color mode from the Scan Type menu in the Scan Control window.

3. Draw the scan selection rectangle around just the portion of the preview image that you want to capture. In my case, I want to capture the Apple logo.

First Adjustment: Auto Adjust

To follow a complete progression from prescan to completed image, let's first look at the starting histogram for the image I'm scanning. In Figure 9.9, note how the highlight and shadow ends are badly in need of adjustment.

> Be aware that the software contains a couple of errors. The Highlight value of 256 that is shown in Figure 9.9 should be 255, as is written here, and the Highlight value of 180, shown in Figure 9.10, should be 179.

The overall contrast and brightness improves from the prescanned image when I click the Auto-Adjustment tool 🔅 in the Scan Control window. However, the contrast between the background and the Apple logo and between the various colors could be improved.

Take another look at the histogram in Figure 9.10. The highlight and shadow sliders have been moved into the beginning and the end of the significant image data. Note in particular that the highlight slider values have been moved from 255 to 179. However, the large peaks

Figure 9.9

Initial histogram and prescan image

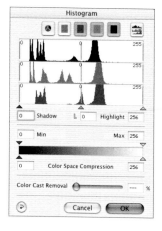

at the highlight end of the histogram are largely the image data in the background surrounding the Apple logo. This background data is superfluous to our goal and in fact is preventing a good clean separation of the logo from the background.

> A multicolored image on a slightly colored background is one of those circumstances where the Auto-Adjustment tool will get you part of the way there but not far enough. The Auto-Adjustment tool does not know that you do not want the background included in the histogram and in its adjustment calculations.

Manual Histogram Adjustment

I move the highlight sliders on all three channels in past the tops of the big highlight peaks and then fine-tune the placement of each channel's highlight slider to emphasize the contrast between the colors in the Apple logo. I have moved the individual channel highlight sliders so that the value of red is 132, the value of green is 126, and the value of blue is 153 (Figure 9.11).

Figure 9.10

Auto adjusted histogram and image results

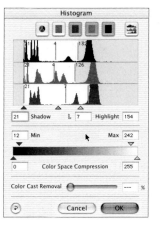

Figure 9.11

Manually adjusted histogram and image results

Figure 9.12

**Initial and adjusted
curve dialogs**

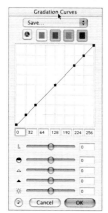

Note how this manual adjustment really brings out an excellent separation of the logo from the background and the separation of most of the colors from each other is better as well. The only colors that are not as clearly separated as we might like are the two colors in the middle, the orange and the red orange.

Fine-Tuning with Curves

The adjustments with the Histogram tool have been pushed about as far as they can be pushed given that it only has three slider control points. To finish our fine-tuning, we will use the Gradation Curve tools, which have six control points along their tonal gradient.

1. Click the Gradation Curve tool ![tool icon]. The master channel Gradation Curves dialog will appear (Figure 9.12).

2. For this image, click the Red channel icon at the top of the Gradient Curves dialog to activate the Red channel ![icon].

3. Click and drag to move the quarter tone point down until the orange and red-orange colors are more clearly separated in the Apple logo.

Now view the final whole image results and compare with the original (Figure 9.13). Also take a look at the image's three component channels (Figure 9.14). You will see how each color can be much more easily separated and selected in the final image when compared with the prescan image's channels.

Remember that your specific adjustments may vary when you were using another image.

You can use the scan techniques shown here to create easy-to-separate complex colored scans. Each image will be a unique challenge that will require slightly different approaches and tool utilization, so it is imperative that you understand the image components and how the various tools affect an image.

Figure 9.13

**Prescan (left)
and final (right)
composite image**

Figure 9.14

(left) Prescan image RGB channels compared with (right) final channels

CHAPTER 10

Power User Tips

SilverFast has a variety of tools, which can help you work faster as well as meet specific needs. If you or those you supervise perform many scans and need to save and repeat scan steps, SilverFast provides you with powerful tools such as batch scanning capabilities, a Job Manager, and a ScanPilot to help you guide your scanning processes and improve your workflow.

The following topics are covered in this chapter:

- **ScanPilot**
- **Using Scan Frames**
- **Batch Scanning**
- **Job Manager**

ScanPilot

In Chapters 4 and 5 we discussed the need to perform the proper adjustments to an image—and the need to perform them in the proper order. In the Scan Overview window, SilverFast's tools are generally set up in the order in which they should be used (left to right).

However, we do not always need to use all of the tools. Further, if we are supervising other operators with various skill levels, we would like to make sure that all of the necessary scanning adjustments are being applied and in the proper order.

SilverFast's ScanPilot allows us to choose the tools we would like to use and then helps guide us through the scanning process so that we perform our corrections in the proper order. The following is a guide to configuring and using the ScanPilot.

The Default ScanPilot

Normally, the ScanPilot will appear automatically when you launch SilverFast. But if the ScanPilot is not visible, click the ScanPilot button located on the vertical toolset on the left side of the preview window. The default ScanPilot appears (see Figure 10.1).

To activate the default set of ScanPilot tools, click the triangular button at the bottom of the ScanPilot window.

The ScanPilot will initiate a prescan of the image employing the type of capture mode that is set in the Scan Type menu choices in the Scan Control window. The ScanPilot will then lead you through the various default sets of tools, requesting your input where necessary, until it initiates the final finished scan.

Customizing ScanPilot

The ScanPilot can be customized to suit your adjustment needs. To change the tools used by the ScanPilot, click the Prefs button at the bottom of the ScanPilot window. The ScanPilot Preferences dialog appears (see Figure 10.2)

This Preferences panel provides you with a set of all the tools that can be accessed through and controlled by the ScanPilot. Check the box next to each tool you would like the ScanPilot to add to its use list. Uncheck any tools you would like the ScanPilot to ignore.

If you would like ScanPilot to include some help text instruction, check the Helptexts check box near the bottom of the window (see Figure 10.3). You will probably want to turn Helptexts off for seasoned users because it will slow down the production process unnecessarily for operators who do not need the instructions.

Figure 10.1

The default ScanPilot toolset

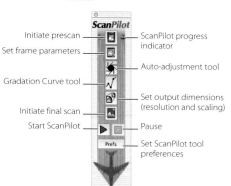

If you would like the ScanPilot to appear with this set of tool preferences each time Silver-Fast is activated, check the Open At Startup check box near the bottom of the window. Once you have the toolset you want, click the OK button at the bottom of the window. The ScanPilot reappears with all of its newly activated tools. Figure 10.4 shows the ScanPilot with a customized set of tools.

Click the activate triangle to initiate ScanPilot and once again it will lead you through the scanning process, pausing where necessary when it needs input information.

> The ScanPilot is useful both as a tool for the operator and as a good tool for a production manger to use. A skilled production manager can guide less-skilled operators by setting up the ScanPilot to perform certain adjustments in a specific order. Using the ScanPilot in this fashion leverages the knowledge and skill of the production manger. The ScanPilot is a terrific training tool as well as a production aid.

Figure 10.2

Check the tools you want to see in the ScanPilot.

Using Scan Frames

Another way SilverFast can help you increase the speed and improve the consistency of your work is by giving you the ability to save scan frames. In SilverFast, much of your image adjustment is controlled through the Scan Control window. The entire setup of a Scan Control window is called a scan frame. Scan frames can be saved and recalled for use at any time. Saving and reusing scan frames is particularly useful if you have a set of scans that will repeatedly utilize the same settings.

Saving a Single New Scan Frame

To create a new scan frame, first perform a prescan on your image using default settings. Then follow these steps:

1. Click to the Frame tab in the Scan Control window.

2. Set up your scan as you normally would, adjusting all the scan parameters such as the size, scaling, resolution image adjustments, and so on as we have discussed throughout this book.

3. Click the Setting menu in the Frame tab and select Save; a Name New Frame dialog appears.

4. Type in the name for this scan frame. All the image adjustment information will now be saved in this frame.

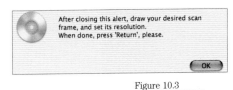

Figure 10.3

An example of help text

Figure 10.4

A customized ScanPilot

Recalling a Scan Frame

To recall the settings saved in a scan frame, click the Setting menu in the Frame tab and choose the desired frame. In Figure 10.5, you can see the changes in various options after I've chosen Portraits_Washington High School from the Setting list.

Once a scan frame setting is saved, it can be recalled at any time to be used again. Saving and using scan frames not only saves time but helps provide consistency from one scan to another.

Managing Frames

You can create multiple scan frames, each with its own setting assigned. Simply click and drag your mouse over another part of an image or another image to create a new scan frame. Be sure that you begin your scan frame selection outside of any existing scan frames (see Figure 10.6). Assign a totally new set of adjustment properties to each new scan frame if you like.

You can see the numbered order in which you created the scan frames by clicking on the right side of the "show brightest/darkest, show scan frame number" icon located at the bottom of the vertical tool palette on the left side of the preview window.

Here are some of the other ways you can use and manage your scan frames:

- **To activate any frame,** simply click the frame.

- **To move a scan frame,** simply click, hold, and drag it. You will notice that when you release the mouse button at the end of the move, the original position of the scan frame flashes momentarily on screen. This is useful for remembering where the original scan frame was located.

- **To duplicate a scan frame,** simply hold down the Option/Alt key and drag the currently active frame to a new location. A plus (+) sign appears indicating that a new frame is being created. This new copy of the frame will have all of the characteristic of the original frame.

Figure 10.5

(left) Default scan frame; (right) new frame settings.

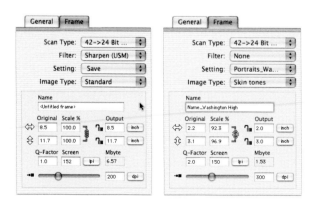

- **To copy the characteristics of one frame onto another,** hold down the Option/Alt key while clicking the frame from which you would like to copy the characteristics. Then click the frame into which you would like to copy them. In some cases, you may have to Opt/Alt-click both the original and the receiving frame for the copy to work.

- **To delete a scan frame,** click the frame you would like to delete to activate it. Click the trash can icon on the left side of the scan preview window ⬚ . You will be able to delete all but one frame. If you try to delete the last frame, you will be warned that you will be deleting the frame as well as all preview images. Always keep at least one scan frame.

Figure 10.6

Multiple scan frames

Saving and Recalling Multiple Frame Settings

Saving and recalling multiple frames, called Frame-Sets, is similar to saving and recalling single frames. The only difference is where we save the settings:

1. Create several scan frames and assign them the characteristics you would like.

2. Click the General tab in the Scan Control window.

3. Click on the Frame-Set menu.

4. Name and save the multiple scan frames (in the Frame-Set menu) just as we did with the single frame setting previously. Remember that when we saved a single frame, we were working in the Frame tab rather than the General tab of the Scan Control window.

5. Recall frame sets by returning to this same Frame-Set menu to select the frame set of your choice.

When the frame set is recalled, not only will all of the adjustment settings be saved, but the position of the scan frames will be preserved as well.

> Saving and using frame sets with multiple positions is a terrific help when you are scanning sets of images that are the same size and in the same position, as with slides on holders.

To scan a specific frame from multiple frames, click the desired frame. Set all the image adjustments you prefer. Then click the Scan RGB Button to create the final scan of that scan frame.

Batch Scanning

Batch scanning allows for the scanning of more than one scan in a single pass. This multiple scan can be of various areas or settings of one image or scans of several images. To capture more than one scanned image in a single pass, click the General tab in the Scan Control window and then click the Scan Mode menu.

If you are scanning using a Photoshop plug-in and want your images to be open and viewable in Photoshop, choose Batch Mode. If you just want to scan your images to disk for accessing them later, choose Batch Mode (File).

Once you choose one of the batch modes, the scan button at the bottom of the Scan Control window will change from Scan RGB (Scan RGB) to Scan Batch (Scan Batch).

When you click the Scan Batch button, each image inside of all the scan frames will be scanned in the order in which they were created. And each image will have its own individual settings applied to it.

> It will be easier to find and manage the images you have later if you take the time to name each scan frame prior to initiating the batch scan. Remember that SilverFast is a bit different from many applications in that you name your image (in the Scan Control window) prior to actually creating the file.

Job Manager

As good as the batch scanning capabilities of SilverFast are, there is an even more powerful tool, Job Manager. And as you will see, Job Manager comes in particularly handy when you are scanning batches of transparencies, dissimilar images, or previously created images.

Job Manager has all of the capabilities of batch scanning, but in addition to scanning multiple, individually adjusted files, it will allow you to do the following:

- Skip images or scan frames

- Scan in both reflectives and transparencies (positives and negatives) in one pass (if supported by the scanner)

- Scan multiple images, on filmstrips for instance, because you are not restricted to images that are in the preview window

- Work with previously scanned images in programs such as SilverFast HDR, SilverFast DC, and SilverFast PhotoCD

- Process entire folders of images in addition to individual files

Working with Job Manager (JM) begins with defining a job. A job is a list of instructions that can be applied to individual images, image files, or a folder full of files. So when working with Job Manager, we focus on defining and configuring a job.

Getting Started with Job Manager

Here is how you can make Job Manager work for you. To activate it, click the Job Manager (JM) icon, which is located near the middle of the vertical tool palette on the left side of the preview window , bringing up an empty JM dialog window. Figure 10.7 shows this window with some jobs in progress.

Now perform the following steps to put the Job Manager to work by setting multiple scan frames with independent scan settings.

1. To create a prescan review, place several images of different types on your scanner. (If you are using a film scanner, try loading a filmstrip.) Then click the Prescan button in the Scan Control window.

2. Define several scan frames by drawing frames around several images or portions of images. Here I have drawn scan frames around three images.

3. Set the scan adjustments for each image as I've shown earlier in this book. For this demonstration, I applied the auto-adjustment tool to each image. Know that you can readjust any scan parameter you set now even after you add this image to the JM.

Figure 10.7

The Job Manager dialog

Creating and Deleting Job Entries

Jobs for JM to process are defined by creating job entries. There are several ways to define a job entry. At the lower-left corner of the JM window are three job entry icons:

- Click the first icon to add individual frames.
- Click the second icon to add multiple frames.
- Click the third icon to add images from an overview set such as a filmstrip.

I clicked the second button to add the previously created scan frames to my job. All three of the scanned frame images are added to the JM window, as shown in Figure 10.7.

> When using a film scanner with a filmstrip adapter, you would click the third job entry tool to select images from an overview preview set, which you would have created from the images on the filmstrip. Scanning filmstrips is explained later in this chapter.

Any job entry can be deleted from the JM entry list. Just click the JM entry and then click the trash can icon at the bottom of the JM window .

You will notice that each image entry has an image preview as well as a list of scan setting characteristics, including icons that show which tools have been used to correct the image so far.

Figure 10.8

Job entries corrected

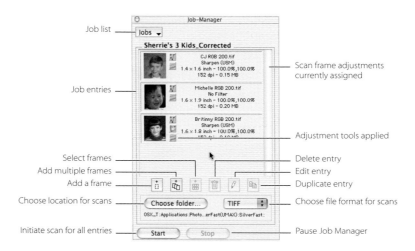

Job list

Job entries

Scan frame adjustments currently assigned

Adjustment tools applied

Select frames
Add multiple frames
Add a frame
Choose location for scans
Initiate scan for all entries

Delete entry
Edit entry
Duplicate entry
Choose file format for scans
Pause Job Manager

Editing Job Entries

Once you have added an image as a scan job entry, you are not tied to any of your initial settings. To change the scan setting for any job entry, follow these steps:

1. Click the entry in the JM window.

2. Click the frame of the image you want to edit.

3. Click the processing pencil tool 🖉 .

4. Make any adjustments you would like to make to the image.

5. Click the processing pencil tool again.

6. A query window appears asking if you want to save changes. Click Yes to apply the changes to your preview image and update the preview.

7. View the changes in the JM window.

Note how each image now has a name assigned to it. I have added a global color correction to the Britinny image and removed the sharpening from the Michelle image (see Figure 10.8).

Saving and Loading Jobs

Once you have included all the images you want and configured the adjustment you would like to be applied during the scan, you will want to save and name the job. Click the Jobs drop-down menu in the upper-left corner of the JM window. Choosing Save will allow you to name the current setup.

Once a job is saved, it can be recalled at any point and reused. Click the Jobs drop-down menu, choose Open, and from the submenu select the setup you want to recall.

Final Job Prep

Once you have finished defining and configuring all of your job images, you should set a few remaining options for how Job Manager will operate:

- **Select a scan job folder.** Click the Choose Folder button to select a location in which to place your finished images.

- **Select a file format for your images.** Click the menu in the lower-right corner of the JM window (the default value is TIFF) and select a file format. The available formats vary with the color space (RGB vs. CMYK) in which you are saving your images. TIFF is a good choice if you want to save your images in an uncompressed format that you can use in many different ways.

See Chapter 11 for more on color spaces.

Select the job images you want to scan. To scan all of the images in the JM list, do not select any job; to scan some but not all of the images, select the ones you would like JM to scan. Use the following keyboard shortcuts to help you make your selections:

Sequential selection	Shift+click the first and last images to be scanned.
Nonsequential selection	Command+click/Ctrl+click each image to be scanned.

Activating the Scanning Process

You are now ready to complete the job; click the Start button (**Start**). The SilverFast Job Manager commences and completes the scanning process for all of the images in the JM list while applying all of the corrections assigned to each image. The resultant files will be placed in the folder you designated.

The scanning process using Job Manager will typically take longer than you may be used to for a standard scan. This is because multiple images are being scanned and processed usually with varying settings. The big advantage here is that the entire process will now occur automatically while you pursue other tasks and interests. If you need to perform many scans and will be using Job Manager frequently, you may want to consider assigning a separate computer to run the scanner and Job Manager.

With Job Manager, you also have the ability to interrupt and monitor the Job Manager's progress.

Stopping/pausing the job You can stop or pause the JM process by clicking the Cancel button in the progress bar or the Stop button (formerly the Start button prior to initiating the scanning process).

Checking job status With a quick glance at the JM window, you can see if your job has been completely processed or not. After JM has run, it will place a small status symbol button, which SilverFast calls an LED (short for light emitting diode), in the lower-right corner of each job entry (see Figure 10.9).

LED Color	Meaning
Green	Process completed successfully
Red	Process not completed successfully
Yellow	Currently in process
Gray	Not yet processed

Figure 10.9

Process status symbol LED

Resetting job status If for some reason you want to rerun a job, perhaps after changing the job parameters, Command+click/right-click the job entry whose status you would like to change. A context menu will appear; select Reset Status.

Scanning Filmstrips with Job Manager

Job Manager is used to control the scanning of multiple images on negative filmstrips, along with scanners such as the Microtek ArtixScan 4000tf, which support the scanning of filmstrips. To scan a filmstrip, follow these steps:

1. Don cotton gloves and clean the images as discussed earlier.

2. Place the filmstrip in the film holder (normally the convex (emulsion) side of the filmstrip images are toward the image collection device, but check the instructions with your specific scanner to confirm this). Follow the instructions for your scanner. Be sure the filmstrip is square in the film holder and that no portion of any of the images is obscured by the film holder.

3. Place the filmstrip holder in the scanner.

4. Access the scanner with SilverFast (through a Photoshop plug-in or the stand-alone application).

5. From the Pos./Neg. menu in the General tab of the Scan Control window, choose Negative.

6. Configure the Film Type And Exposure in the NegaFix dialog. (See Bonus Chapter 2 for a complete description of these settings.)

7. Click the Job Manager button located on the left side of the preview window ▦. The Job Manager window will appear.

8. Click the third button, Add Images ▦, to activate the preview window for the filmstrip.

Alternatively, you may find and click an alternate button, Add Single Image From Film Strip (located above the Job Manger icon in the toolset on the left side of the preview window ▦) if you would like to add a single preview image from the filmstrip and *not* proceed through Job Manger to set up and scan multiple images.

An Overview window will appear. If this is your first scan with this filmstrip, the preview will appear with a blank set of filmstrip images (Figure 10.10 shows this window after a pre-scan). Note that the size and number of image spaces will depend upon the scanner and film sizes you are using.

In the upper-right corner of the Overview window are three buttons. The first button is for printing preview images. The second is for adding or refreshing preview images to this window. The third is for pausing the add or refresh process.

Click the second button, Add Preview. The scanner will create preview images of all the images in the film holder, like the ones in Figure 10.10.

To add one frame to the Job Manager, click the first preview image and then click the Add button (**Add**). A settings window appears.

Because there have as yet been no adjustments assigned to the preview image, SilverFast provides us with the option of applying an automatic correction to our image. Check the check box next to Adjust Image Automatically and SilverFast will assign the auto-adjustment correction (discussed in Chapter 4). This of course can be further modified, as discussed in Chapter 5.

Click the OK button and this image will be added to the Job Manager window.

Multiple images from the filmstrip preview can be added by Shift+clicking sequential images or Command+clicking/Ctrl+clicking nonsequential images in the filmstrip preview window prior to clicking the Add button.

Once an image or images have been added to the Job Manager window, they can be modified, managed, and processed with the procedures and techniques described earlier in this chapter.

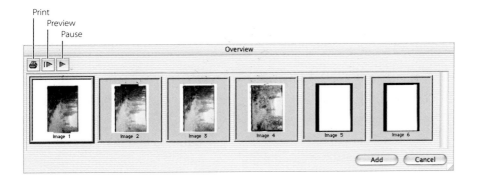

Figure 10.10

The filmstrip Overview window

CHAPTER 11

Getting a Grip on Color Management and Output

Perhaps the greatest challenge we have faced in open platform computer-based publishing is color management. Historically, color professionals captured, manipulated and output color images on proprietary, closed systems. Color was very good and predictable. All that has changed with the advent and subsequent explosion of desktop publishing. Now most color is captured and manipulated by operators with little or no professional color training who work on open systems where color files are being transferred into many different environments. The challenges of controlling color in open environments are substantial. This is the task we tackle with color management. Whole books (and many of them) have been devoted to this topic, but we will hit the important high points here.

- A color management overview
- Creating an ICC profile in SilverFast
- Acquiring and accessing ICC profiles
- SilverFast color management workflows
- Output tips

A Color Management Overview

As we capture, manipulate, and output color images on various devices, the color characteristics of the images tend to change. The reason for this is that each device has different color capabilities. Our challenge is usually to minimize the changes and match colors as closely as possible; this is called color management. Today's approach to controlling color reproduction on multiple devices is known as ICC color management because it complies with the specifications published by the International Color Consortium (ICC), the recognized authority on color standards. This approach allows for a uniform method of identifying color values and the application of a consistent approach to the conversion of these color values (such as the conversion of an RGB scan to CMYK mode).

To gain the benefits of an ICC color management workflow, you'll need to obtain ICC profiles for your scanner, monitor, and output devices. These profiles express the reproduction characteristics of each particular device and can then be used in conjunction with any ICC-compliant CMM (color management module, also known as color matching method or color manipulation module) to convert the color data for accurate display or output. CMMs that are widely used in today's desktop publishing workflows include Apple's ColorSync CMM (Mac only), ICM CMM (Windows only), and the Adobe Color Engine CMM (Mac and Windows).

SilverFast 6 offers the option of creating ICC scanner profiles using a supplied color target. The rest of your devices can be profiled through the use of a spectrophotometer coupled with color management software, or less demanding users could use generic ICC profiles supplied by their device manufacturers. In this chapter, we'll take a closer look at how SilverFast can work within an ICC color management workflow.

To get a better idea of what the challenges are, how we meet them, and how SilverFast fits into the color management scheme of things (also known as workflow), there are three key concepts to understand: color spaces, color gamuts, and color profiles.

Color Spaces

A *color space,* also known as a color model, is used to describe and manipulate color and is defined by the *color components* we are using. Two of the most common color spaces we use are RGB and CMYK, but there are others, such as Lab, HSL, and HSB. Often the type of device we are using—at least initially—determines the color space in which we are working. For instance, most digital capture devices such as scanners and digital cameras utilize RGB as their primary color space. In printing, CMYK is the preferred color space.

Yet the two most common color spaces—RGB and CMYK—handle color completely differently from each other. RGB is an additive light-based color space that creates colors by adding various percentages of red, green, and blue to create color. In contrast, CMYK is a subtractive ink-/toner-based color space that creates colors by mixing various percentages of inks or toners together, which subtracts various portions of light. (Refer back to Chapter 1 for more explanation and illustrations on additive versus subtractive color.) In addition, RGB images are typically viewed on glass or plastic monitors, while CMYK images are typically reproduced on various paper substrates. Because these two different color models use different colorants, substrates, and methods for creating colors, matching the colors in an image created in one color space (RGB) with those reproduced in another (CMYK) can be quite a challenge.

Color Gamuts

The term *color gamut* refers to the range of reproducible color a given device can create. There are dozens of variables that influence the range of reproducible color. Color spaces, colorant, and substrates are some of the major ones. Devices such as high-quality RGB-based color monitors have much larger color gamuts than devices such as CMYK-based commercial printing presses. This type of common mismatch means that we can capture and view a wider gamut of color on a monitor than we can reproduce when we print that same image on a CMYK printing press. This often creates unattainable expectations for the final print. On top of the gamut mismatch, all sorts of color shifts can occur when we convert an image from an RGB gamut to a CMYK gamut (see Figure 11.1). One of the most important tasks in color management is to be able to define the color gamut for all of our input and output devices so that we can match them as closely as possible. We record a device color profile through the creation of a color profile.

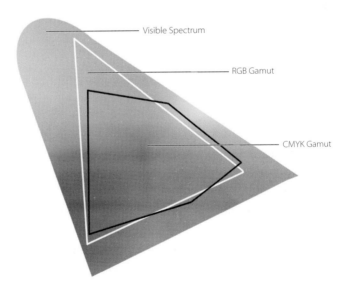

Figure 11.1

Different devices have different color gamuts.

Visible Spectrum

RGB Gamut

CMYK Gamut

Color Profiles and Color Management Modules

A *color profile* is a file that contains information about the color gamut of a device. There are various levels and qualities of color profiles: generic, model-specific, and device-specific, with the device-specific profile being the most accurate. Color profiles are exchanged through a color management module (CMM) in an attempt to match the colors from one device to another. SilverFast provides us with the means for creating high-quality device-specific profiles that can be used in a color management system that will exchange the color gamut information of your scanner with other color devices you are using. Applications such as Photoshop allow you to read and utilize color profiles and determine which CMM will be used when profiles are exchanged (see Figure 11.2).

Creating an ICC Profile in SilverFast

As mentioned, if you want to be able to keep control of color as you move images from one device to another, you must be able to acquire or create and transfer the color profiles of all the devices that your file will encounter. SilverFast allows either utilizing previously created profiles or making your own color profiles, which will be unique to your scanner. Let's discuss making your own profile first and then cover how to access and work with profiles.

As we discussed earlier, there are several types of color profiles, including generic profiles that specify general color space. Adobe 1998 represents a common *generic profile.* There are also *model profiles* that contain color gamut information about the average color characteristics of a certain model of device, such as a certain model of scanner. Model profiles contain more specific information about a certain device than the generic profile. And finally, there are custom profiles. Custom profiles are made with and for not just a model but a specific device, which in this case will be your scanner. Custom profiles, if they are properly constructed, represent the most specific, and therefore most accurate, information about the color characteristics of your scanner or any other device you choose to profile.

Creating a custom scanner profile always involves scanning a scan target with known values. The creation of a scanner profile begins with the calibration procedure I described in Chapter 4. I'll outline that again briefly:

1. Create a preview scan of an IT8 target.

2. Carefully select the target area.

3. Click the IT8 Calibration button on the left side of the preview window ![icon]. The IT8 Calibration dialog appears (see Figure 11.3).

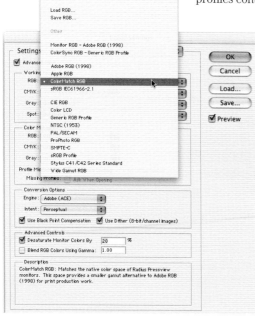

Figure 11.2

Photoshop color profiles (here, the RGB profiles) and CMMs (here, the Adobe [ACE] CMM)

4. Click the Start button.

5. You will be asked to find and select the target data file that matches the IT8 target. Browse to the proper file and select it. (Upcoming versions of Ai will have embedded bar codes to automatically recognize and select the proper target data file.)

In Chapter 4, we stopped at this point by clicking OK, satisfied that our scanner was now calibrated. In this case, let's take our calibration data another step:

6. Click the Export ICC button.

SilverFast will create an ICC profile labeled with the name of your scanner and place this ICC profile in the SilverFast color management folder (located in Photoshop's `Import/Export` folder if you are using a plug-in). Later in this chapter, I'll show you how to access these profiles when you set up your color management preferences.

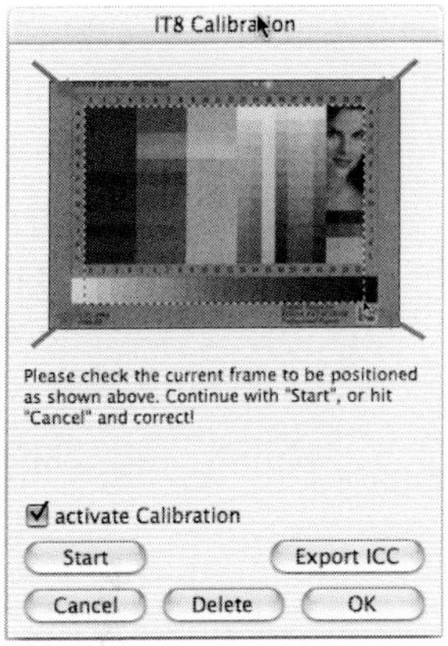

Figure 11.3

IT8 Calibration dialog

Acquiring and Accessing ICC Profiles

Once you have created an ICC profile, you must tell SilverFast how you want this color data to be handled with your image during and after the scan.

> Only plug-in technology provides full two-way color management communication and control, and particularly with Photoshop. TWAIN technology does not provide this functionality.

To access the color management controls, click the Option or Options button on the Scan Control window, to bring up the Defaults window; then click the CMS (color management system) tab (Figure 11.4). You will see that there are four sections to this dialog. We will start at the top of the CMS tab and work our way down.

Color Management Pane

By default, SilverFast does not employ any color management tools. The first pane of the CMS window is where we initially activate SilverFast's color management and determine the basic type of color management system to be utilized.

Scanner -> Internal

This setting controls what happens to your scanned image data once it leaves your scanner and is stored as a file.

None Choose this if you want no color adjustment at all (the default setting). I don't recommend this option because all color control is forfeited.

Calibration This option is automatically selected if you have calibrated your scanner using the IT8 target (see Chapter 4); use it if you want your scanner to deliver consistent calibrated results but do not intend to use color profiles.

ColorSync or ICM Choose ColorSync (on a Mac) or ICM (on Windows) if you intend to have both a calibrated scanner and the use of color profiles later in your workflow. We will assign a specific color profile for use in the next pane.

If you choose Calibration, you will want to configure the remainder of this Color Management pane but no other adjustments will be needed. If you intend to manage your color with profiles on other devices, select ColorSync or ICM here and complete the other panes in this window (see the following).

> You must calibrate your scanner to use either the Calibration or ColorSync/ICM menu choices. I recommend using at least the Calibration choice to be sure that you will be receiving consistent calibrated results from your scanner. Remember, not all versions of SilverFast have IT8 targets and/or support calibration. You can upgrade to a version that does or perform a manual calibration as outlined in Appendix A on the companion CD.

Internal -> Monitor

This setting controls what happens to your scanned image data when it is opened on a monitor.

None Choose this if you want no color adjustment at all when your file is displayed on a monitor. Not recommended for use in most cases.

Figure 11.4

The CMS tab of the Defaults dialog

Automatic Choose this if you have selected Calibration from the Scanner -> Internal menu but do not have a specific profile and/or monitor to which you would like to map your color image data. If you choose Automatic and will be moving your image into Photoshop, you will be leaving the display color matching to Photoshop. You can maintain control of the display colors by assigning (from the Internal menu in the Profiles For ColorSync/ICM pane, described shortly) the same color spaces, such as Adobe RGB, that Photoshop will be using. These settings will take advantage of SilverFast's built-in capability to match colors with Photoshop. Automatic is a good choice if you are not using specific color profiles past the scanning step but want to display the best, and most predictable, calibrated results possible in Photoshop.

ColorSync or ICM Choose ColorSync or ICM if you intend to use an ICC monitor profile to control the display of your image data on a monitor. You will assign a specific color profile for use in the next pane.

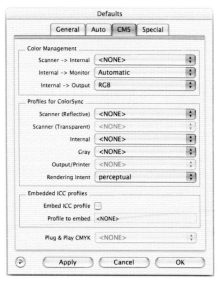

Internal -> Output

This setting controls what happens to your scanned image data when it is sent to and used on an output device other than a monitor, including in some cases output for editing.

RGB Choose this if you have selected Calibration and Automatic for the previous settings and/or if you want to create a generic RGB file. If you will be outputting on an RGB device such as a film recorder and you do not have any profile information about that device, use RGB as well.

ColorSync Choose this if you want to assign a specific color profile for use in the Profiles For ColorSync pane.

ICM Choose this if you are working on a Windows computer and you want to assign a specific color profile for use in the Profiles For ICM pane.

CIELab Choose this if you want your file placed in the Lab color space for either conversion or editing. Some color editing programs and color management systems work best when working with Lab-based colors.

P&P CMYK Choose this (it stands for Plug & Play CMYK) if you want your color imaged data converted on-the-fly to CMYK data. You would choose this if you were planning to convert your file immediately to CMYK for output on a CMYK device such as a commercial printing press.

> If you intend to multipurpose your images—that is, to use them for many different output devices—it is generally best not to confine the color space of your images to just one device early on. This is particularly true about converting your image to the relatively small CMYK gamut immediately from your scanner. If you are working in a print-only (CMYK) workflow with only one output device, you may, for workflow speed reasons, want to convert your image to that color space and gamut early. But doing so will limit your ability to take advantage of the varied, and often larger, gamuts of other output devices. For more flexibility, save your images initially in a larger color space (such as an RGB space) and then convert a copy of that image to CMYK later on.

Profiles For ColorSync or ICM Pane

This pane is where you will assign the specific color profiles and spaces you would like to apply or assign to your images. If you have selected any ColorSync or ICM menu choice in the Color Management pane and/or Automatic from the Internal -> Monitor menu and want to control the display of colors when opening the image in Photoshop, configure the various profile choices made available here.

Scanner (Reflective) and Scanner (Transparent)

If you have created a color profile for your scanner, as we did earlier in this chapter, this is where you will assign that profile to your images and color workflow. If you chose ColorSync or ICM from the Scanner -> Internal menu, this is where you assign the color profile to be used by those systems.

Click the Reflective or Transparent menu, depending upon which type of image you will be scanning. Select the scanner profile from the menu.

If you have loaded a manufacturer's scanner profile or created and saved a scanner profile, as we have in this chapter, it will appear in this list. Remember that the custom profile you create will nearly always be more accurate than a generic or model profile provided by a manufacturer.

Internal

If you chose ColorSync or ICM from the Internal -> Monitor menu, this is where you assign the color profile to be used by those systems. This is also where you can assign the color space to match the one used by Photoshop if you chose Automatic from the Internal -> Monitor menu.

Click the Internal menu; a list of Monitor profiles will appear (see Figure 11.5). Select the profile that matches your use. I have chosen AdobeRGB1998.icc but there are many to choose from. While space does not permit me to cover them all, I'll describe a few of the more common profiles and their uses.

AdobeRGB1998 This is a good choice for images that you intend to multipurpose. The Adobe RGB color space is large enough to encompass most of the output devices to which you might want to convert you image's colors in the future. This is the match to the color profile of the same name in Photoshop.

Note in some circumstances your profile may have the suffix.icc (such as AdobeRGB1998.icc). The "icc" stands for "international color consortium" which represent an industry standard profile format.

ColorMatch This ColorMatch color space attempts to match a Press-Match 21 CMYK simulation monitor. This is a common choice among commercial printers that will be using their image mostly for prepress output. If your commercial printing company uses this color space in its workflow, you may want to choose it as well to match its color management as closely as possible.

Color LCD This would be a possible choice if you were creating images to be used exclusively for presentations rendered on LCD projectors. This is a device-specific color space.

Figure 11.5

Internal Profile menu

NTSC1953 If you were creating images for display on standard television sets, this would be your choice. Be aware, however, that with the emergence of the many new types of television technologies such as LCD, HDTV, and plasma display, there is no longer just one television standard.

PAL_SECAM This profile can be used for images that are bound for video recordings. Here again, as in the world of TV, new technologies such as CD and DVD are broadening and changing the presentation color gamut choices.

sRGB A general monitor color space. A good choice if you intend to use your images just on the World Wide Web. A poor choice, due to its restricted gamut, if you intend to print your images and particularly if you intend to output them in CMYK PostScript (commercial printing). Note that sRGB is the default color space in most versions of Photoshop.

Gray

If you are scanning grayscale images you can select either the Generic Gray Profile.icc or a custom profile if you have created one. I recommend at least using the generic gray profile rather than leaving this as None because most desktop scanners will capture grayscale images darker than they should if they are not calibrated (linearized). (See the manual calibration information and instructions in Appendix A on the companion CD for a more in-depth discussion of linearization.)

PHOTOSHOP AND SILVERFAST PROFILE MATCHING

sRGB is not a good color space if you intend to use your images for printing as well as other uses. But sRGB is the default color space in many versions of Photoshop. If you choose Adobe RGB 1998 (or a non-RGB color space) from the Internal menu, be sure to change Photoshop's color space as well. SilverFast's color management system is designed to communicate and match directly with Photoshop's color management, so it is important that the color space you choose here be the same in Photoshop, otherwise color may shift unpredictably and often with unpleasant results. These Photoshop color profile controls are configured in the Color Settings dialog in Photoshop.

A good rule of thumb in the world of profiles is, if you are not sure where the images will be used, choose a fairly wide gamut profile (like Adobe RGB) for your initial color space. The Adobe RGB colors can always be remapped into a more specific output color space on later copies of the image.

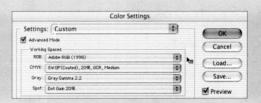

Output/Printer

Here you choose the specific print output device. If you have chosen ColorSync or ICM under the Internal -> Output menu in the Color Management pane, you must choose an output device here. If you are not prepared to choose a specific output device, then you should choose a non-print-specific setting under Internal -> Output menu, such as RGB or CIELab.

Click the Output/Printer menu and select the specific output device for which you are preparing your image. I have chosen USSheetfedCoated here (see Figure 11.6), which would be used for printing on a commercial CMYK printing press on coated stock. If you were printing this image to a desktop printer, such as an Epson S-C42 inkjet printer, then you would choose the profile for that printer. Note the profile labeled S_C42_Standardf.icc.

Any application that allows you to create and make ICC-compliant profiles, including Photoshop, can be used to create profiles, which can be placed in the SilverFast profile folder and accessed through this menu.

Rendering Intent

So far we have designated the capture (scanner), viewing (monitor), and output (printer) profiles. Now we need to tell the CMS our preferences in terms of how we would like the colors fit or mapped from one color space and gamut into another. This is what we do when we assign an "intent" to this mapping. For some images, we may want to retain as much color saturation as possible, and with others, maintaining the relative differences in original and final colors may be more important. SilverFast provides us with four possible intents.

Figure 11.6

Output/Printer menu

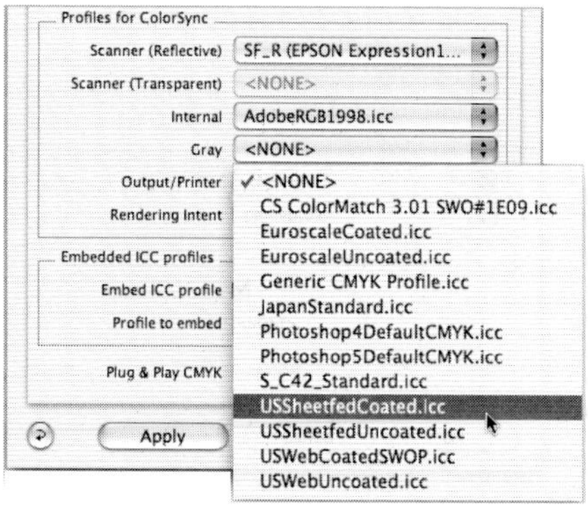

Perceptual This is the most common choice for scanned images of contone photographs. This intent will maintain the relative difference between the colors in an image as they are moved and mapped from one color space to another. Smooth transitions from one color to another are given preference over color saturation.

Rel. colorimetric (relative colorimetric) This choice is used when you want to maximize the color gamut reproduction of colors that may tend to be out of gamut on a printed piece relative to their original colors. This method maximizes color gamut rather than matching colors from one paper or device to another. An example would be if you were trying to maximize the reproduction of bright spot or neon colors in CMYK.

Saturation Choose this method if you want to maximize the saturation of your colors. This method emphasizes color saturation over color matching. Business graphics such as pie charts and graphs would be good candidates for this method.

Abs. Colorimetric (absolute colorimetric) This method is similar to the relative colorimetric in that color gamut tends to be maximized, but in this case color fidelity from one paper or device to another is emphasized over pure gamut maximization. So if you are trying to match wide gamut colors, such as bright spot colors, from one device to another, this is a good choice.

I chose Perceptual here because we are primarily discussing the reproduction of color contone images.

We have now finished configuring our color management profiles and choices. If any of our devices (scanner, monitors, or printers) or types of images or uses (color contones to business graphics) are changed, the CMS choices should be modified.

Profile Setup Comparison

Figure 11.7 shows a comparison of how you would set up the Color Management pane for the creation and delivery of just a calibrated image and one that will be created and delivered ready for full use of ICC profiles. Note, however, that even in the calibration-only setup, the Internal profile (under Profiles For ColorSync) is set for Adobe RGB 1998 so that when I take my images into Photoshop, they will display properly (assuming that I have configured Photoshop with the same profile).

Figure 11.7

Color management setups

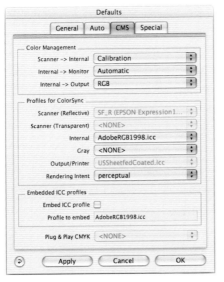

Calibration-only CMS configuration

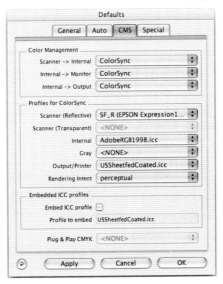

Calibration and ICC profile CMS configuration

Embedding Profiles

Once you have configured your color management system (CMS) profiles and gamut mapping preferences, you can decide whether to embed the output profile in the image. Embedding a profile means that the profile of your choice will be sent along with the image. This profile can then be read by another CMS and used to process the image.

To embed a profile, check the Embed ICC Profile box. The profile that will be embedded is clearly indicated in the Profile To Embed field. (Compare these data fields in the two CMS setups in Figure 11.7.)

Not all workflows call for the use of embedded color profiles. In fact, sometimes embedding profiles gums up the works when images are being printed (as in some PDF workflows). If you control all of the input and output devices and your workflow is fairly linear, you probably do not need to embed profiles. Profiles are most useful when files are being sent out for output on outside devices. If you work with service bureaus and/or printing companies, ask them if they want to use embedded profiles and seek their guidance on which ones.

Plug & Play CMYK

At the very bottom of the CMS tab is an area labeled Plug & Play CMYK. If you choose P&P CMYK under the Internal -> Output menu, this area becomes active. Plug & Play CMYK is for production of on-the-fly conversion from RGB to CMYK files during the scanning process; this is typically used when an image is destined to be output on only one CMYK output device.

Using Plug & Play CMYK can help speed up your workflow and provide you with high-quality device-specific color conversions. In addition, by using the same reference Lab color space used by Photoshop, Plug & Play CMYK will provide you with preview consistency from SilverFast through Photoshop. However, if you intend to perform edits or additions to your images and/or output your images to multiple devices, then Plug & Play CMYK is typically not recommended.

To take advantage of the speed and CMYK preview and output color accuracy afforded by the use of Plug & Play CMYK, set up SilverFast with the values shown in Table 11.1 and Figure 11.8. It is important that you use the same color profiles and rendering intents in SilverFast as you will be using in Photoshop if you want the preview to look (and print) the same as you move your image from SilverFast to Photoshop; Figure 11.8 also shows how to set Photoshop.

Table 11.1

SilverFast Plug & Play CMYK Setup

MENU	VALUE
Scanner -> Internal	Calibration
Internal -> Monitor	ColorSync (Mac) or ICM (Windows)
Internal -> Output	P&P CMYK
Internal	Same as working RGB color space in Photoshop Color Settings
Rendering Intent	Same as Intent setting in Photoshop Color Settings window
Plug & Play CMYK	Same as working CMYK color space in Photoshop Color Settings window

When you choose Plug & Play CMYK, the Profile To Embed field will automatically update to the P&P CMYK choice.

> If you do not have the same profile available in the Plug & Play CMYK menu as you are using in the Working CMYK menu in Photoshop, you can export the working CMYK profile from Photoshop (Color Settings → Working CMYK → Export) and place it in the Profile folder being used by SilverFast (ColorSync folder on Mac OS, ICM folder on Windows).

Finishing Up

Once you have made all of your color management choices, you can exit the CMS tab. Click the Apply button to test your setup value. If you forget to configure one of the menus, Silver-Fast will remind you with a warning screen like the one in Figure 11.9. If you get a warning, click OK to approve and set the changes to the CMS tab.

If you have selected either P&P CMYK or any CMYK-based ICC profile, the scan button in the Scan Control window will change from Scan RGB to Scan CMYK to reflect the new color management instructions you have given SilverFast.

When SilverFast or any software indicates a "CMYK scan," it does not literally mean that the scanner will be capturing a CMYK image. The scanner will still initially capture the image in RGB mode and then convert the image to CMYK using the CMS preferences and profiles you have selected. This will restrict the image's color gamut and therefore its flexibility. It's usually better to capture your image in RGB mode and save an archived RGB image to which you can always return.

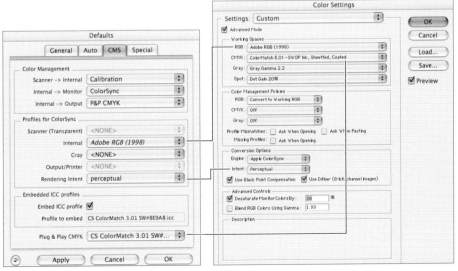

SilverFast Plug&Play CMYK Settings   Photoshop Color Settings

Figure 11.8

Make sure these choices in the SilverFast Plug & Play CMYK setup match those in the Photoshop Color Settings window.

SilverFast Color Management Workflows

There are many varieties of workflows, or paths, your images can take through a production process. There are simple ones in which you scan the image on one scanner and print it on one output device. More complex workflows may involve multiple input and output devices. SilverFast's CMS system allows you to control how the color data in your images is captured, viewed, and output on various devices. Figure 11.10 shows several different workflow paths that an image may take and how the profile setup values might vary with each.

Note that in some workflows, ICC profiles will be embedded along with the file; in others, the profiles will be used in the preparation and/or conversion of the file, such as from RGB to CMYK, but not embedded in the file itself. Also note that if you intend to scan a 48-bit image with the intent of processing it in SilverFast HDR, a color profile can be embedded during the scan and utilized by HDR to process the image (see Chapter 12 for more on HDR).

Output Tips

Today we have access to an ever-increasing number of output devices, including monitors, desktop printing devices, large format printers, and commercial printing presses. And the dividing line between desktop and commercial printing devices is becoming increasingly blurred. Many printing companies, for instance, use desktop proofing devices for creating color proofs to represent their press output. It is always a good idea to know what kind of output device will be used prior to capturing your images. If you are outputting to many devices, it's a good idea to make sure your images can be used on all of them. You should know the image size, resolution, color space/gamut, and screening technology requirements of your output device(s). Because it is not practical to capture a separate image for each output device, we are often required to make compromises. Following are some specific guidelines for creating images for use on various types of output devices.

General rule 1: Start large and go small. If you will be multipurposing your images, capture them at the largest image dimension, highest resolution, and largest color space in which they will be used. You can then, on copies of your original images, reduce the size, resolution, and color space for the less demanding output. Reducing image size, resolution, and color gamut is typically less harmful to your image than attempting to enlarge dimension, resolution, and color space.

General rule 2: Create archive images. Create and save general-purpose archival images to which you will return time and again to make copies for various uses. My typical general purpose images are 8″×10″, 300 ppi, Adobe 1998 RGB TIFF images with little or no unsharp mask applied.

Figure 11.9

Profile Warning window

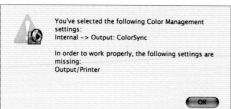

You've selected the following Color Management settings:
Internal –> Output: ColorSync

In order to work properly, the following settings are missing:
Output/Printer

OK

Figure 11.10

Workflow and profile paths

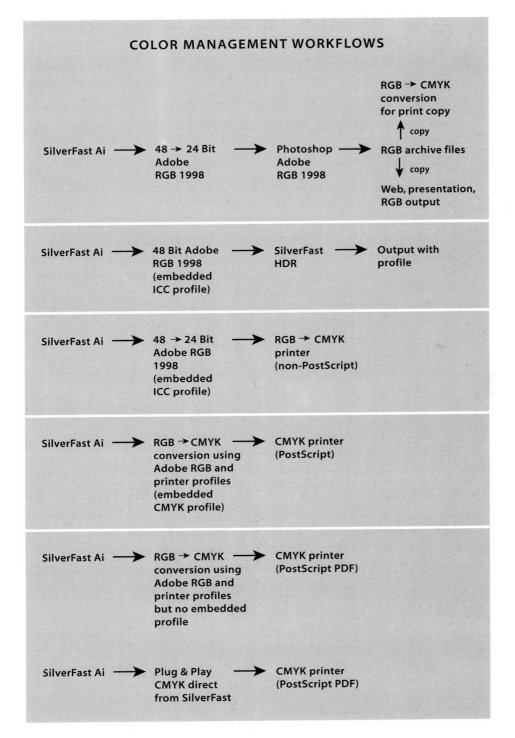

COLOR MANAGEMENT WORKFLOWS

Commercial printing Commercial printing is probably the most demanding purpose, in terms of image quality and resolution, for which you use your images. Images that may look just fine on screen, such as low-resolution JPEG images, often do not print nearly as well. This is due to the processing, know as RIPping, that occurs when your image is printed. RIPping often exposes quality and resolution problems that are not immediately apparent on screen. Low-resolution monitors are more forgiving than print devices. Here are the scan characteristics I recommend for commercial printing:

Setting	Value
Image dimension	Largest to be used (8"×10" if I am not sure).
Resolution	300 ppi.
Color space	RGB or Lab. (I may perform a Plug & Play CMYK conversion if I am printing the image only on one device and I have its color profile.)
Sharpening	I capture an unsharpened image and sharpen (a copy) when I am done editing. My standard sharpening setting for faces is amount = 100%, Radius = 1, threshold = 3 to 5.
RGB -> CMYK conversion	I perform this just before I print on a copy of the original image.
File format	TIFF or EPS.
Archive image	I save an unsharpened, full size and resolution, RGB, TIFF as an archive image to which I can return to make copies for other uses in the future.

Desktop printing Desktop printing devices are not as demanding as commercial printing devices in terms of resolution requirements. In addition, many desktop printers prefer to receive RGB rather than CMYK color space images if they possess in-RIP RGB-to-CMYK conversion capabilities. My image capture approach to desktop printing is very similar to that of commercial printing, with the following changes:

Setting	Value
Resolution	200 ppi instead of 300 ppi.
Color space and RGB -> CMYK	Nearly always capture in RGB, and if my desktop printer has built-in (in-RIP) RGB-to-CMYK conversion, I may not convert the image color space to CMYK but rather allow the printer's RIP to perform the conversion.

E-mail and World Wide Web use Images to be used on the Web should always be in RGB color space and never converted to CMYK. The standard resolution is 72 ppi (although some prefer to use 96 ppi for higher-resolution monitors); image dimensions are typically smaller, 3"×5" (216×360 pixels) or smaller. JPEG (medium quality) is the preferred file format for contone images. I *do not* sharpen images that I am saving as JPEGs because the JPEG compression algorithm tends to posterize the sharpened high-contrast edges in the images, thereby destroying them.

PowerPoint (and other presentation applications) Images that will be used in PowerPoint presentations have similar dimension and resolution requirements to those used for e-mailing and the Web. The difference may be in the file format choice and the amount of compression applied for the PowerPoint images. File size is not as important a consideration for PowerPoint presentations, so you may not have to compress your images and you may be able to use somewhat larger images. File formats such as BMP, PICT, and WMF are acceptable here; just check to see which file formats your version of your presentation program supports. But remember that if you plan to print your PowerPoint presentation, you will want to use images that conform to the images size, resolution and file format requirements of your output device rather than the minimal requirements of PowerPoint.

PDF files PDF files can be used for a wide variety of output environments, from commercial printing to the Internet. Create images with the dimension, resolution, color space, file format, and sharpening requirements for the intended output device. Images can be down-sampled and compressed in the PDF creation ("distilling") process, so create multipurpose images for the highest-quality device you will be using.

Multipurpose images For images that will be used for more than one purpose, I tend to capture them as if they will be used for commercial printing (the most demanding use) to create a multipurpose archive image. I then make copies of these images and downsize, sample, and compress the color space and make file format changes based upon their various uses.

CHAPTER 12

Using SilverFast HDR, DC, and PhotoCD

SilverFast Ai is designed specifically to work with a scanner when capturing an image. The big advantage to working with the scanned image as it is captured is that the scanned image data can be adjusted during the image capture process when there is maximum image data available.

But this is not always possible. We often are faced with the challenge of correcting images for which we have no original hard copy, an image that has been captured by another scanner, or increasingly, digital photography images that have no hard original because they are digital to begin with. And in some circumstances, we may not know all the adjustments we want to make on an image when we initially capture it and would like to have the option of making high-quality corrections in the postscan.

LaserSoft Imaging provides us with three tools that allow us to work with images after they've been captured: SilverFast HDR, DC, and PhotoCD. Most of the SilverFast Ai tools and techniques we have learned apply to these applications as well, but there are some features and processes that differ from SilverFast Ai, so it is on these that we will focus in this chapter.

The following topics are covered in this chapter:

- **Getting Images into SilverFast HDR**

- **Adjusting Images in SilverFast HDR: HiRePP and SC2G**

- **SilverFast DC and DC-VLT**

- **SilverFast PhotoCD**

Getting Images into SilverFast HDR

HDR is short for "high dynamic range." This refers to HDR's capability, and in fact preference, for working with images that have large amounts of image data. HDR can work with images saved in either 24-bit or 48-bit RGB mode. However, the best results will be obtained from working with images that have the higher (48-bit) bit depth (see the section labeled "Capture Bit Depth, Channels, and Shades of Gray" in Chapter 1). If you have a choice, you should obtain 48-bit images to work with in SilverFast HDR. Higher-quality digital cameras and scanners can capture images in 48-bit mode. SilverFast Ai can also capture images in 48-bit mode.

Capturing HDR Images

If you are using a SilverFast controlled scanner to create an image to be used in SilverFast HDR, you will want to create one that contains as much data (48 bits) as possible and is specifically created for use in HDR. The main setting difference you will make compared with a regular SilverFast scan will be in the Scan Type menu in the Scan Control window. Follow these steps to create an HDR-readable image:

1. Perform a clean preview scan.

2. When configuring the final high-resolution scan setup, choose 48 Bit HDR Color or 16 Bit HDR Grayscale as your scan mode.

3. Configure your scanner's resolution and scaling settings using the tools and techniques discussed in Chapters 4 and 5.

You will notice that when you choose one of the two HDR settings, most of the prescan adjustment tools are inactive. In fact, only the scaling and resolution controls are active. This of course is because, by choosing an HDR scan type setting, you are choosing to perform all of the image adjusts in the postscan using the HDR tools.

> If you will be using your images at various sizes and at multiple resolutions for various output devices, the best approach is to capture the image at the largest dimension and highest resolution at which you intend to use it. Reducing the dimensions or down-sampling the resolution in the postscan is far less harmful to your image than sizing or sampling up.

By choosing one of the HDR Scan Type settings, you guarantee that the scanner will deliver an image with as much raw image data as is possible—data for HDR to use in the adjustment of your image.

Activating SilverFast HDR

SilverFast HDR can be launched as either a stand-alone application or as a plug-in in Photoshop. Using HDR as a plug-in gains the convenience of the built-in interoperability with Photoshop (see Chapter 11 on color management), as well as immediate access to Photoshop's editing tools once your work in HDR is done.

To start SilverFast HDR as a Photoshop plug-in, launch Photoshop and choose File → Import → SilverFast (HDR), as shown in Figure 12.1. The HDR Scan Control window appears (Figure 12.2).

You will notice that the HDR Scan Control window and tools look very similar to the normal SilverFast Ai ones. Most of the differences are minor simplifications to the tools and choices. For instance, the Scan Type menu on the Frame tab has become Image Mode menu, in which you will only find two choices, 24 Bit Color and 8 Bit Grayscale. Also, there is no Prescan button (because the image capture has already occurred).

The only slightly confusing thing in some earlier versions of SilverFast may be the button labeled Scan RGB at the bottom of the window. More recent versions use the more appropriate label of "Process" rather than scan. When you click this button in HDR, you will not really be scanning an RGB image but rather processing the RGB image you opened in HDR. So just don't take that button too literally; go along with the scan analogy and all will be well!

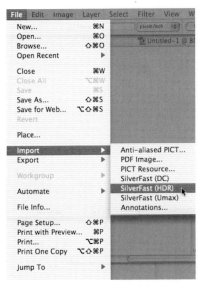

Figure 12.1

Launching SilverFast HDR from within Photoshop

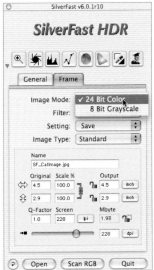

Figure 12.2

The HDR Scan Control window

Opening Images in HDR

There are three ways to open an image for processing in SilverFast HDR:

- Using the Virtual Light Table (VLT), which provides thumbnail, expanded thumbnail, and full size preview, allow you to see all of the details in an image. (See the next section "SilverFast DC and DC-VLT" for instructions on using the very cool SilverFast virtual light table.)

- The Open button on the HDR Scan Control window General tab

- The Image drop-down menu on the General tab

- The context menu from the Preview window title bar

The most direct way to open an image in HDR is to click the Open button, which takes you to a traditional Open dialog. The Virtual Light Table, however, provides you with a wide range of image management tools and controls.

Opening from the Context Menu

You can also use the mouse to access the Open Image and Overview functions. Control+click or right-click the top of the preview window. A context menu appears that gives you the choice of opening an image, using the Overview window, or opening a recently opened image.

Opening from the General Tab

You can also use the Image menu in the General tab of the HDR Scan Control window to access the Open Image and Overview options.

Although SilverFast HDR can open both TIFF and JPEG format images, whenever possible you should create or request TIFF images rather than JPEG. JPEGs have varying amounts of damaging lossy compression applied to them; TIFFs will be free of these degradations and will therefore provide you with better final image results.

Adjusting Images in SilverFast HDR: HiRepp and SC2G

Once you have opened an image in HDR, you can use all of the standard SilverFast Ai tools, techniques, and processes we have discussed in previous chapters. The only difference is that you will be applying them to an image that has already been scanned.

"When you work in HDR, two aids that can help you work faster and improve the quality of your images are specifically available to you The first tool, HiRepp, allows you to open and work with very large files quickly and easily, thereby saving lots of production time. The second tool, called SC2G, allows you to control the adjustment of a color image into a grayscale image, thereby saving you from having to perform that chore in Photoshop.

HiRepp

HiRepp is a proprietary image format technology that allows for a dramatic decrease in the time that is required to open large pixel-based image files. One example will serve to make the point. Opening a 500 MB image in Photoshop 6 required 90 seconds compared with 2.5 seconds using HiRepp in HDR. That is 36 times faster, or a time savings of 97 percent.

Taking advantage of such savings is easy; just make sure that the files with which you are working are saved in a HiRepp-capable format. If you have captured your image with SilverFast, in Version 5.52 or higher, and saved your image in either 48 Bit HDR Color or 16 Bit HDR Grayscale, your image is HiRepp-capable.

To work with an image not already saved in HiRepp format, such as a file from a digital camera or an image captured on another scanner, simply open the image in HDR and select either 48 Bit HDR Color or 16 Bit HDR Grayscale from the Image Mode menu.

SC2G

SC2G is short for "selective color to grayscale." This is a little-known and little-used Silver-Fast capability available in all versions of SilverFast including HDR. But for those of us constantly in need of converting RGB images to grayscale and routinely disappointed in the low-contrast images that result when default conversions are used, this is indeed a most powerful and useful tool.

In many color images, objects are clearly distinguished when they are viewed in color. But when these images are converted to grayscale, many of the image components have poor contrast separation. This is because in the color image, the object may have very different hue values but luminance values may be very close. The flower picture in Figure 12.3 is just such an image. In the color version of the image (see the color section), all of the flowers and particularly the gladiolus in the front are clearly distinguished. But in the initial default grayscale image the gladiolus is murky and poorly distinguished from the rest of the image elements. What we want to be able to do is adjust the luminance values of the various colored objects separately to create a grayscale image in which each of the flower elements exists in contrast to the others. This is where SC2G shines.

Open the gladiolus image from the companion CD in SilverFast HDR, and follow these steps to grayscale success:

1. Convert the image to 8-bit grayscale using the Image Mode menu. Note the poor appearance of the flower.

2. Click the Selective Color tool ![tool]. A special version of the tool appears (Figure 12.4) that allows us to adjust the luminance of the various fundamental colors (red, green, blue, cyan, magenta, and yellow) in an image.

Figure 12.3

We'll convert this image to a more interesting grayscale.

3. To get an overall sense of the amount of red, green, and blue in your image, click the Factors tab in the Selective Color tool window (Figure 12.5).

As you can see, the relative amounts of red, green, and blue are indicated by the values red = .30%, green =.59%, and blue = .11%, indicating that there is twice as much green as red and three times as much red as blue.

4. Click the Gray Matrix 6 tab again to proceed.

5. Click the gladiolus to select the color in the gladiolus for adjustment. Because the gladiolus is basically red, the red column in the Selective Color tool is activated (a small gray triangle appears above the red column indicating that it is active).

6. Click the top of the red column until the contrast of the flower reaches your desired level. I have raised the luminance level to a −44 here.

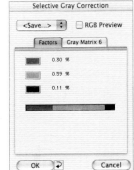

Figure 12.4

The initial selective color settings

Figure 12.5

The Factors tab

7. To adjust the contrast of other portions of the image, click those image areas and adjust their luminance values. You can click the RGB Preview button to see the original color version of the image as an aid when selecting colors. Here are the adjustments I made to the gladiolus:

Click	Adjust to
Gladiolus (red color column)	−44
The blue mum (blue color column)	+30
The dark green grass (green color column)	+30
The light green grass (yellow color column)	+30

Note the dramatic change in the contrast of the various elements in the image we have adjusted (Figure 12.6).

SilverFast DC and DC-VLT

The DC stands for "digital camera." This version of SilverFast image adjustment software was designed specifically for opening and adjusting low-bit-depth images that were captured by lower-quality digital cameras. Opening and working with images in SilverFast DC is just like working with SilverFast HDR, except that you are limited to working with a maximum of 8-bit grayscale and 24-bit color images. (In fact, the DC Scan Control window looks just like the HDR one, shown back in Figure 12.1.)

> If you work with both high- and low-bit-depth images, you may want to work in SilverFast HDR exclusively because it supports both types of images.

Shasta_Raw 16bit.tif

If you attempt to open a higher-bit-depth image, such as a 48-bit color image, you will receive a warning message, "Error: Unallowed number of bits per pixel." If you receive this message, or if you see the red bar-and-circle icon in a preview window, open the image in SilverFast HDR instead.

SilverFast DC-VLT

The newest version of SilverFast DC is called DC-VLT, which stands for Digital Camera-Virtual Light Table. (Owners of DC versions can upgrade to DC-VLT through the LaserSoft website: `www.lasersoft.com`.) This VLT version provides a sophisticated, quick, and easy-to-use set of tools for viewing, sorting, orienting, and even printing sets of images. Like the other SilverFast software modules, DC-VLT is available as a stand-alone application or as a Photoshop plug-in; it can be used with any set of digital images and is not limited to digital camera images.

Figure 12.6

The adjusted image and the settings that achieved it

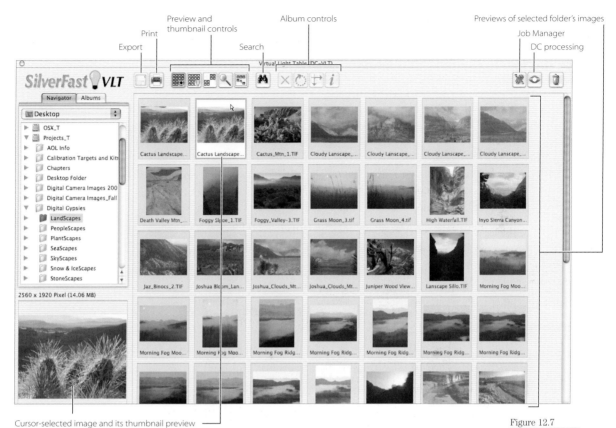

Export

Print

Preview and thumbnail controls

Search

Album controls

Previews of selected folder's images

Job Manager

DC processing

Cursor-selected image and its thumbnail preview

Figure 12.7

The VLT, showing initial previews

Accessing Images

When DC-VLT is launched, the Virtual Light Table appears (see Figure 12.7). In the upper-left corner of the window are two tabs, a Navigator tab and an Albums tab. The Navigator tab is used for finding the folder on the hard disk or other storage media that contains the images you would like to view. Handy folder tabs allow you to easily locate nested folders.

Click the folder containing the images you want to view. Previews of all the images in your selected folder will appear in the main Overview window to the right. Move your cursor over the various images in the Overview window (no clicking required). Larger previews will appear in the thumbnail preview in the lower-left corner of the VLT window.

Creating Albums

Images from various folders can be organized into albums. Here's how:

1. Click the Albums tab (Figure 12.8).

2. Click the + button to create a new album.

3. Type the album name in the naming window that appears. A new album will appear in the Album tab.

4. Drag images from the Overview window into the Album icon.

Using Albums and Overviews

You can manage and manipulate your albums and overviews in several ways:

- Click the album folder icon to display the contents of the album.

- Click the show/hide album button ▦ found in the horizontal toolset at the top of the Overview window.

- Click the show/hide overview button ▦ to control the display of the Overview.

- Click the magnifier icon 🔍 to activate the Magnifier menu, which allows you to control the sizes of the overview, album, and preview images.

Note that when an image is selected for preview, by double-clicking its thumbnail, a full size image preview appears in which you can see all the detail in the image.

- Click the sort icon ▦ to activate the menu, which allows us control how the image will be sorted in view windows. Note specifically the last menu choice, Snap Album Thumbnails To Grid, which will redistribute the stacked album previews into the standard tiled grid view.

- Click the search icon 🔍 to conduct a search for images.

- Click the four album control tools ✕ ⟳ ⇄ 𝑖 to mark, rotate, flip, or get info on any selected album images.

- Click the disk or printer icons 🖫 🖨 to either export or print any selected images. Note that the print function will create and print a PDF sheet of images.

Once you are finished viewing and organizing your images, you can proceed directly to either Job Manager (if you would like to process multiple images) or the SilverFast DC application (for processing individual images). Click either the Job Manager or SilverFast icons 🎆 ◉ located at the far right end at the top of the VLT window. Once you are in either Job Manager or SilverFast DC, you will have access to all the standard SilverFast tools.

SilverFast PhotoCD

PhotoCD is a proprietary multiresolution file format developed by Kodak. PhotoCD image libraries are usually initially written to a CD from which they can be accessed directly or transferred to another type of media such as a hard drive. There is a complete set of preview images included with each library of images stored on a PhotoCD, CD, and they can be used for rapid review of all the images include in the PhotoCD library. A good method of managing many PhotoCD images is to only access and transfer the images you want to use, leaving the remainder stored on the CD.

Accessing PhotoCD Image Libraries

SilverFast PhotoCD provides us with the ability to access PhotoCD images either directly from the CD or from other storage media if they have been transferred. Here are the several methods for accessing PhotoCD images.

Place the PhotoCD disk in your computer's CD-ROM drive and launch SilverFast PhotoCD, either as a plug-in to Photoshop (recommended) or as a stand-alone application. Click either the Open or Overview buttons or use the preview window context menu to initiate access to the PhotoCD images.

> See the earlier section on SilverFast HDR for details about using the Overview button and the preview window menu to access images.

SilverFast PhotoCD will automatically search for a loaded PhotoCD disk and a file named `OVERVIEW.PCD;1`. Once this is located, SilverFast presents you with an Overview window showing thumbnails of all of the images in the PhotoCD library.

If a disk and the `OVERVIEW.PCD;1` file is not found, SilverFast PhotoCD will present you with a window asking you to locate a folder containing PhotoCD images. Navigate through your hard drive to locate your PhotoCD library folder and SilverFast will use that folder to create its overview.

Figure 12.8

The Albums tab, with preview and thumbnail

Selecting PhotoCD Images

PhotoCD images can be selected singly, consecutively, or non-consecutively. To open an image in the SilverFast Prescan window, click it in the Overview window and then click OK. To open multiple images, click the first image and Shift+click the last image of a continuous set or Command/Ctrl+click individual images until all the desired images are highlighted; then click OK.

Menu Selection of Images

You will probably find using the Overview selection method the easiest and most convenient method because lists of PhotoCD images are merely sequentially numbered filenames that provide no clue as to their content.

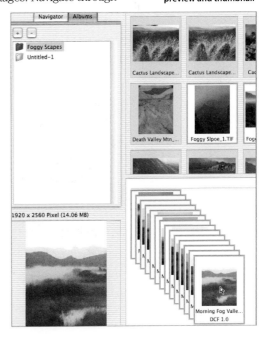

However, as an alternative to using the thumbnails in the preview window for selecting images to open, the Prescan window context menu may also be used to open PhotoCD images. Control+click or right-click the title bar of the SilverFast Prescan window.

Here are descriptions of the choices on the resulting context menu:

PhotoCD Overview This choice provides an Overview window containing thumbnails of all the images in a PhotoCD library (as explained earlier).

> This PhotoCD Overview menu choice will be available only if there is a PhotoCD disk in the CD-ROM drive and an OVERVIEW.PCD;1 file is present on the disk.

PhotoCD Folder This choice can be used for manually searching and selecting folders named Images without using an Overview window. This allows you to access PhotoCD images when OVERVIEW.PCD;1 is not present or if you just prefer to access the images without using the overview feature.

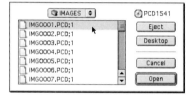

PhotoCD Open Image This is used for manually accessing single PhotoCD images from a list of PhotoCD images.

PhotoCD *image name* This choice provides access to the most recently opened image.

Previous Image/Next Image This choice switches from the currently selected image to either the previous or next image in the prescan preview window. This allows you to access images in the order in which they appear on the CD without regard to whether you have previously selected them.

Previous Selection/Next Selection This one switches from the currently selected image to either the previous or next selected image in the prescan preview window. This allows you to access images that you have previously selected. Images must have been previously selected in order to be accessed in this manner.

Printing a Thumbnail Sheet

Once you have activated an overview display of thumbnail images, you can print a copy of this sheet to your printer. Click the printer icon ⊟ to activate the standard print dialog box and print a sheet of small low-resolution images.

Editing PhotoCD Images

Once you have opened the image(s) that you would like to correct, you can use all the same SilverFast tools discussed previously to edit and correct your images.

Index

Note to the Reader: Throughout this index **boldfaced** page numbers indicate primary discussions of a topic. *Italicized* page numbers indicate illustrations.

Open Your Eyes to
Photosh👁p

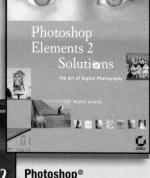

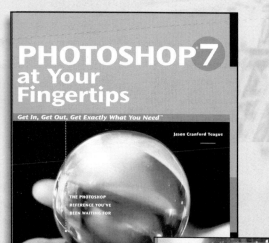

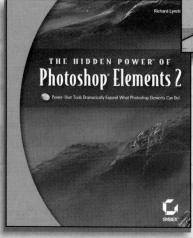

Photoshop® Elements 2 Solutions: The Art of Digital Photography
ISBN: 07821-4140-4 · $40

The Hidden Power™ of Photoshop® Elements 2
ISBN: 07821-4178-1 · $40

Photoshop® 7 at Your Fingertips: Get In, Get Out, Get Exactly What You Need™
ISBN: 07821-4092-0 · $40

Photoshop® 7 Savvy™
ISBN: 07821-4110-2
$40

Photoshop® 7 Learning Studio™
ISBN: 07821-4185-4
$119.99

Coming Soon
Photoshop Tennis: The Secrets of Winning Digital Design
ISBN: 07821-4191-9 · $44.99

Style. Substance. Sybex.

SYBEX®

Get Savvy™

Sybex introduces Savvy,™ a new series of in-depth, premium graphics and web books. Savvy books turn beginning and intermediate level graphics professionals into experts, and give advanced users a meaningful edge in this competitive climate.

In-Depth Coverage. Each book contains compelling, professional examples and illustrations to demonstrate the use of the program in a working environment.

Proven Authors. Savvy authors have the first-hand knowledge and experience to deliver useful insights, making even the most advanced discussions accessible.

Sophisticated Package. Savvy titles have a striking interior design, enhanced by high-quality, coated paper for crisp graphic reproduction.

Flash™ MX Savvy
by Ethan Watrall
and Norbert Herber
ISBN: 0-7821-4108-0
US $50

Photoshop® 7 Savvy
by Steve Romaniello
ISBN: 0-7821-4110-2
US $50

Maya™ 4.5 Savvy
by John Kundert-Gibbs
and Peter Lee
ISBN: 0-7821-4109-9
US $60

Dreamweaver® MX/ Fireworks® MX Savvy
by Christian Crumlish
ISBN: 0-7821-4111-0
US $50

SYBEX®

www.sybex.com

Style. Substance. Sybex.

Soluti👁ns FROM SYBEX®

iMovie 3 Solutions brings high-end visual effects to the iMovie community with easy-to-follow projects, step-by-step instructions, and companion sample videos. Whether you're a hobbyist, a budding producer, or a dedicated video prosumer, *iMovie 3 Solutions* will help you create unique and breathtaking videos on a budget.

- Adding logos and watermarks to your movies
- Producing exciting picture-in-picture effects
- Creating larger and more dynamic title sequences
- Combining animated elements with your iMovie footage
- Making slide shows with great special effects, including camera pans
- Designing interactive QuickTime skins that surround your iMovie videos
- Converting your PowerPoint presentations into iMovie form
- Authoring captions and subtitles for your movies

The companion CD is packed with project videos, as well as a 30-day fully functional version of Photoshop Elements.

iMovie™ 3 Solutions:
Tips, Tricks, and Special Effects
by Erica Sadun
ISBN: 0-7821-4247-8 • US $39.99

Photoshop Elements 2 Solutions makes Photoshop Elements 2 approachable and offers instruction and professional advice on all its features.

- Getting Photoshop Elements 2 up and running
- Sharpening out-of-focus pictures
- Straightening a crooked scan
- Improving product and real estate shots
- Removing unwanted objects
- Optimizing photos for the web and e-mail
- Touching up faces
- Making realistic-looking composites

The companion CD comes with utilities to make your work easier, plus trial versions of fun and useful plug-ins.

Photoshop®
Elements 2 Solutions
by Mikkel Aaland
ISBN: 0-7821-4140-4
US $40.00 full color throughout

SYBEX®

www.sybex.com